IMAGES
of America

POMFRET

On the cover: This photograph shows the corner of Forest Place and West Main Street during the 1930s. Today this portion of Main Street houses a Subway restaurant, B. J.'s Downwind Café, and Coughlins. The second-floor porches that look so elegant became unsafe and were removed gradually over the 20 years after this photograph was taken. This area looks much different today. (Courtesy of the McClaren Collection, Darwin R. Barker Museum.)

IMAGES of America

POMFRET

Todd Langworthy

ARCADIA PUBLISHING

ISBN 978-0-7385-5547-8

Published by Arcadia Publishing
Charleston SC, Chicago IL, Portsmouth NH, San Francisco CA

Printed in the United States of America

Library of Congress Catalog Card Number: 207933084

For all general information contact Arcadia Publishing at:
Telephone 843-853-2070
Fax 843-853-0044
E-mail sales@arcadiapublishing.com
For customer service and orders:
Toll-Free 1-888-313-2665

Visit us on the Internet at www.arcadiapublishing.com

This book is dedicated to the citizens of the town of Pomfret and the Pomfret Town Board, who are celebrating the town's bicentennial in 2008. This book is also dedicated to my wife, Judy, and my children, Maitland and Travis. Thank you and I hope you enjoy the book.

Contents

ACKNOWLEDGMENTS

For the creation of this book, I needed to utilize photographs from others, as I have very few of my own concerning our town history. Thus I spent a great deal of time scrutinizing collections from a number of sources in the area. First, I wish to extend my sincere gratitude to curator Nancy Brown and her staff at the Darwin R. Barker Museum in Fredonia. The museum's McClaren Collection and the Mason Collection formed the basis for this book. Without their help, I could not have completed this project in any way. I also wish to thank archivist Jeremy Linden from the archives and special collections department at the Daniel A. Reed Library at the State University of New York College at Fredonia. He helped me construct a pictorial history of the schools in our town, which includes the university campus. Special thanks also go to Mary Benner for helping me research a number of photographs in chapters 1 and 3. I would also like to thank the Chautauqua County Historical Society and James O'Brien, as well as Ellen Schwanekamp and the McClurg Museum in Westfield for the use of a number of unique photographs that I included in this book. The photographs in their collections made this book much more interesting and I am deeply grateful for the ability to use them. My sincere thanks also go out to Andrea Andrews and Dale Mirth from Brookside Manor Bed and Breakfast for the photographs of their wonderful establishment and the history of the surrounding area. I would be remiss not to thank my editor Tiffany Howe and the staff at Arcadia Publishing for taking on my project and being such a great help in making this book come to fruition. Finally I wish to thank three members of my family that are members of the historical society in Sheridan, Richard and Mary Langworthy and Traci Langworthy. Without the help and encouragement of my parents and sister, I would not be half of the historian I am today. Thanks to all and I hope the book meets with your approval.

—Todd Langworthy

Introduction

The town of Pomfret was part of the Holland Land Company purchase from Robert Morris in 1791. By 1800, a number of settlers had begun buying plots of land near where the town is located today. Eventually one settler, Zattu Cushing, came to the area to purchase land and make his permanent home. He has since been recognized as the founder of the town. The story of how Cushing came to know about the area and decide to settle in it is one of the most exciting in the town's history.

In 1795, Cushing married Rachel Buckingham in Saratoga County. Cushing was born in Plymouth, Massachusetts, and learned the trades of shipbuilding and farming from his father, Nathaniel. In 1799, Cushing took a job supervising the building of a ship in Presque Isle (Erie, Pennsylvania). The ship was called the *Good Intent* and was said to be the first large ship built on Lake Erie. On his way home from Presque Isle, Cushing traveled through the area and stayed overnight near Canadaway Creek in what later became Fredonia. He was impressed by the land and vowed to return and settle in the area with his family as soon as he was able. That time came in February 1805, when Cushing and his family made the journey to the area from their home in Oneida County. Upon arrival, he found that Thomas McClintock had already taken the land he wanted to buy, so he settled in a log cabin near the mouth of the Canadaway Creek that had been partially built by Low Minegar the previous year. By the fall of 1807, Cushing had cleared about 50 acres in the area of the mouth of the creek. At this time, he was able to sell this land and buy the land he had originally wanted from McClintock. Cushing built his house and barn on the new land, located near the Canadaway Creek at what is now 171 Eagle Street. The young town flourished in the first two decades, with many settlers coming from the east to establish new homes. Many of these prominent settlers are described in chapter 1.

With growth came the birth of a village that was called Fredonia. The name seems to have come from the idea that the new village needed to have a sophisticated, European-inspired name that would attract the best settlers to the area. So the old name Canadaway that had Native American origins was replaced with the name Fredonia. The village was officially recognized in 1829. Many famous individuals visited Fredonia, including the Marquis de Lafayette in 1825, Mark Twain, and many others. By the beginning of the 20th century, the town of Pomfret had become a bustling center for education, the arts, and commerce.

Much of the growth during the 20th century was attributed to education with the emergence of the Fredonia Normal School, which eventually grew into what is today the State University of New York College at Fredonia. Education spawned further growth in commerce and an appreciation of the arts fueled by facilities such as the Fredonia Opera House. Pomfret's proximity to Chautauqua Institution, Buffalo, Jamestown, and Lake Erie made it a favorite stop of many travelers who wished to visit the famous little town and take in some of the beautiful scenery and special events. Even through the Great Depression, Pomfret survived and flourished when many other small towns began to fade. It is the special quality of the town of Pomfret that allowed it to survive and even prosper when other towns nearly vanished.

It is impossible to guess what plans Zattu Cushing had for the town 200 years ago. Did he simply hope the town would attract a few good settlers and become a village, or did he want Pomfret to achieve greatness and notoriety like his boyhood home of Plymouth, Massachusetts? As the town celebrates its bicentennial in 2008, Cushing would likely be very happy with how things turned out in the little spot he picked out to raise his family. As the county's first judge, Cushing became famous for his excellence in making fair decisions in a court of law. It is hoped that readers will enjoy this brief glimpse into the town's past and feel encouraged to learn more about what the town has accomplished and what it might accomplish in the future.

One

Famous Fredonians

As the town of Pomfret grew in the early years, the village of Fredonia was born within that town. Fredonia attracted many talented individuals that became permanent residents and contributed a great deal to its history. Many of these individuals became famous regionally and sometimes nationally. On the following pages are just a few of the people that have achieved notoriety throughout history as famous Fredonians.

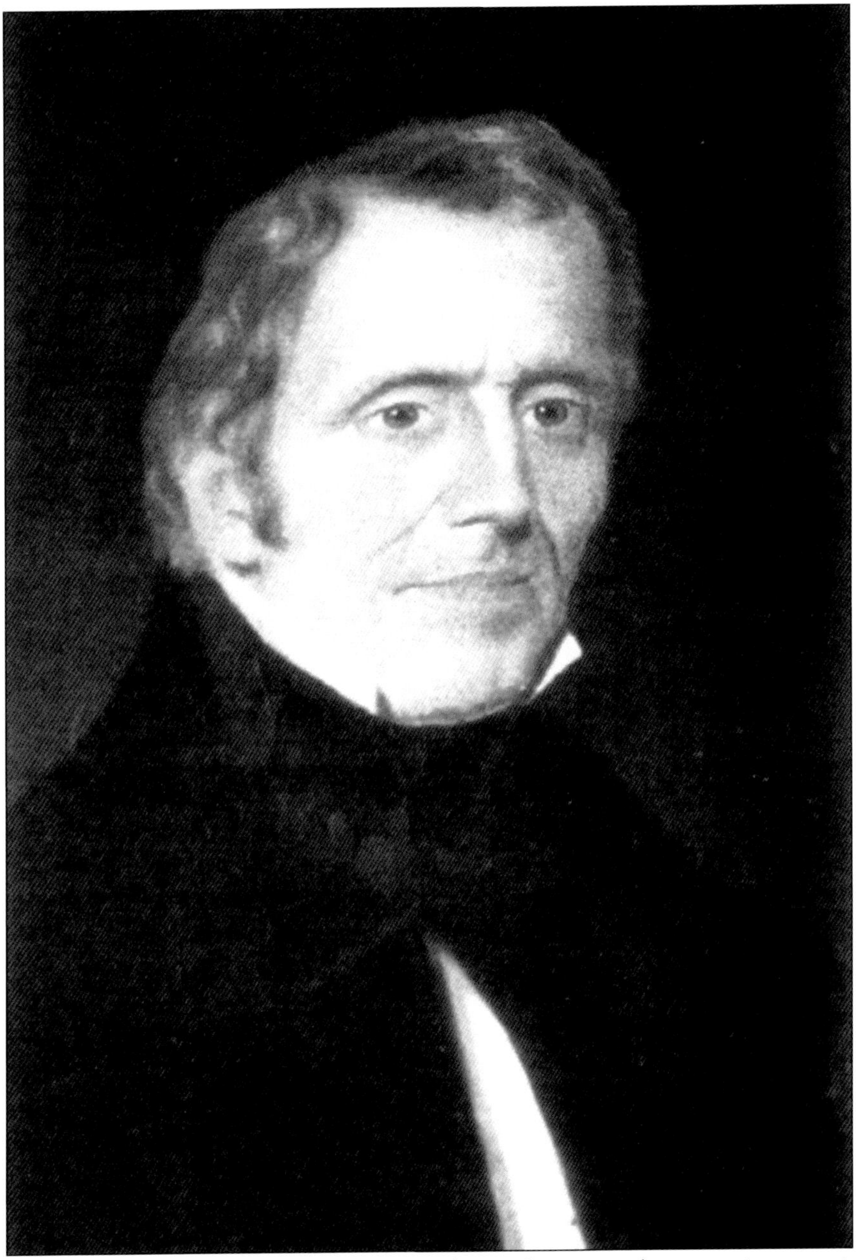

Zattu Cushing was a man who possessed outstanding judgment and courage in every situation he encountered. As the first permanent settler in Pomfret, Cushing became the leader of the young community in the early years. Settlers looked up to him as a man they could both count on and trust. Those qualities served him well as Chautauqua County's first judge in 1811. This is a portrait of Cushing that today hangs in the Chautauqua County courtroom. Throughout the history of Chautauqua County, judges have heard difficult cases in the county capital of Mayville, just as Cushing did in the early years. The portrait has served as a reminder that even a person without professional training such as Cushing is capable of being a good judge if they stick to the facts and use the sound intellect that brought them to the service of the people in the first place.

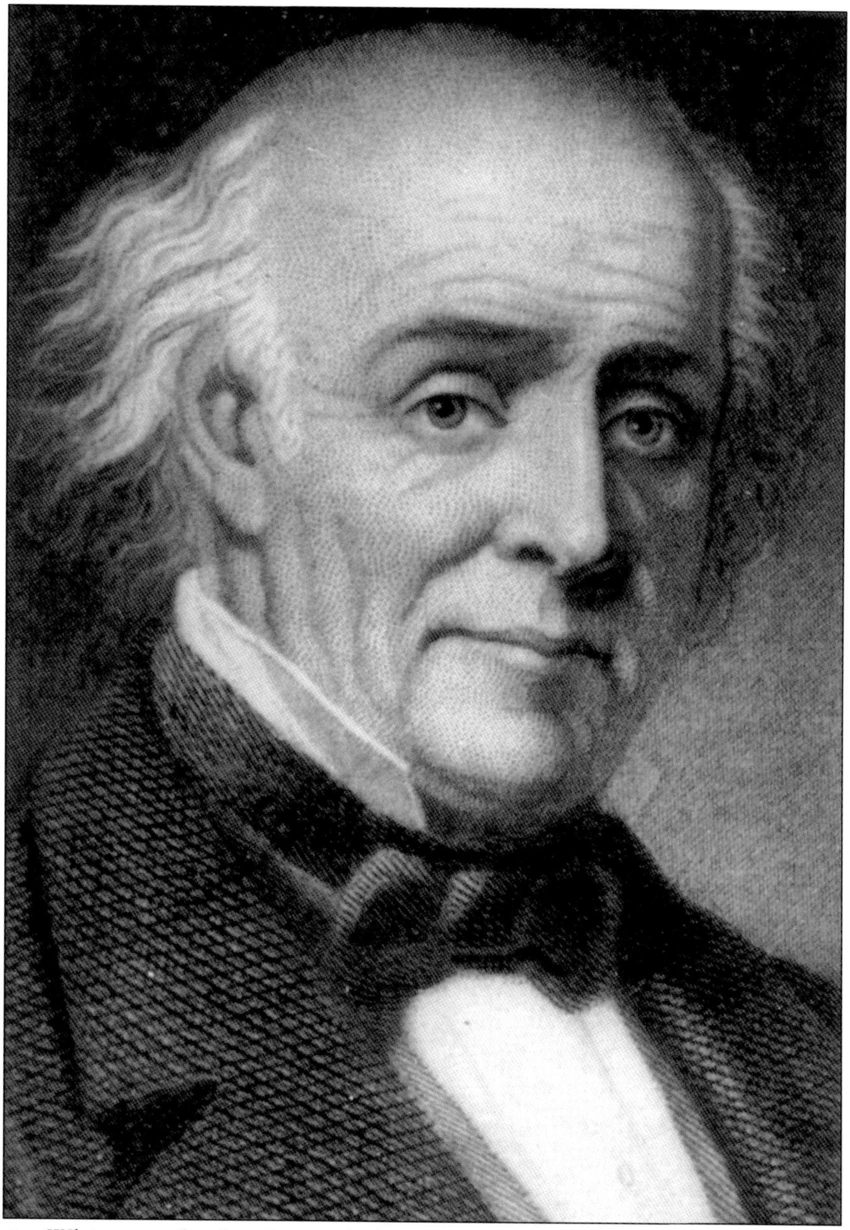

Dr. Squire White was the first licensed physician in Chautauqua County, having settled in Pomfret in 1809 after a brief stint as a teacher in the neighboring town of Sheridan. White immediately became an important part of the young community. He married Hezekiah Barker's daughter Sarah in 1813 and had four children before her untimely death in 1823. White later married Cushing's daughter Lydia and had three children with her. White was very active in the community, serving as town supervisor in 1838 and 1839. He purchased 25 acres of land from Barker, his father-in-law, at the corner of what is today Main and White Streets. On that site, White built a beautiful home that was eventually demolished years after his death in 1857. White's son Devillo constructed a new home on this original site and lived in it for 45 years. In 1919, White's granddaughter Isabelle White sold the home that is now known as the White Inn Hotel and Restaurant.

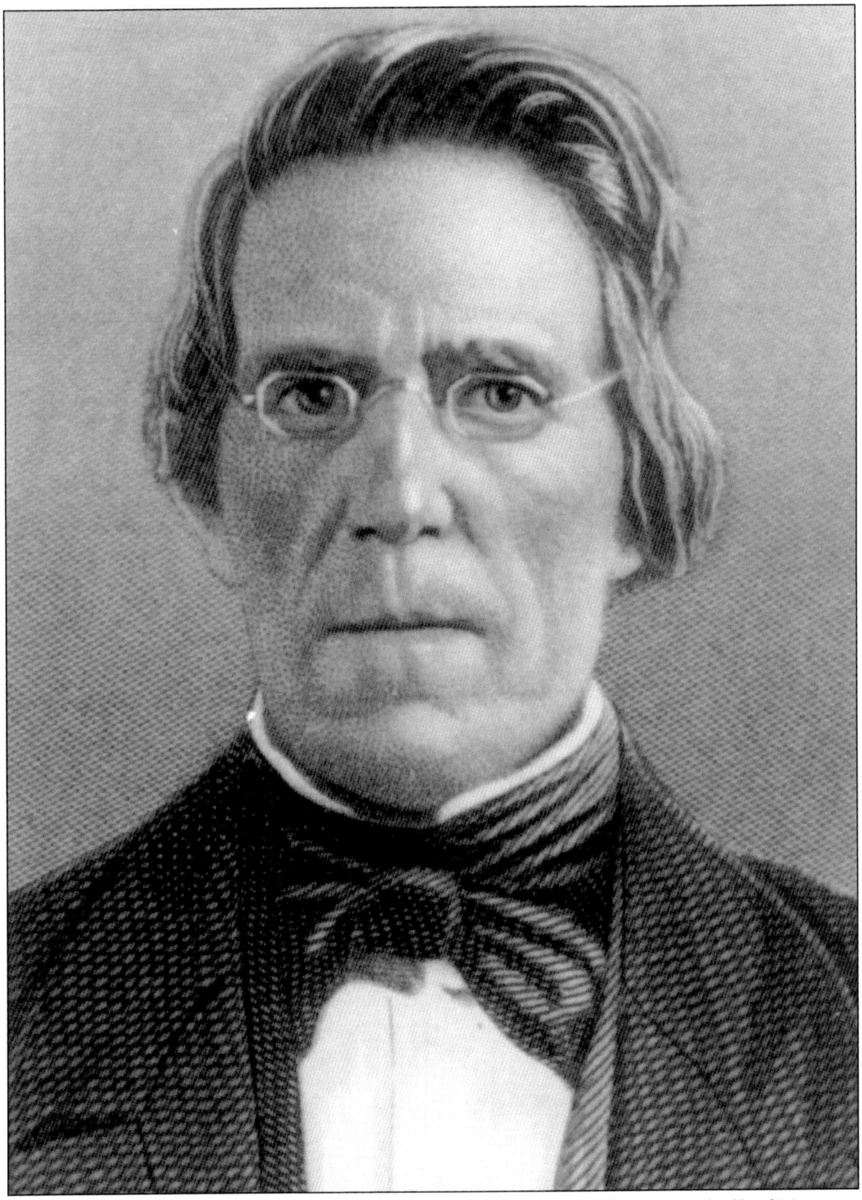

Thomas G. Abell was the son of one of the town's first settlers, Thomas Abell of Vermont, who came here in 1813. The elder Abell was a Revolutionary War veteran, having fought in the battles of Bennington and Fort Ticonderoga. Thomas G. purchased the land where the Russo building now stands and built a hotel that faced the commons. The hotel was later known as Johnson House, Taylor House, and eventually the Columbia Hotel. Thomas G. was also involved in bringing the first stagecoach service to Chautauqua County with the hope of enhancing his hotel business. He was also interested in education, serving as one of the founders of Fredonia Academy. Thomas G. was the builder of the house that is currently the Larson-Timko Funeral Home on Central Avenue. As with many of the early prominent families, the Abell family was related through marriages to other founding families. Most noteworthy was the fact that Thomas G.'s granddaughter was Katherine Cushing, wife of William Barker Cushing, the grandson of Zattu Cushing.

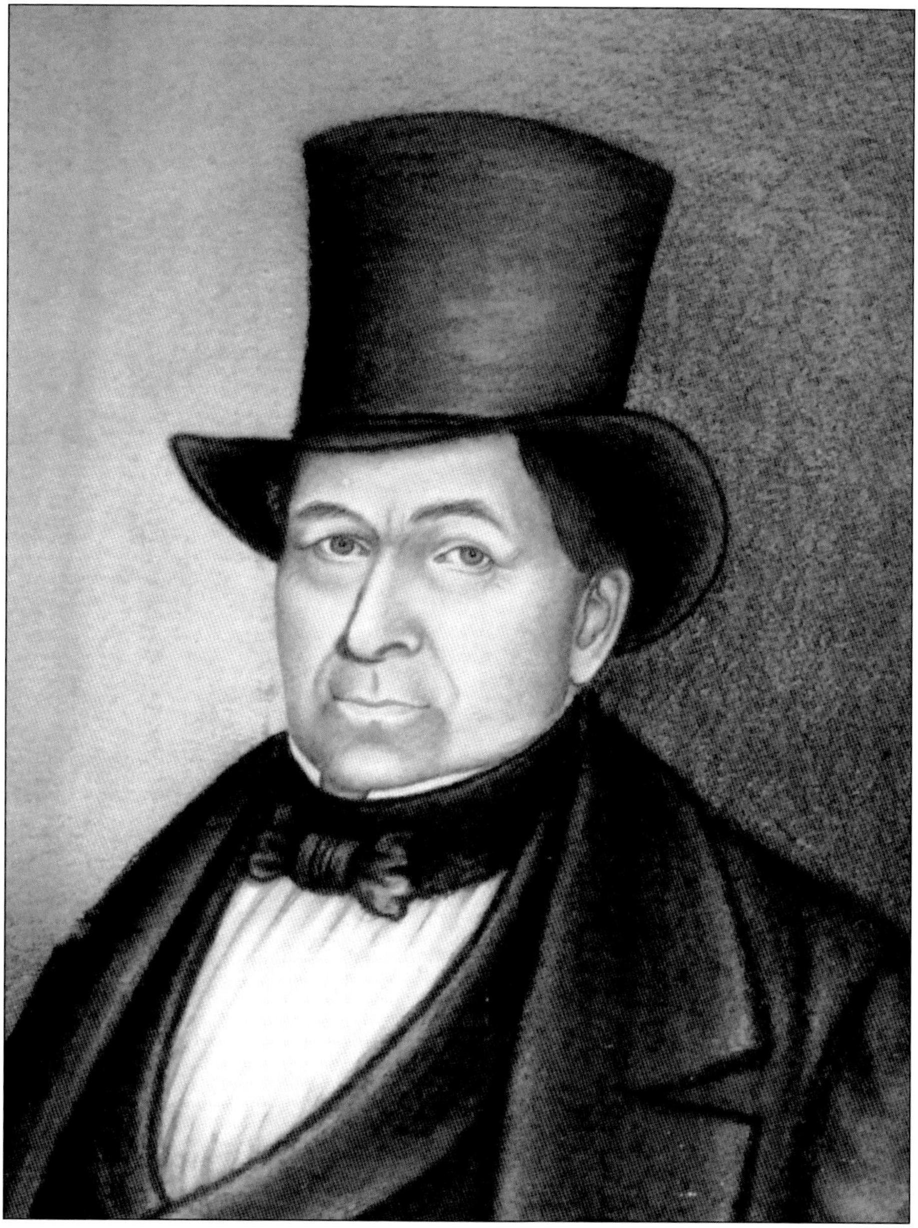

Leverett Barker came to Pomfret in 1809 with Squire White and became another important member of the early community. In 1811, Barker married Desire Barker, who was the daughter of Hezekiah Barker. The two Barker families were not related prior to the marriage. Leverett was a tanner and currier by trade, so upon his arrival, he proceeded to set up his own tannery on Main Street, which became very successful. He also became involved in the community and served as town supervisor for seven years. He was active in the state militia, rising eventually to the rank of major general of the 26th Infantry Division. He also built a beautiful brick home on the corner of Main and Day Streets in 1821. This home was eventually given to the community by his son Darwin R. Barker to be used as a library beginning in 1884. Today the home has become the Darwin R. Barker Museum, with a connection to the newly constructed library in the rear of the home.

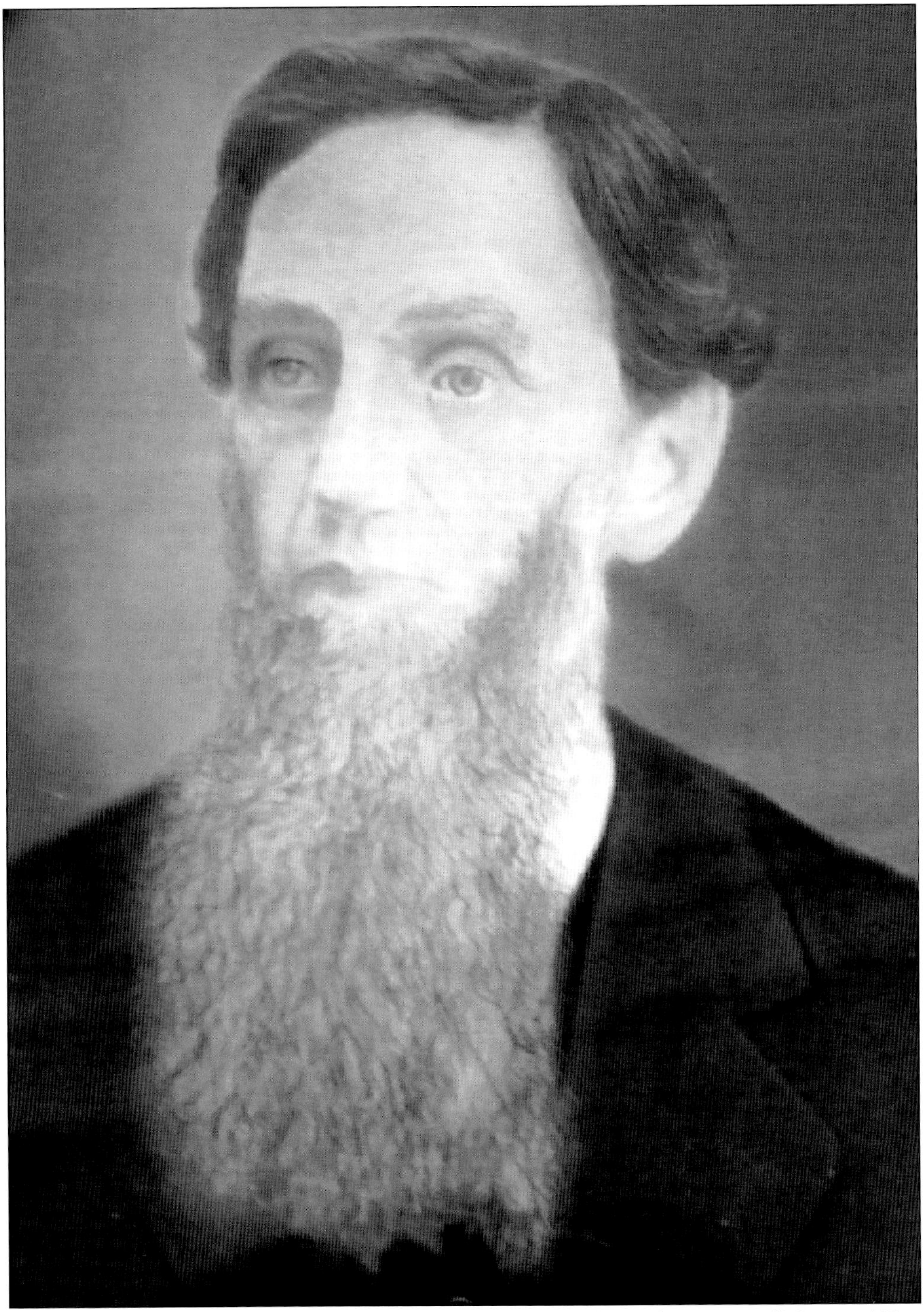

Darwin R. Barker donated the house his father, Leverett, built on the corner of Main and Day Streets to the community to be used as a library. The only stipulation was that the portraits of his parents always be hung in the front room above the mantle. They are still displayed there today as part of the Victorian parlor re-creation.

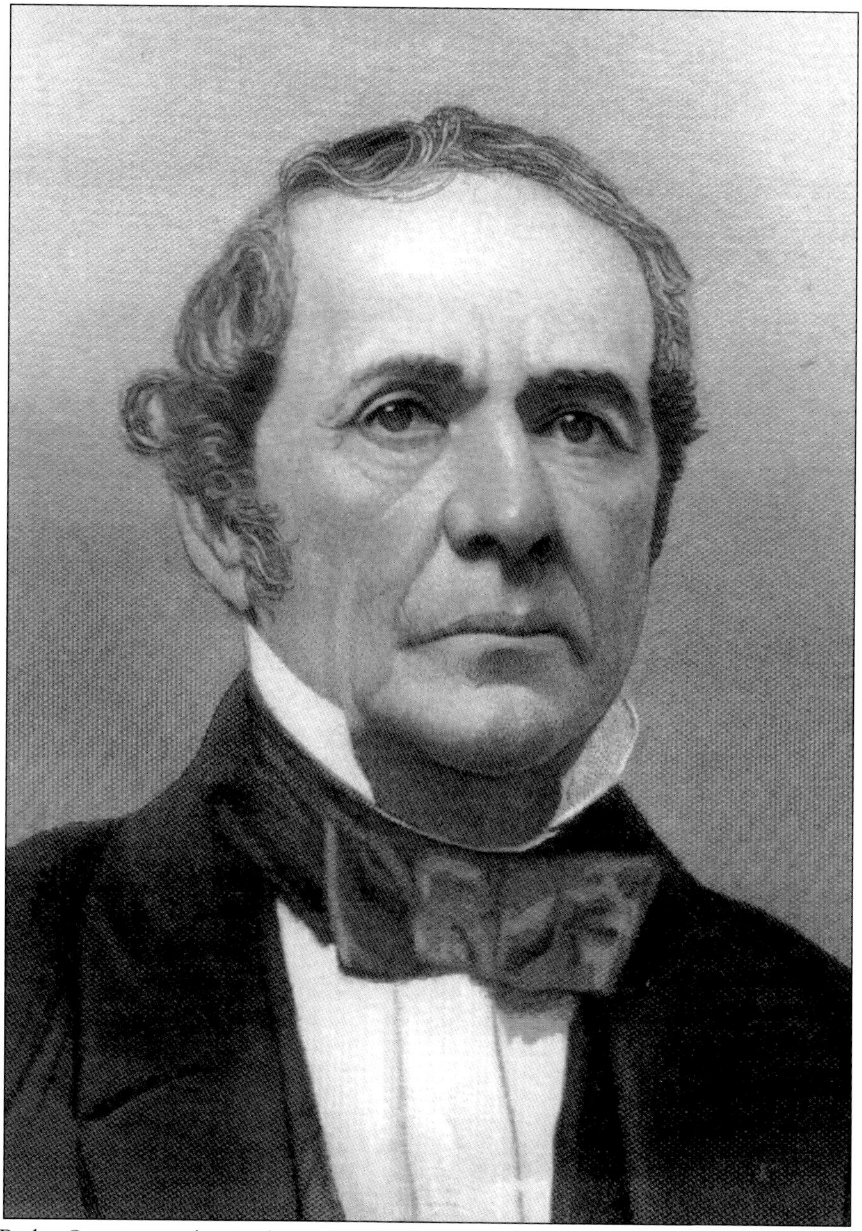

Elijah Risley Sr. was another early settler who had a profound impact on the young community. He was a Revolutionary War veteran with the rank of major general. He built a modest home near the top of West Main Hill at what is today the entrance to Berry Road. In his first few years in Pomfret, Risley built a gristmill and sawmill on the western bank of Canadaway Creek. These businesses helped the community grow very quickly as they attracted both commerce and new settlers to the area from many miles away. Risley also had three sons, Elijah Jr., William, and Levi, who lived in the area where today Risley Street remains and had a major impact on the town's future. The brothers were active in business, with Elijah Jr. opening a store in town that made him the first merchant in Chautauqua County. The three brothers also became known for their Risley Brothers Seed business that gained them fame and fortune throughout the northeastern United States.

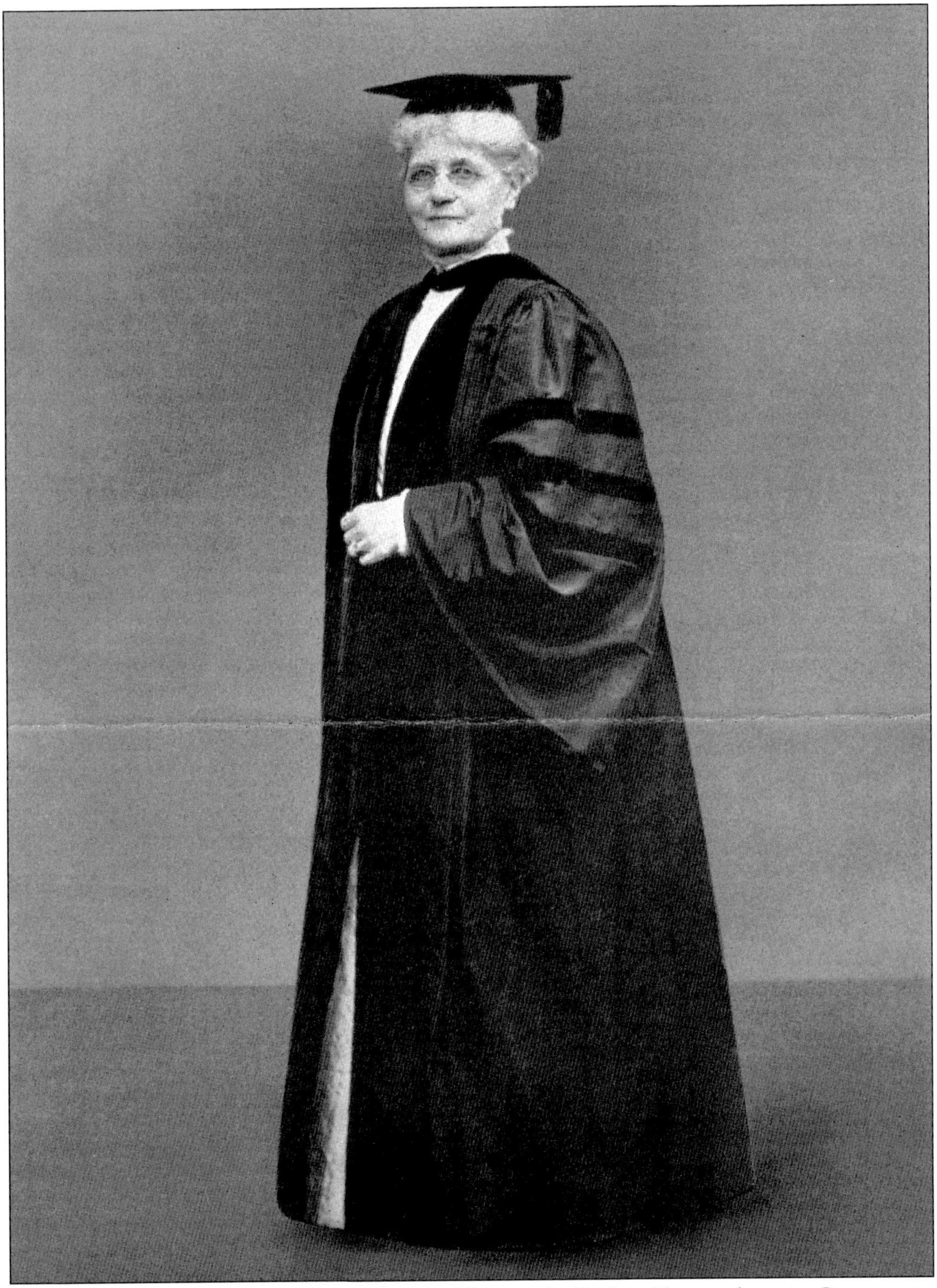

Dr. Emilie Jones Barker was the second wife of Darwin R. Barker. She was born in Germany in 1840, 20 years after her future husband was born in Pomfret. She was a graduate of Wellesley College in 1886 and the first female physician there. She passed away on October 8, 1941, in Sacramento, California.

Hon. George Barker was one of a number of highly respected judges from Pomfret in the 19th century. He moved to Fredonia to establish his law practice shortly after being admitted to the bar. He served as president of the village for two terms and was elected justice of the New York State Supreme Court for the eighth judicial district in 1867.

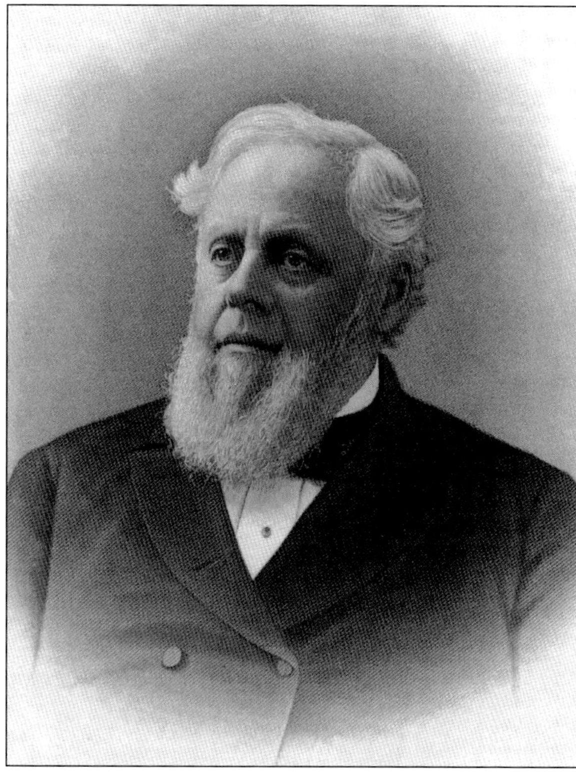

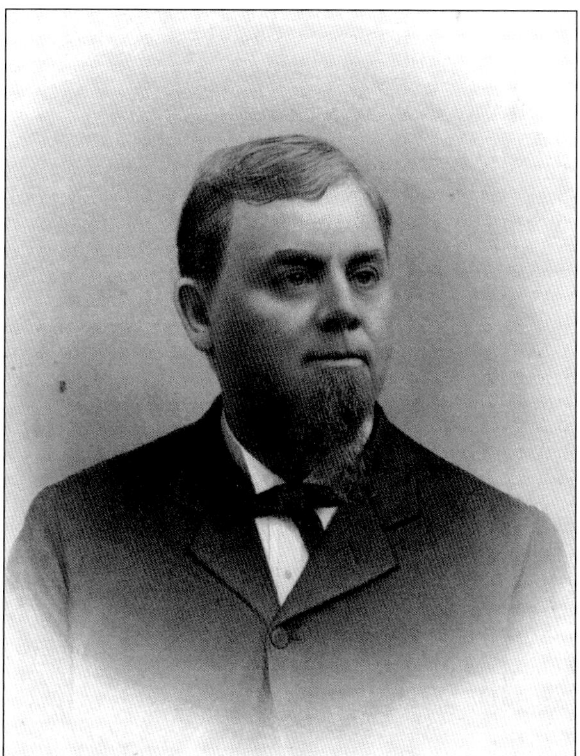

Milton M. Fenner volunteered for service in the Union army at the beginning of the Civil War and rose through the ranks very quickly. He eventually became assistant surgeon of the navy in 1864. In 1869, He opened his practice in Fredonia. Eventually a remedy known as Fenner's Golden Relief was sold all over the eastern United States, making him one of the wealthiest town residents.

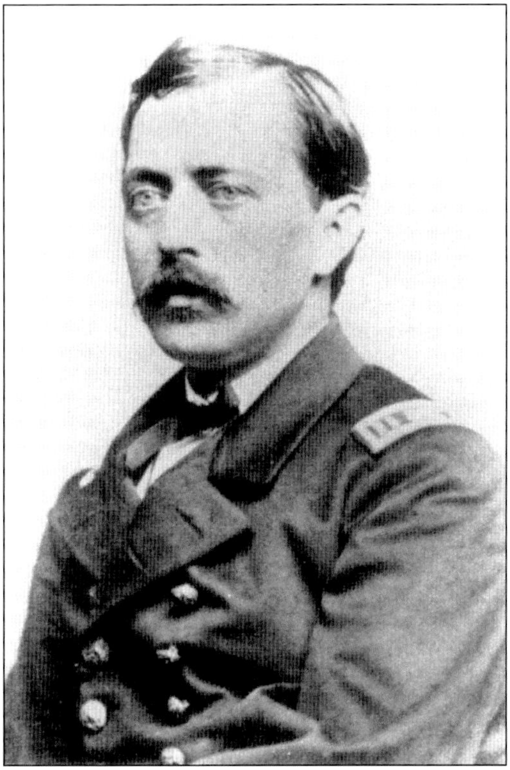

Milton Buckingham Cushing Jr. was the oldest son of Milton Buckingham Cushing Sr. and Mary Barker Cushing. His grandfather was Pomfret's first settler, Zattu Cushing. Milton was trained to be a pharmacist but eventually joined the navy and was assigned to the department of the navy's office in Washington, where he served throughout the Civil War. He passed away on January 4, 1887, in Dunkirk.

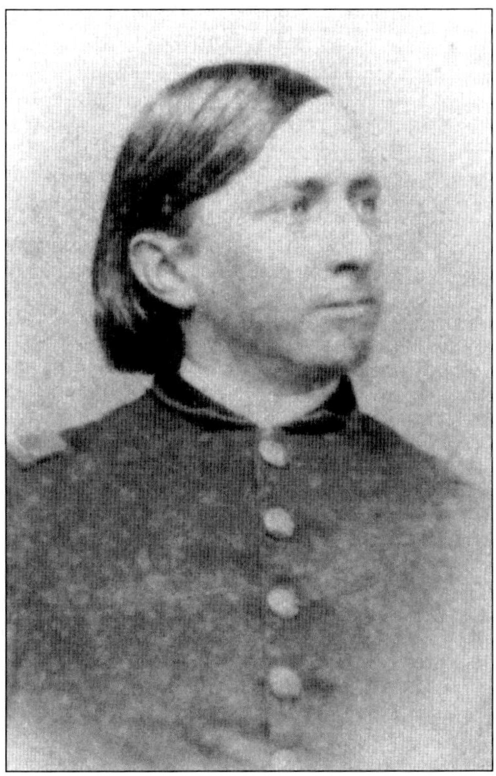

Howard Bass Cushing was the second oldest of the four boys born to Milton and Mary. Shortly after the start of the war, Howard joined Battery B of the First Illinois Light Artillery. He was killed by the Apache in a battle in Arizona in May 1871. He is buried in Arizona.

Alonzo Hereford Cushing was the second youngest of Zattu's four grandsons that served in the Civil War. Alonzo graduated from West Point in June 1861 and began his active duty the following month. He was the commander of Battery A, 4th U.S. Artillery during most of the major engagements in the eastern theater during the first two years of the war. During the Battle of Gettysburg on July 3, 1863, he was the defender of "the angle," which was the objective of the confederate attack named Pickett's Charge. During the last moments of the charge, he was wounded three times before falling dead at the last of his unit's operational guns. His body was taken from the field by his oldest brother Milton and transported to West Point where he was buried on July 12, 1863.

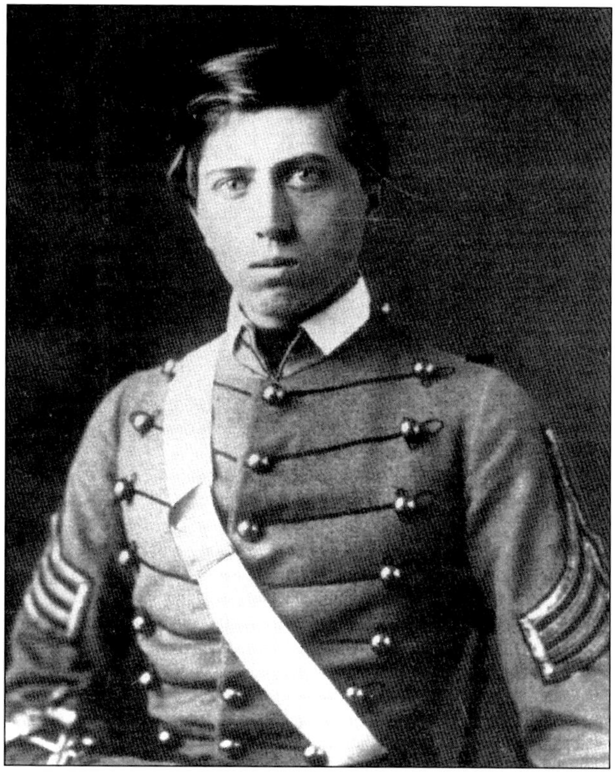

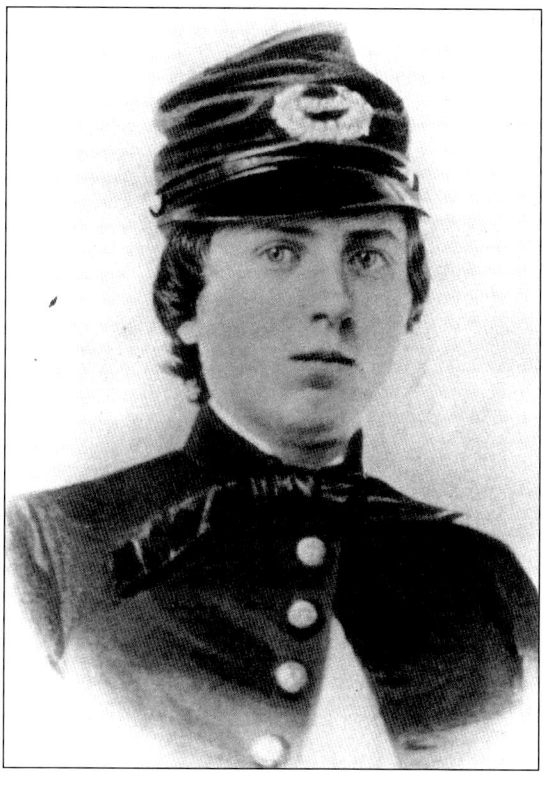

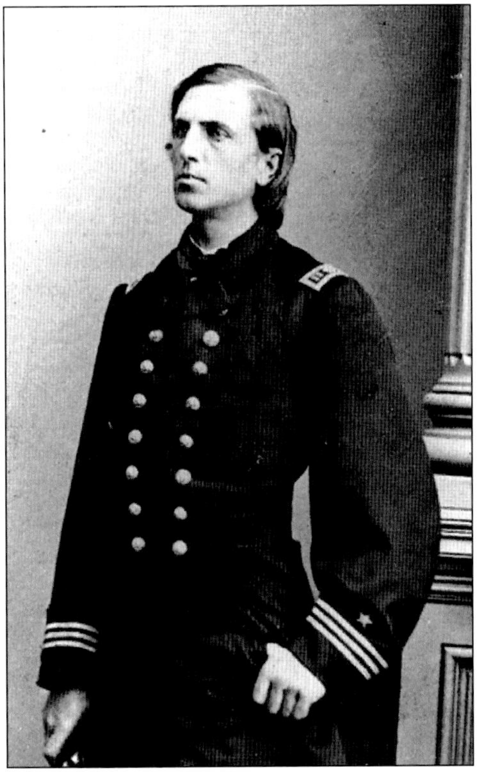

William Barker Cushing was the youngest of the four grandsons of Zattu to serve in the Civil War. In 1857, he entered the U.S. Naval Academy in September as the youngest cadet at age 14. His behavior often brought him problems at the academy until he was eventually forced to resign a few weeks before the start of the Civil War. Secretary of the Navy Gideon Wells saw something in the brash youth and granted his request for an appointment in the U.S. Volunteer Navy after his resignation from the academy. He was given an assignment in the summer of 1864 to devise a plan to sink the CSS *Albemarle*, a new ironclad ship stationed in North Carolina. On the evening of October 27, 1864, he led his group of volunteers up the Roanoke River to attack it. He attacked the ship and detonated a torpedo under the wooden hull, sinking it. Shortly after the successful attack, he was promoted to the rank of lieutenant commander in a letter written by Pres. Abraham Lincoln.

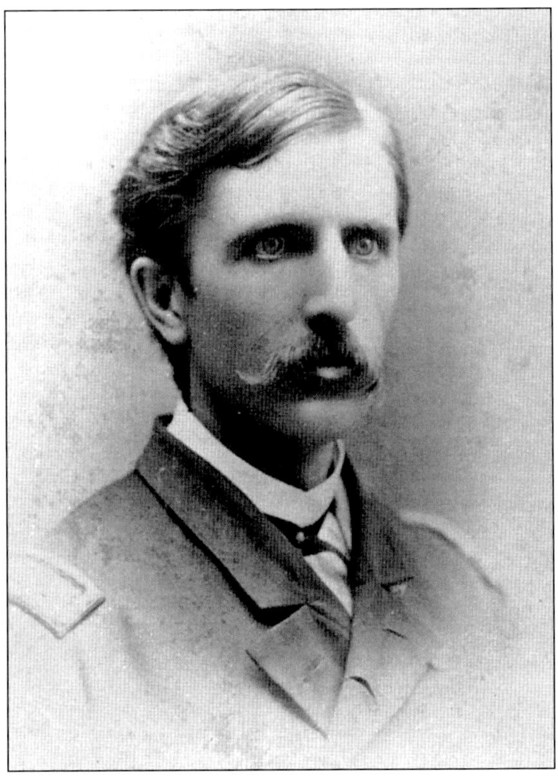

Katherine Louise (Kate) Forbes Cushing met Civil War hero William Barker Cushing when he was home on leave after the war. He was very taken with the girl who became his wife on February 22, 1870. His duties in the navy kept him away from home most of the time in the years after the war. After his death in 1874, she remained at home and never remarried.

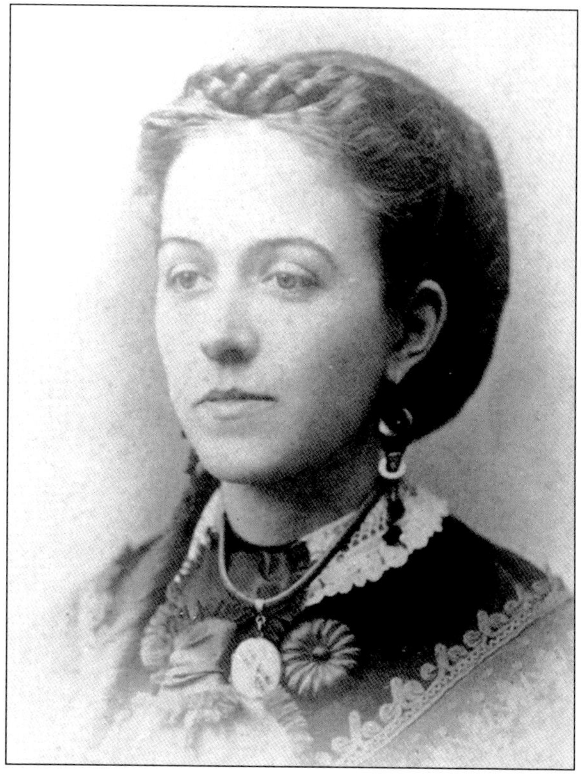

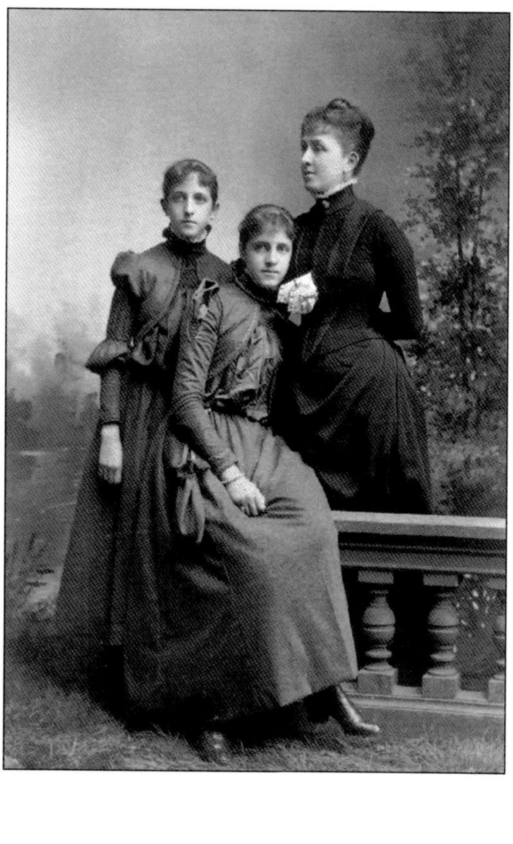

This photograph shows Kate Cushing with daughters Katherine and Louise while living in Fredonia years after William's death. The Cushing women were very proud of the accomplishments of their husband and father. Katherine and Louise remained in Fredonia, never marrying. The girls both became teachers and taught in Fredonia for many years into the 20th century.

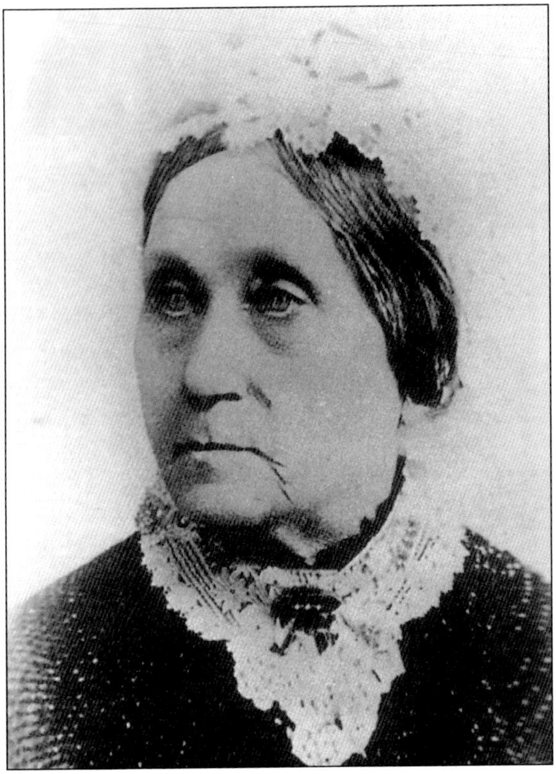

Mary Barker Cushing was the wife of Dr. Milton Buckingham Cushing Sr. and the mother of Milton Jr., Howard, Alonzo, and William. Mary worked extremely hard to support her family when she brought them back to Fredonia in 1847 after her husband's death. She operated a small nursery school in her home to pay the bills, while the boys worked odd jobs to assist in making ends meet.

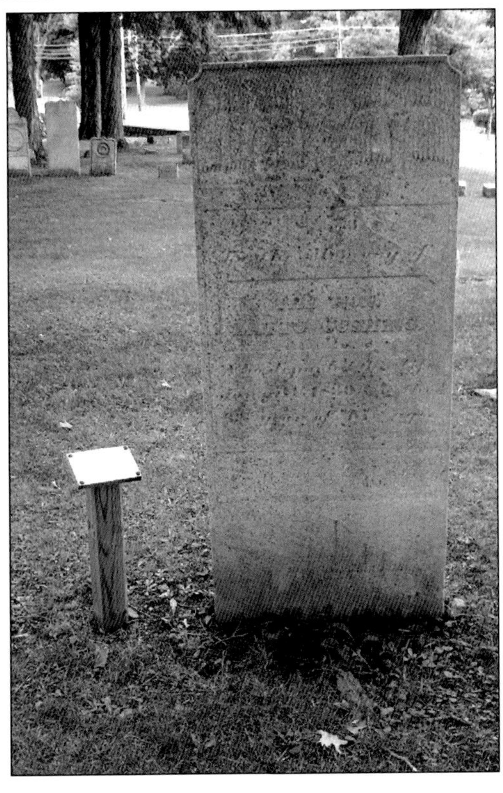

This photograph of Zattu Cushing's grave has been under discussion in recent years. There is currently a project underway in the town to repair many of the gravestones in the Pioneer Cemetery, where this grave is located.

Philip Phillips Sr. was born in Stockton on August 13, 1834. Phillips was known to have a unique musical ability at an early age, according to his choir teachers in Cassadaga. He eventually studied music and became a famous singer of gospel songs, traveling throughout the world. He became known as the "singing pilgrim," achieving fame by performing the song "Your Mission" in Washington for Pres. Abraham Lincoln in 1865.

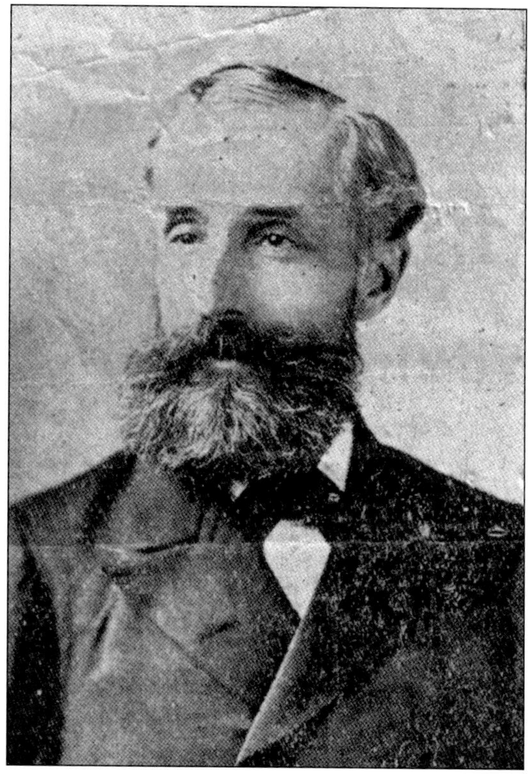

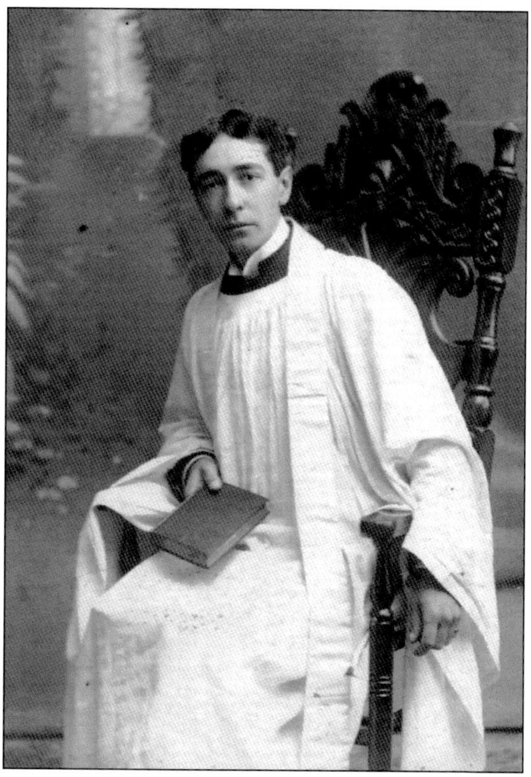

Philip Phillips Jr. also had an extraordinary talent for music and a love of gospel. He was the youngest son of Philip Phillips Sr., having graduated from Ohio Wesleyan University in 1890. He entered the ministry of the Methodist Episcopal Church and published *Our New Hymnal* with his famous father in 1894.

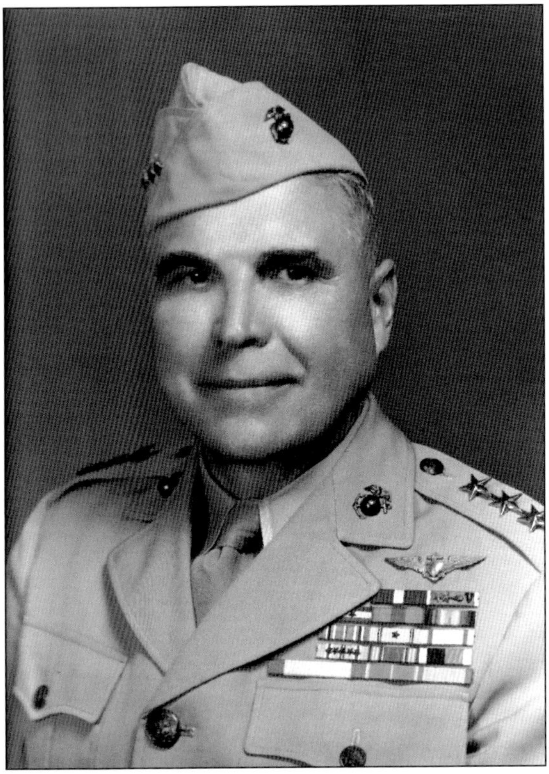

Lt. Gen. Louis E. Woods, who enlisted in the U.S. Marine Corps in April 1917, served throughout World War I on the USS *Georgia* and the USS *Pittsburgh*. During his famous career in World War II, Woods was promoted to brigadier general in 1942 and awarded the Distinguished Service Cross for his leadership in the Battle of Guadalcanal. In 1944, he was promoted to major general and received the Legion of Merit award.

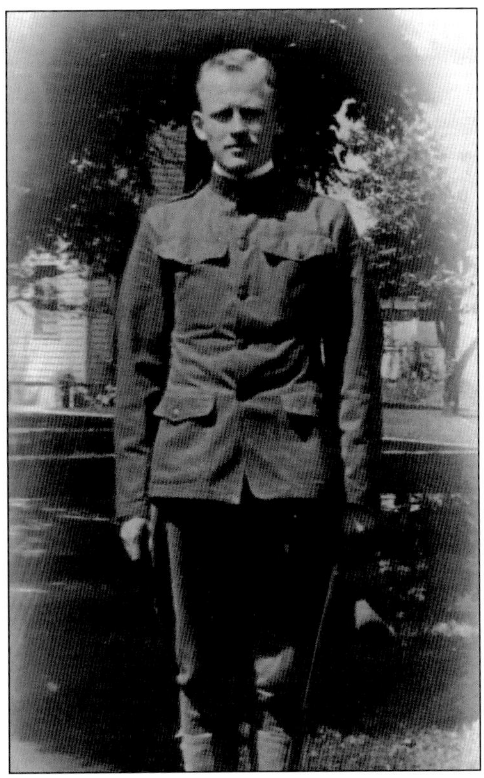

Like many young men in 1917, 1st Lt. Jack Wilder was anxious to get to Europe to defeat the Germans in World War I. This photograph was taken just before he left for France on August 12, 1917, in front of his home at 194 Temple Street. He was killed in Tours, France, on August 19, 1918. He is buried at Arlington National Cemetery in Arlington, Virginia.

Lorenzo Morris was a prominent attorney who moved to Fredonia in 1852 after practicing law for a brief time in Mayville. Morris was active in the state militia, reaching the rank of colonel before resigning in 1842. In 1868, he was elected as a democratic state senator for the 26th district. He was very active in the workings of the state normal schools while in the senate, eventually becoming president of the board of trustees of the Fredonia Normal School in 1873. At the beginning of the 20th century, he lived at 67 East Main Street.

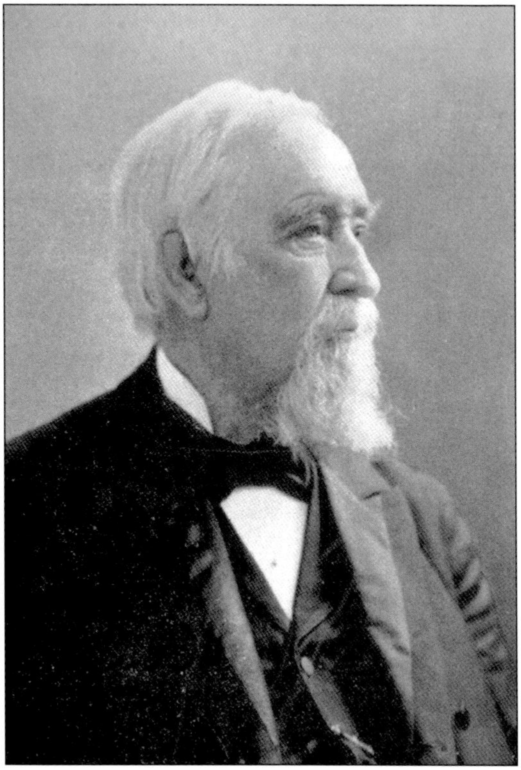

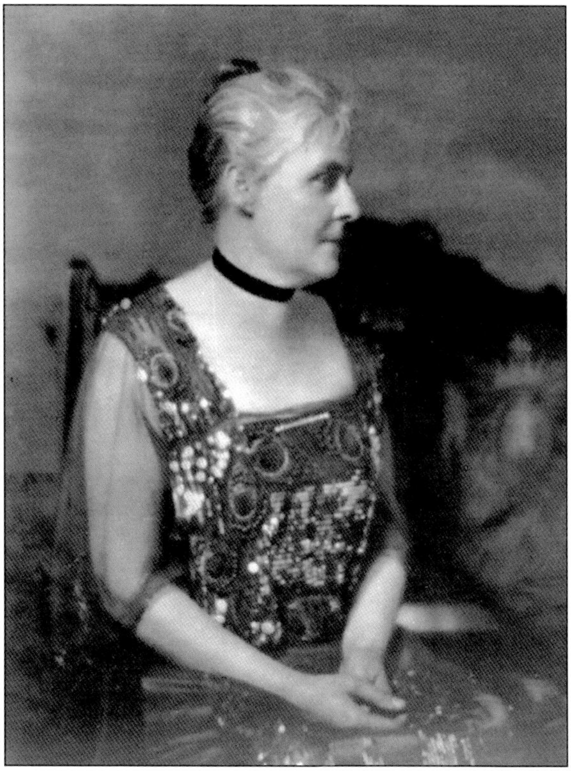

Winifred Lambert was the wife of John Lambert, the daughter of Williston Phillips, and the niece of Philip Phillips Sr. Like her uncle, she was known locally as an extremely talented musician who possessed a lovely soprano voice. Her husband, John, was a former state supreme court justice. This photograph was taken in 1937, and it shows a startling resemblance to her cousin Philip Phillips Jr.

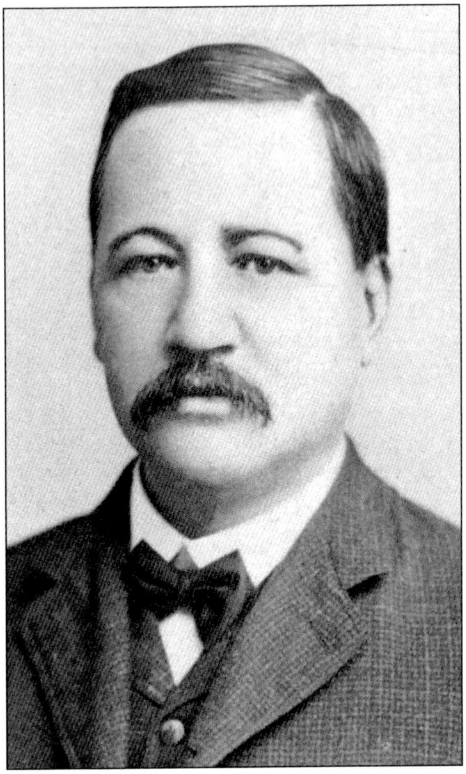

Henry Leworthy came to Fredonia in 1875 and entered the Fredonia Normal School. He had roots in Europe, where his great-grandfather fought under Arthur Wellesley, Duke of Wellington, at the Battle of Waterloo. Leworthy was known as an astute businessman, having opened the Belden and Leworthy store in 1890 with his partner, Bert Belden. Leworthy was very active in the community and in the Methodist Episcopal Church.

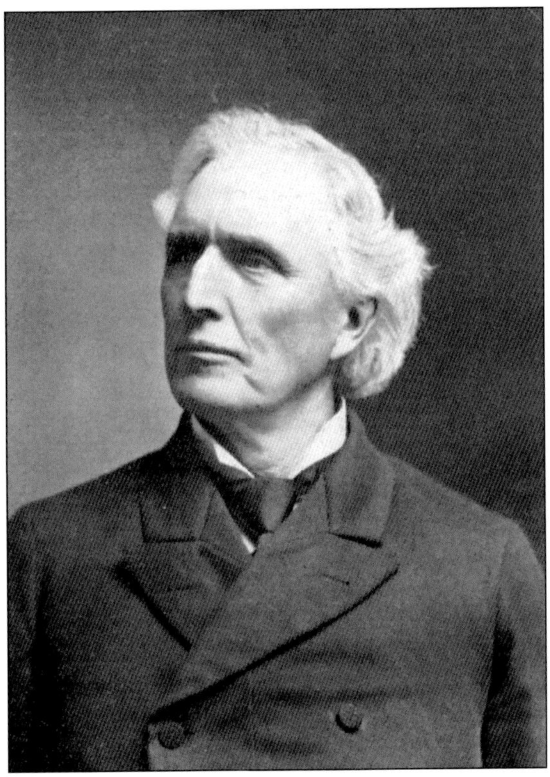

Dr. Darius G. Pickett was born in Stockton on December 9, 1841. He graduated from Buffalo University in 1874 and practiced medicine in Stockton until he moved to Fredonia in 1885. His home and office were located at what was then known as 42 West Main Street. He was very interested in politics, having been the Town of Stockton's supervisor before moving to Fredonia. He was the Town of Pomfret's supervisor in 1891 and a member of the village board in 1892 and 1893. He was also involved in a number of profitable business ventures involving the providing of waterpower from Canadaway Creek and its tributaries.

Charles L. Mark was born in Fredonia on August 12, 1822. He attended the Fredonia Academy until 1837. He was engaged in a very successful mercantile business in town as well as the manufacture of pot and pearl ashes. He was a member of the board of mangers of the state normal school starting in 1877. He also made sizeable donations to the Darwin R. Barker Library and the village. His greatest gift to the community was the two fountains that currently adorn Barker Commons, having been donated in 1901 and maintained ever since.

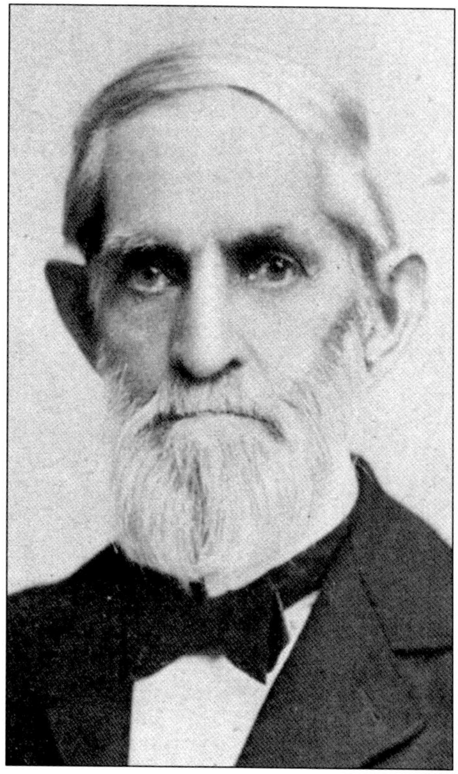

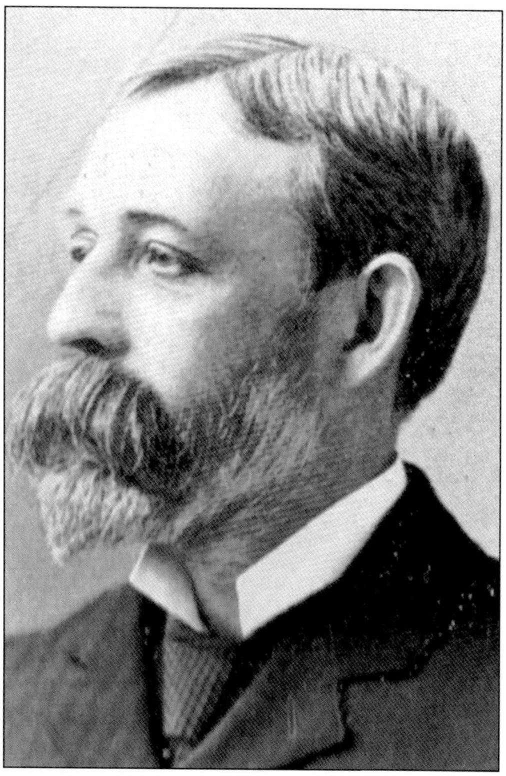

Mark's son Dr. Edward Mark was born in Fredonia on May 30, 1847. Edward attended the Fredonia Academy until he was 20 years old and then the University of Michigan. He then studied in Germany before returning to accept a position at Harvard University to be the chairman of the zoological department there. One of his most famous and enthusiastic students was future president Theodore Roosevelt.

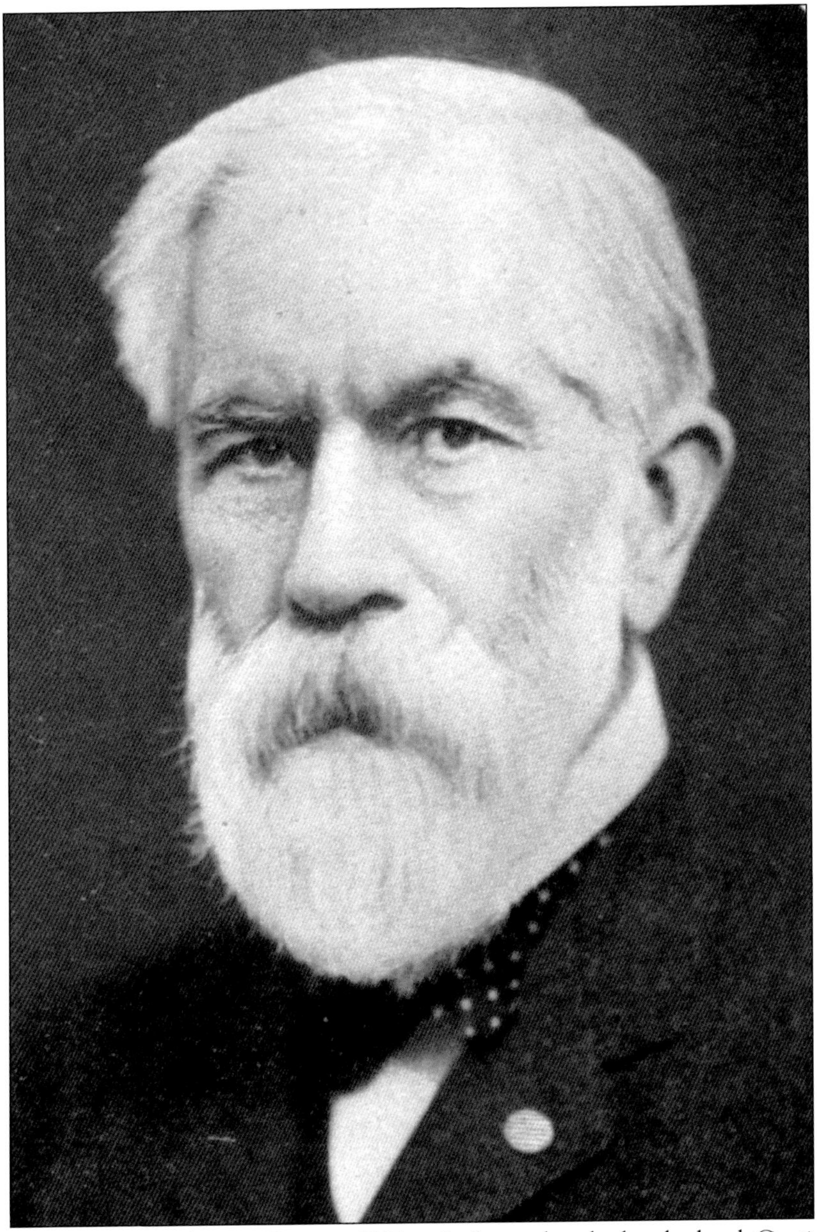

Maj. Enoch A. Curtis was born in Busti in 1831 and educated at the local school. Curtis realized as a young man that he enjoyed and had a talent for building, and he pursued it. In the spring of 1862, he enlisted in the Union army and was elected captain of Company D, 112th New York Volunteers. His bravery was evident in a number of battles but no more so than the Battle of Cold Harbor, where he was seriously wounded on June 1, 1864. Upon his discharge, he proceeded to set up his residence in the growing village of Fredonia. After a few years as a successful businessman in the mercantile business, Curtis decided to pursue his old dream of becoming an architect. A few of his designs include the Fredonia Village Hall, the Gate House and chapel at Forest Hill Cemetery, the Columbia Hotel (current site of the Russo building), the old Brooks Hospital, the Pavilion at Point Gratiot (which burned), and many private residences, including the Horace White home.

Two

Early Schools and the State University of New York College at Fredonia

Education has always been an important part of life in Pomfret. From the early log cabin schools to Fredonia Academy's opening in 1826, children in Pomfret had access to a solid education in the early years. The Fredonia Normal School that began in 1867 was a stepping-stone to bigger and better opportunities that manifested themselves in the establishment of the State University of New York (SUNY) College at Fredonia. SUNY Fredonia survives today as the legacy of the importance of education to the town's early settlers.

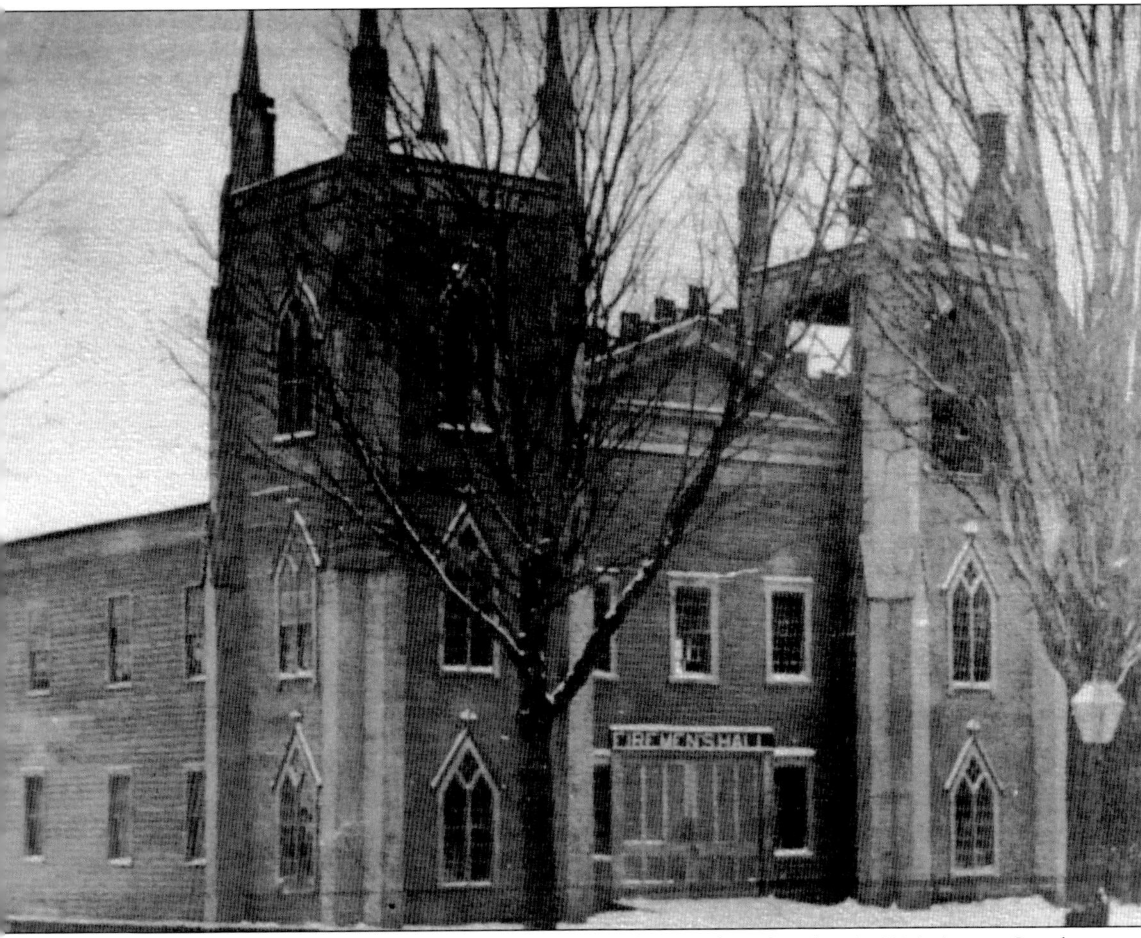

The Fredonia Academy was incorporated in 1824 and opened on October 4, 1826. Austin Smith served as the first principal of the school, which was located where the village hall is currently located. The land was donated by Hezekiah Barker as a way to expand the school system he had begun when he arrived in Pomfret. Barker had built a log cabin school near the commons area shortly after setting up his residence, so his interest in education was very high. The Fredonia Academy was no doubt his pride and joy, as his dream of providing a top-notch school for the children of Pomfret came to fruition. Many prominent residents attended the academy, which eventually came upon poor economic times and was absorbed by the normal school.

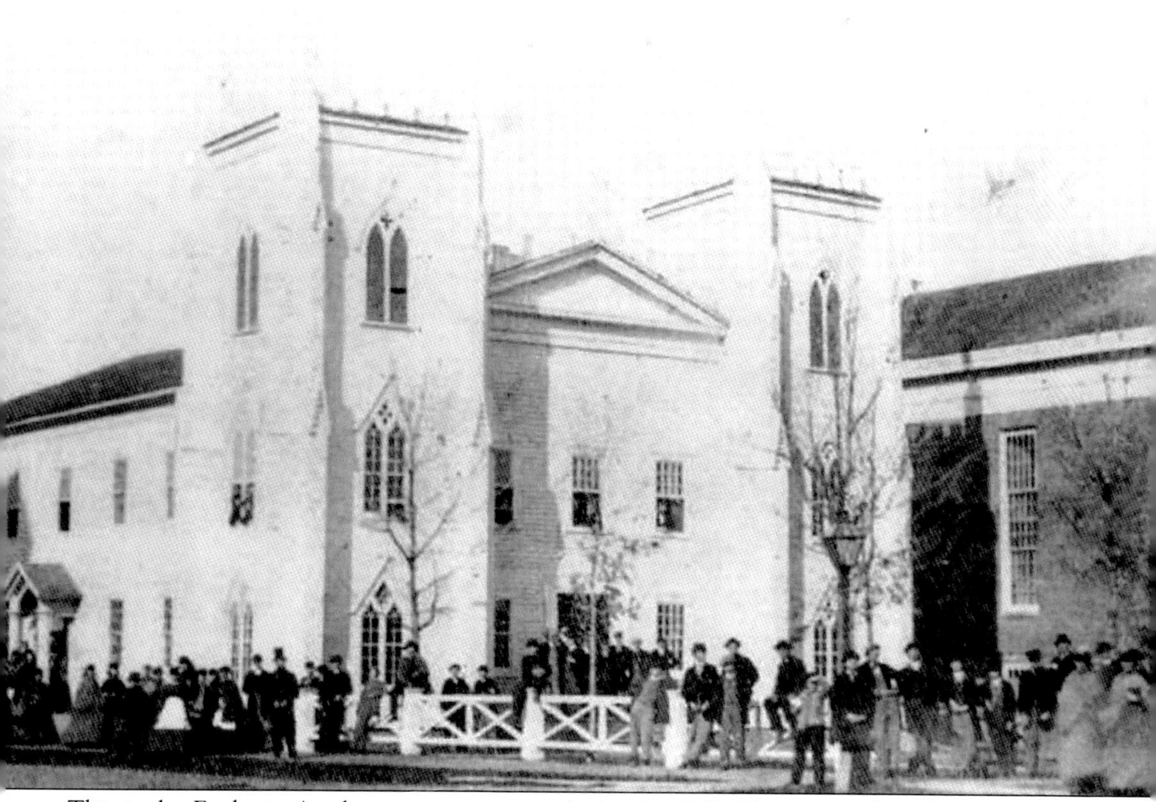

This is the Fredonia Academy as seen at a gathering in 1865. The principal at this time was Homer T. Fuller, who presided over the proceedings that included a visit to the Presbyterian church nearby. This period was the beginning of difficult economic times for the school, which saw enrollment drastically increase and then decrease from year to year after the Civil War. The plight of the academy became a major concern of most people in the town, as it was the educational pillar of the community. A number of prominent residents had already made substantial donations to keep the school going, but it was feared that the school could not survive.

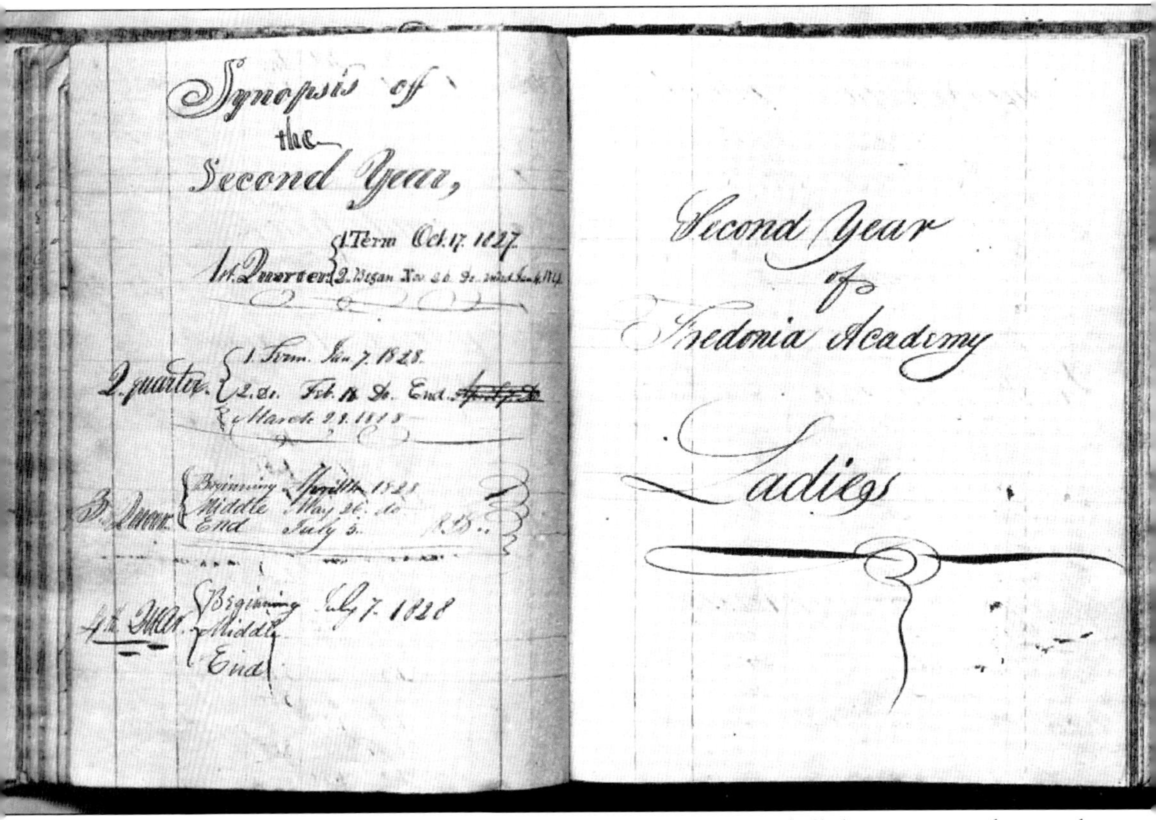

The synopsis book of the Fredonia Academy from 1828 represented all the important dates and events that had taken place during the second full year the school was open. Also included was a list of students, benefactors of the school, and staff. Students at the academy were expected to attend classes all day and then study and recite verses for anywhere from three to five hours each night. All the standard subjects were taught, including basic religious instruction. Students had very little free time during a typical day at the academy.

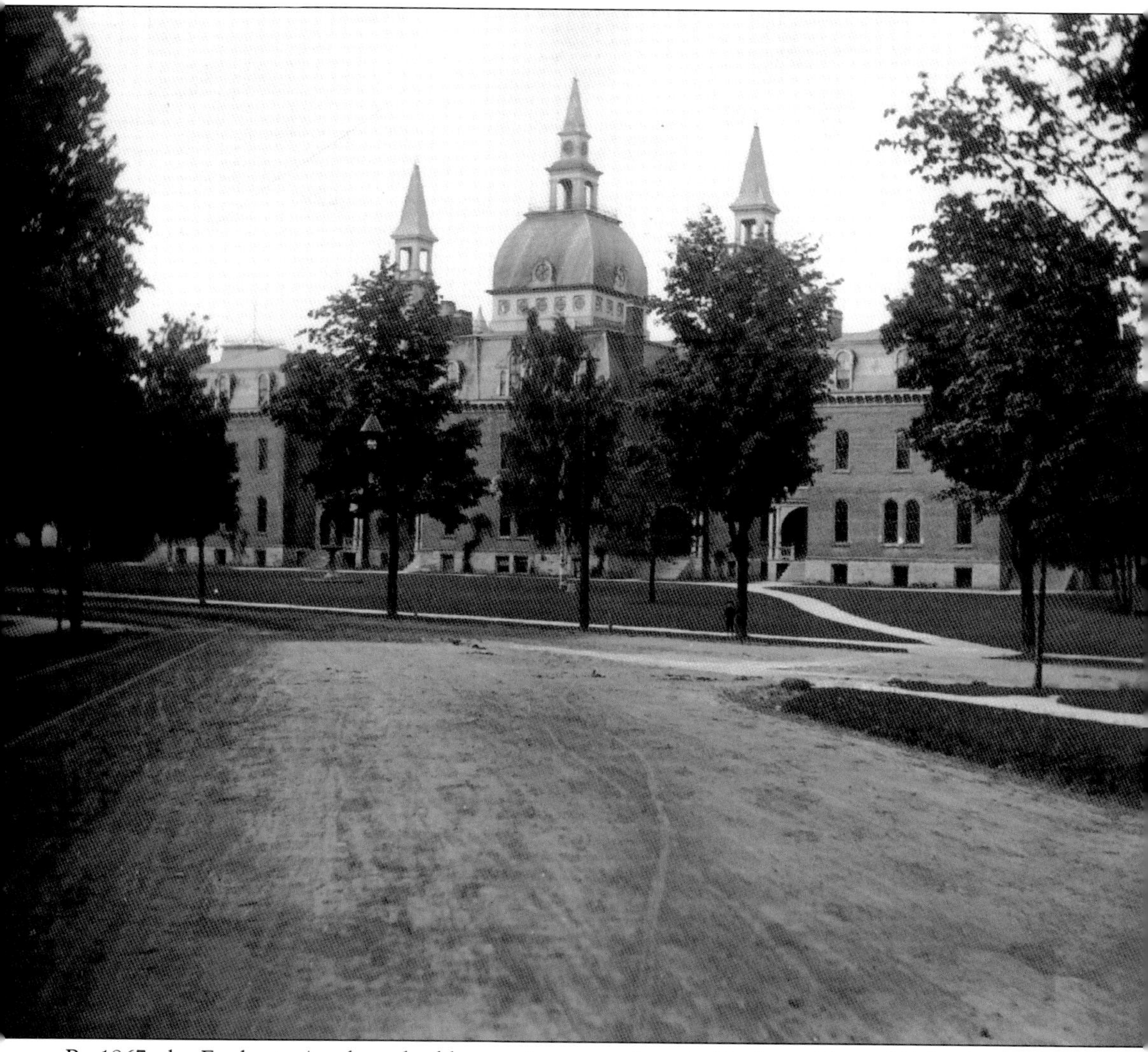

By 1867, the Fredonia Academy had been reincarnated as the Fredonia Normal School, which was part of the normal school movement in New York State. The movement was aimed at training teachers that would remain in the state and teach upon graduation. Instruction began in kindergarten and continued through the college level, with classes offered to prepare teachers. There was no tuition or fees for textbooks, but students were required to sign a declaration that they would teach in New York State upon graduation. Special certificates were also offered in art and music. The site of the normal school, as seen in this 1892 picture, was at the corner of Temple Street and Central Avenue. This eventually became the site of "Old Main" and today's One Temple Square.

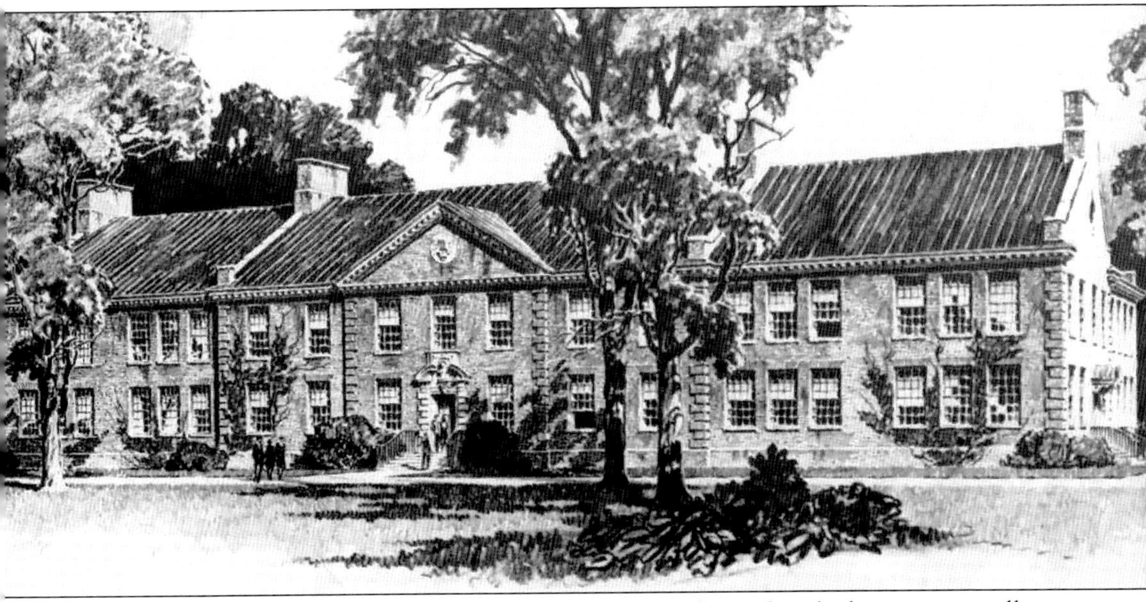

The first 70 years of the normal school saw a devastating fire, a sharply decreasing enrollment, and an uncertain future in the New York State legislature. Then in 1930, 58 acres of land were purchased on Central Avenue in the hope that one day the normal school might become a much larger campus. In 1938, the music building, seen in the photograph, was built on that plot of land and later named Mason Hall. This building was the start of what became an even bigger transformation in the history of Pomfret education.

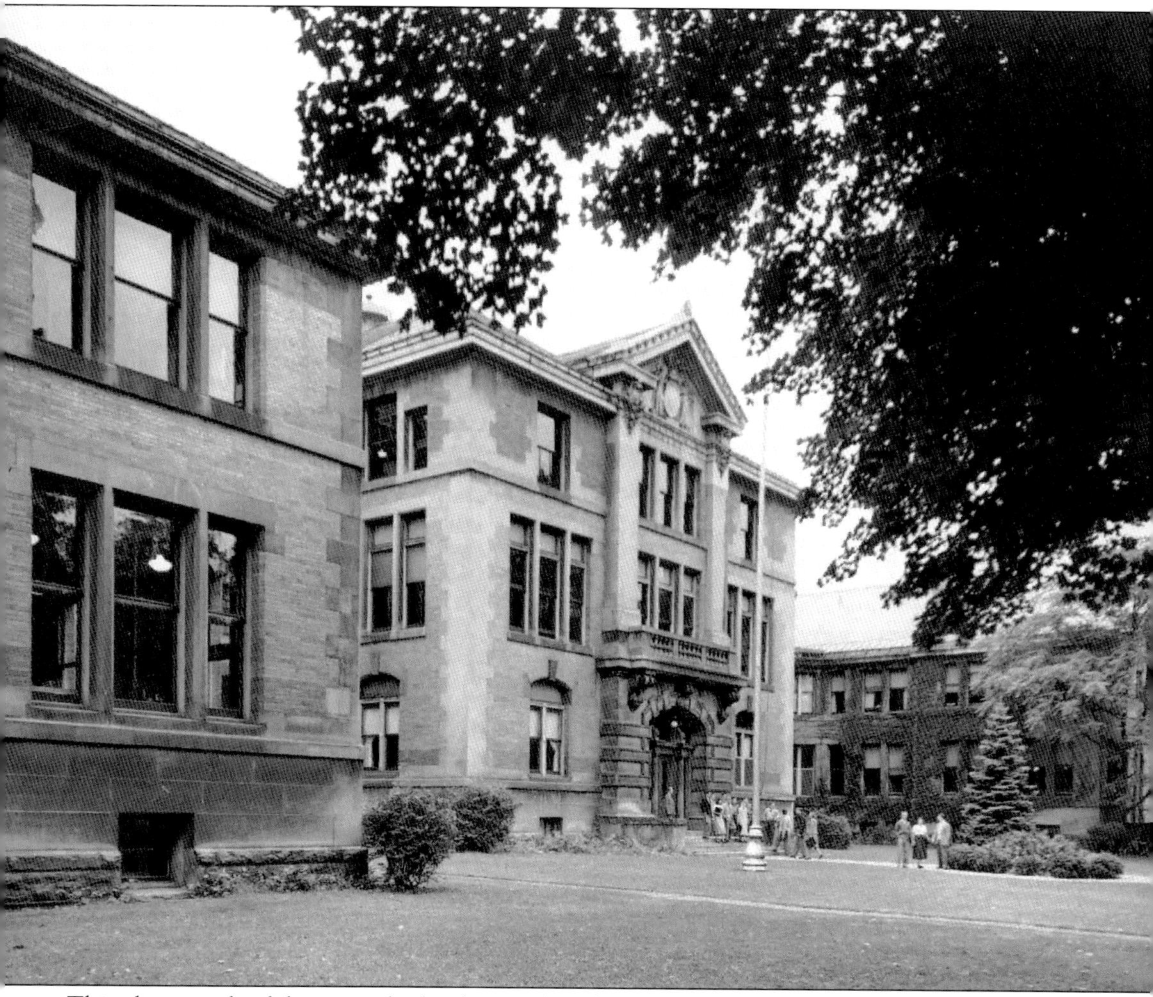

This photograph of the normal school was taken during the 1930s at about the time the music building was being built on Central Avenue. This building is actually the second normal school building, as the first one was destroyed by fire in 1900.

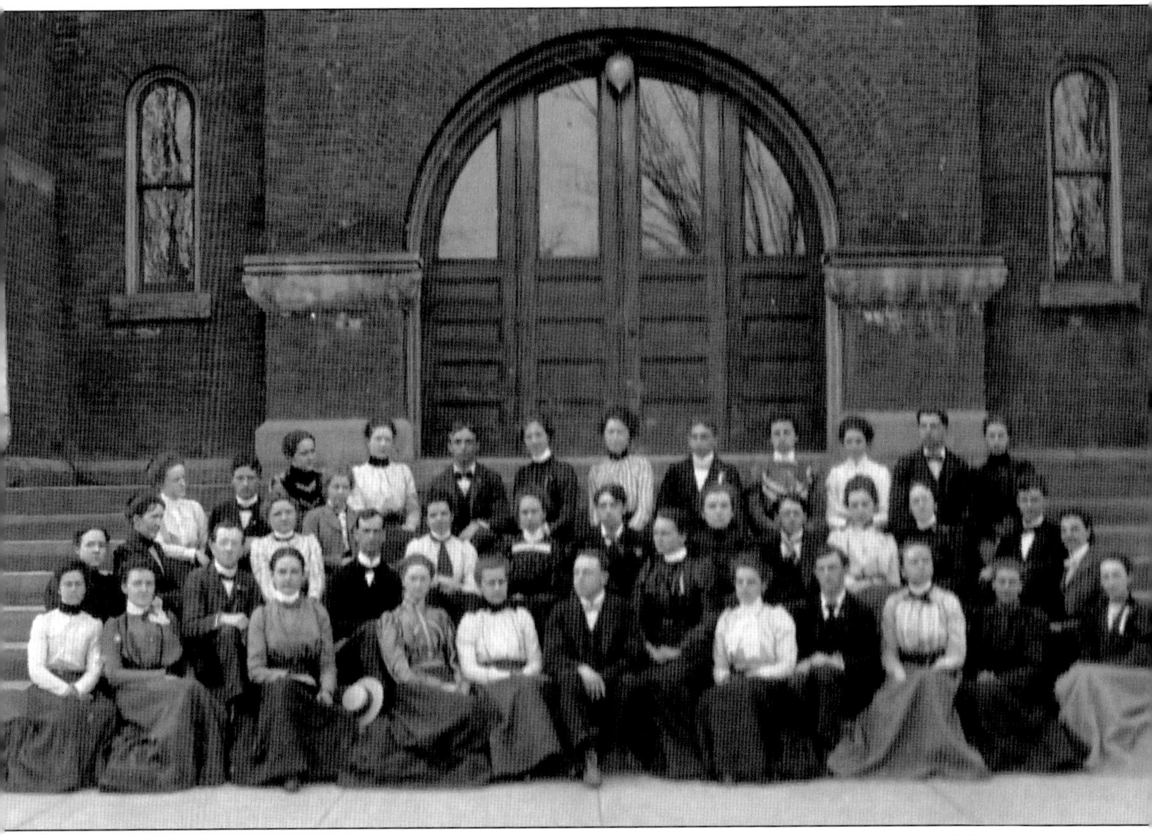

This photograph is of the last graduating class at the original normal school building in the summer of 1900. This was about the average size of graduating classes at the time, although the number fluctuated greatly. All of the men and women pictured in this photograph were expected to teach in the state due to the signing of their declarations. Some did not, but it seems that little was done to those that did not follow through on the declaration.

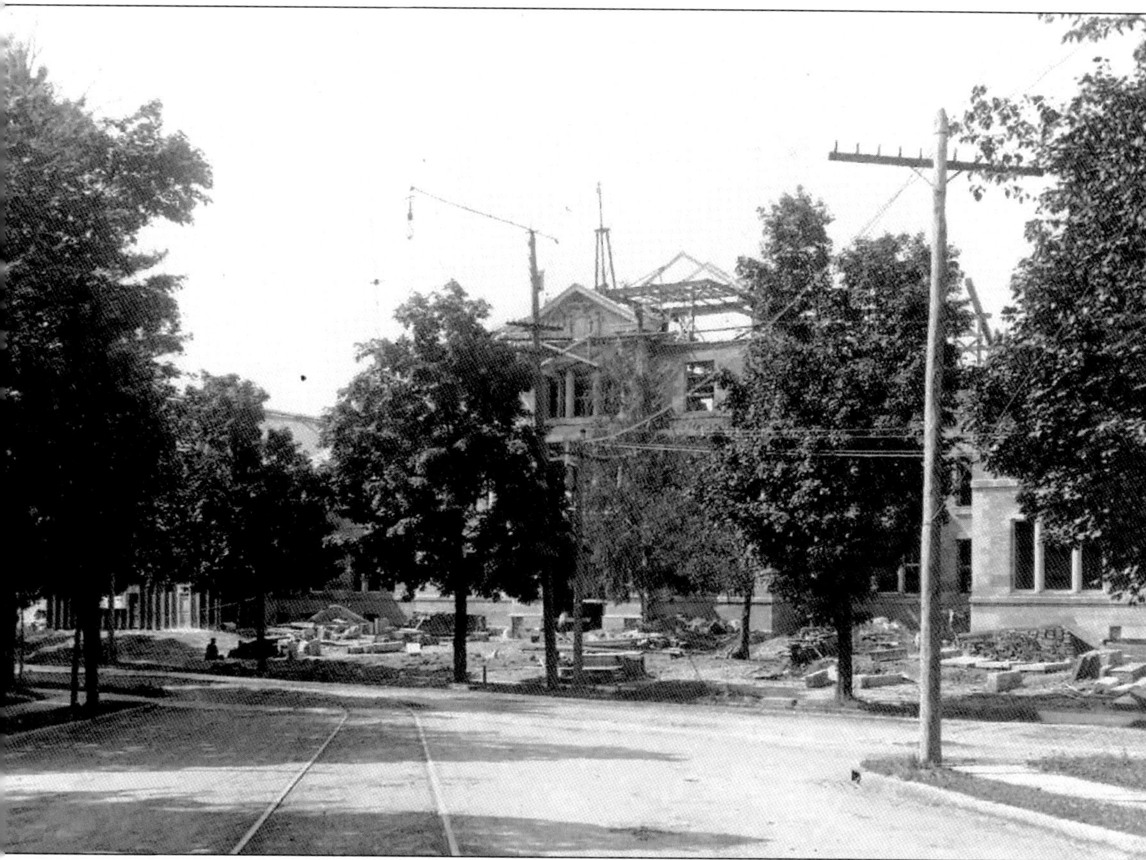

After the devastating fire at the normal school in December 1900, construction quickly began on a new building on the site of the old one. This photograph is one of few in existence that shows the new building under construction in 1901 and 1902. This building still exists today and is known as One Temple Square.

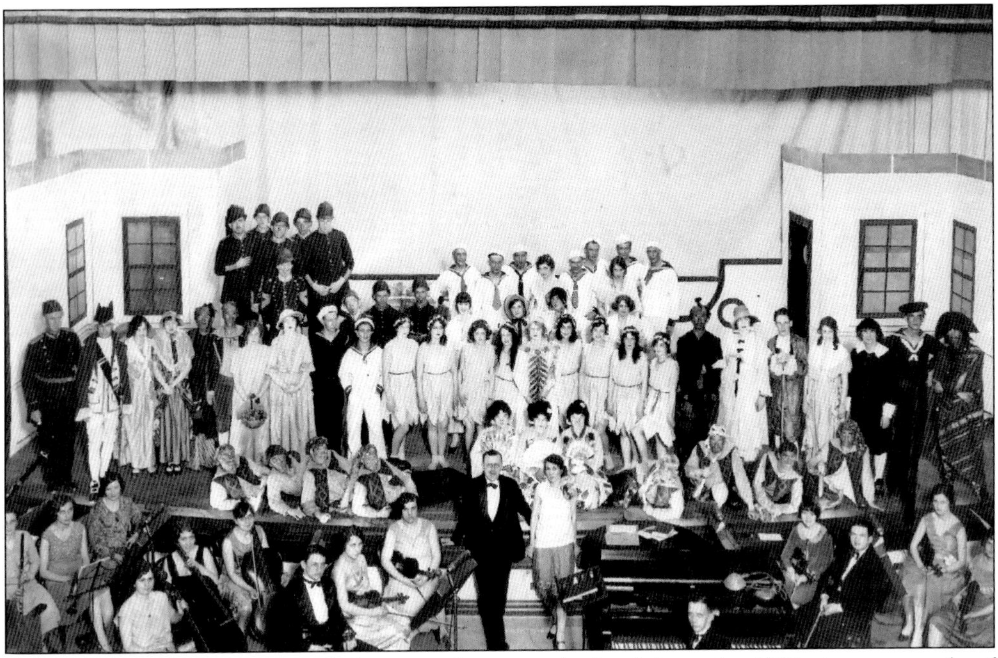

This photograph of the festival chorus at the normal school from the 1920s is an example of how important music was to the students at the school. Long before SUNY Fredonia came into existence, the normal school had a fine reputation for excellence in music. The festival chorus performed regularly in the community.

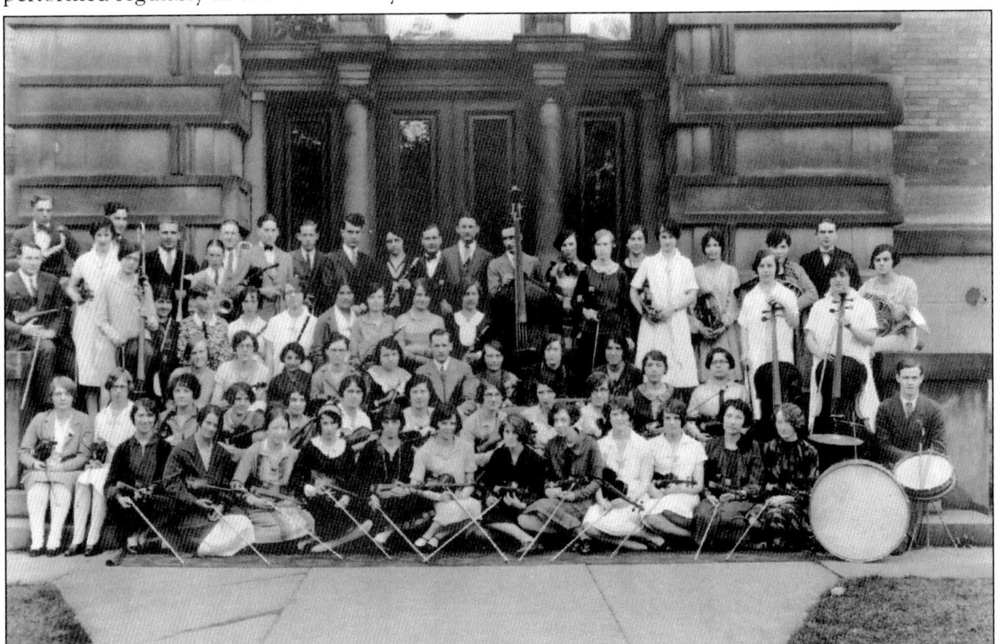

The Fredonia Normal School orchestra had a reputation as one of the finest in western New York in May 1927, when this photograph was taken. The pride in musical excellence did not die with the normal school, as SUNY Fredonia's reputation as a music school has continued to this day.

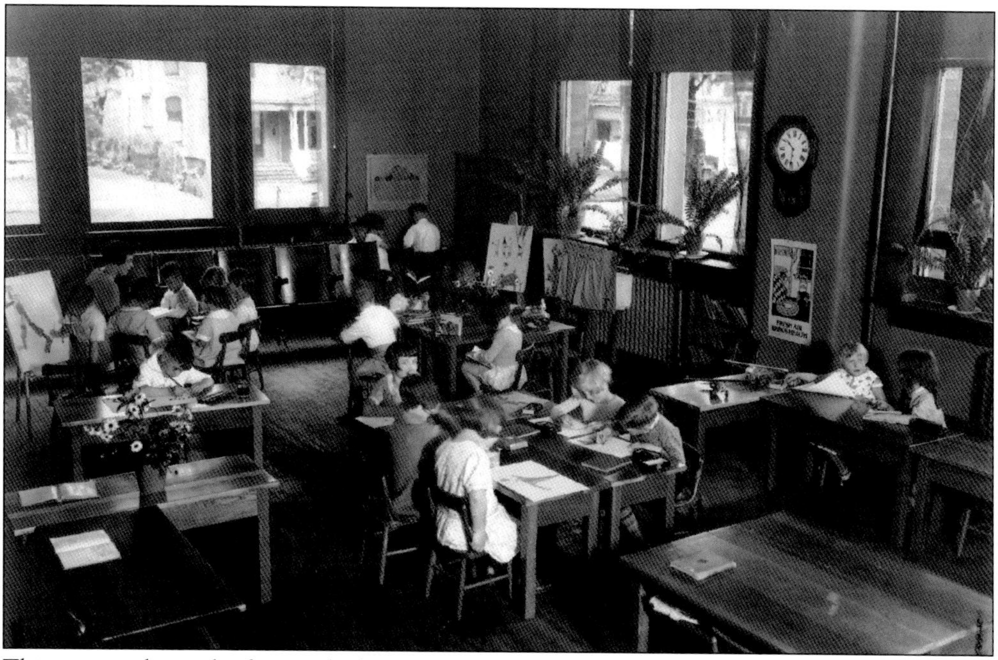

This picture shows the first grade demonstration room at the normal school. This room was one specifically used to train teachers in a hands-on environment with students. The teachers-in-training did not go out into area schools to teach as often as they do today. These rooms were used to help future teachers hone their skills and put into practice what they learned.

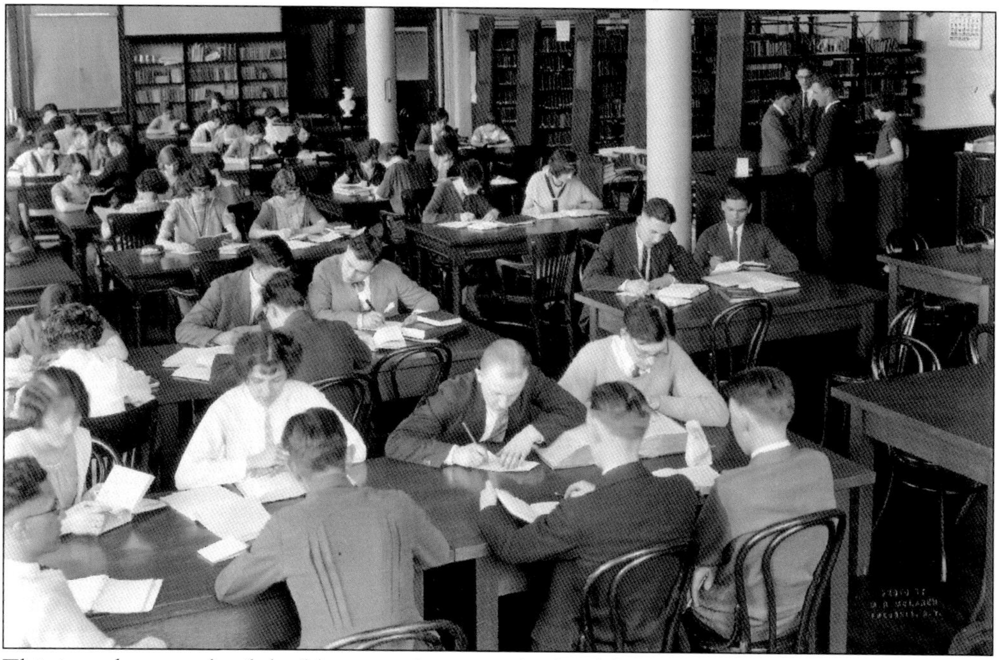

This is a photograph of the library at the normal school from 1925. The students often spent many hours writing and researching topics in the library during their training. Teacher education at this time revolved more around theory and academic study than on the practices of classroom management and learning strategies that are taught today.

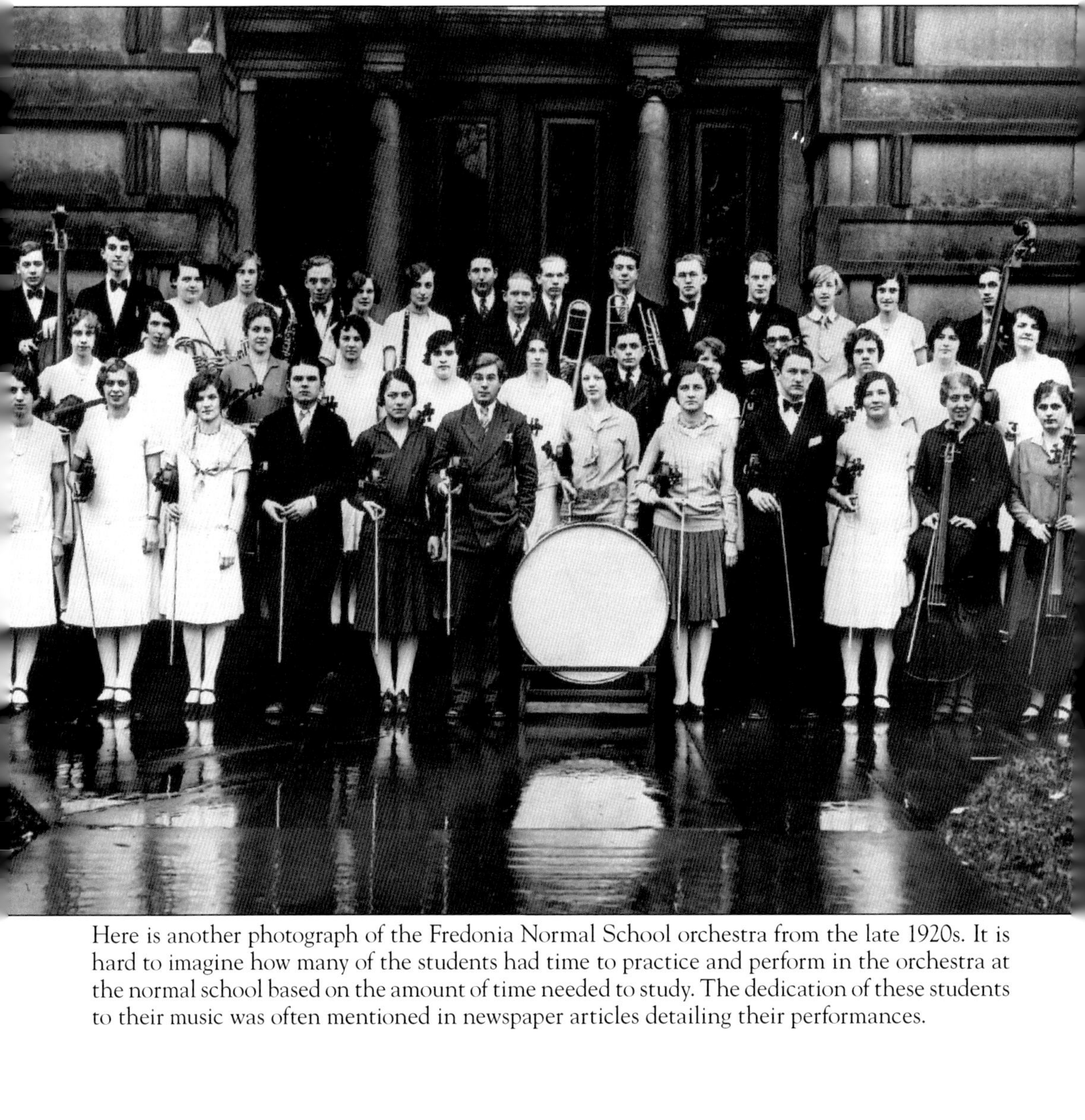

Here is another photograph of the Fredonia Normal School orchestra from the late 1920s. It is hard to imagine how many of the students had time to practice and perform in the orchestra at the normal school based on the amount of time needed to study. The dedication of these students to their music was often mentioned in newspaper articles detailing their performances.

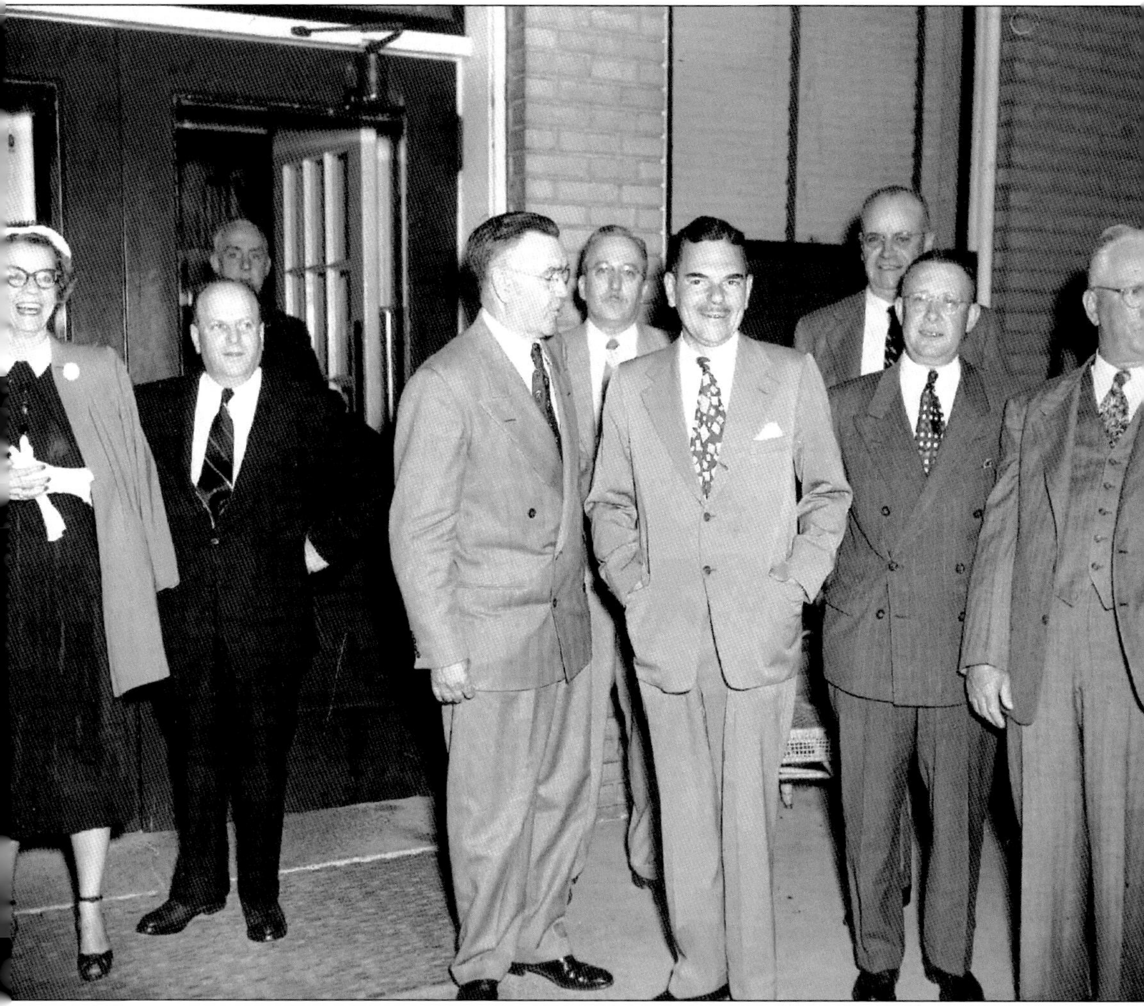

The new music building for the normal school began with the cornerstone-laying ceremony held on July 11, 1939, as seen in this photograph with Gov. Thomas Dewey. The building was completed two years later in 1941. The building was later called Mason Hall, named after American music education pioneer Lowell Mason.

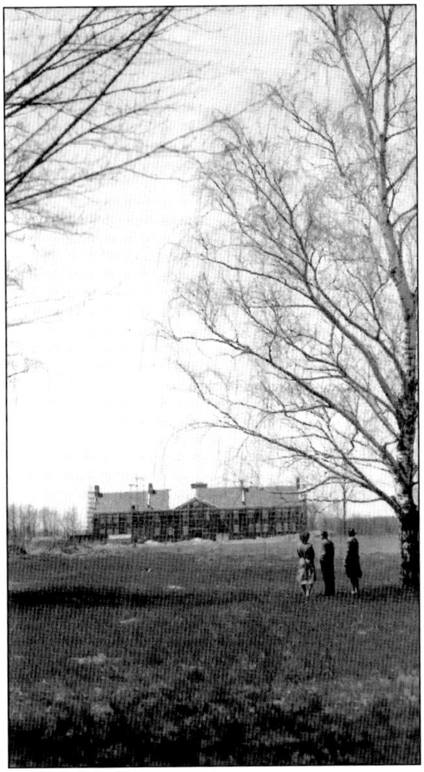

This picture of the new music building being completed in 1941 represents the first building on the site that became the future home of SUNY Fredonia. The building seems odd by itself compared to how it looks today in the center of the bustling campus with buildings all around it. Music became such a large part of the curriculum at the new state university beginning in 1948 that this building (later named Mason Hall) needed an addition 30 years after being finished.

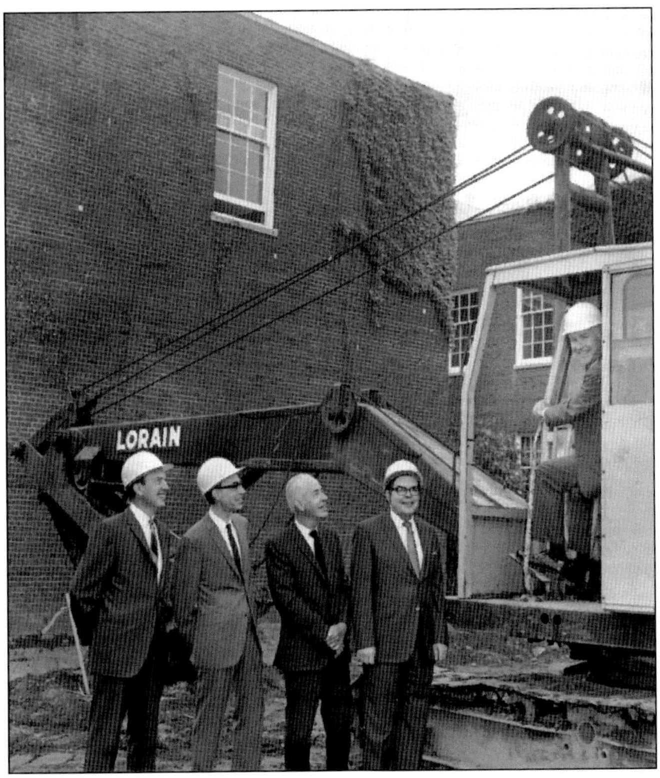

Dr. Oscar E. Lanford operates the controls during the groundbreaking of the new addition to Mason Hall in this June 17, 1970, photograph. Lanford was president of SUNY Fredonia during a major construction period of the college from 1961 to 1971. Also in the picture, from left to right, are Doug Carter (assistant vice president for administration), Dr. Richard Sheil (acting chairman of the music department), Howard E. Marsh (associate chairman of the music department), and Dr. Robert Marvel (dean for fine and performing arts).

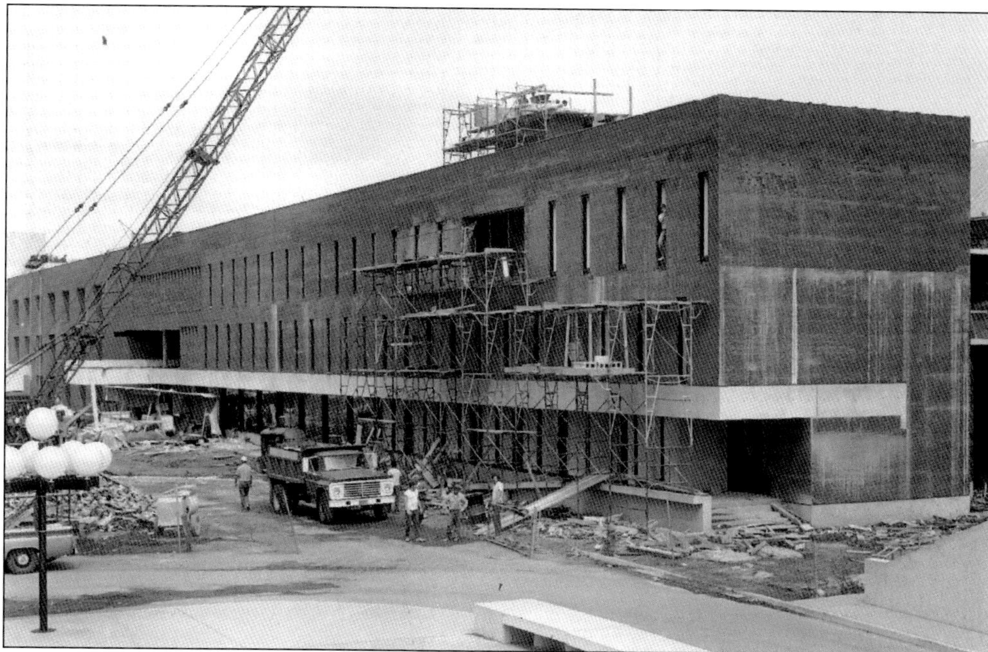

The addition to Mason Hall, shown here in August 1971, included personal practice rooms and space for small recital halls and storage. The building's construction was to be completed the following year. The addition became known as "new" Mason Hall, while the original became known as "old" Mason Hall, despite the fact that the two were connected.

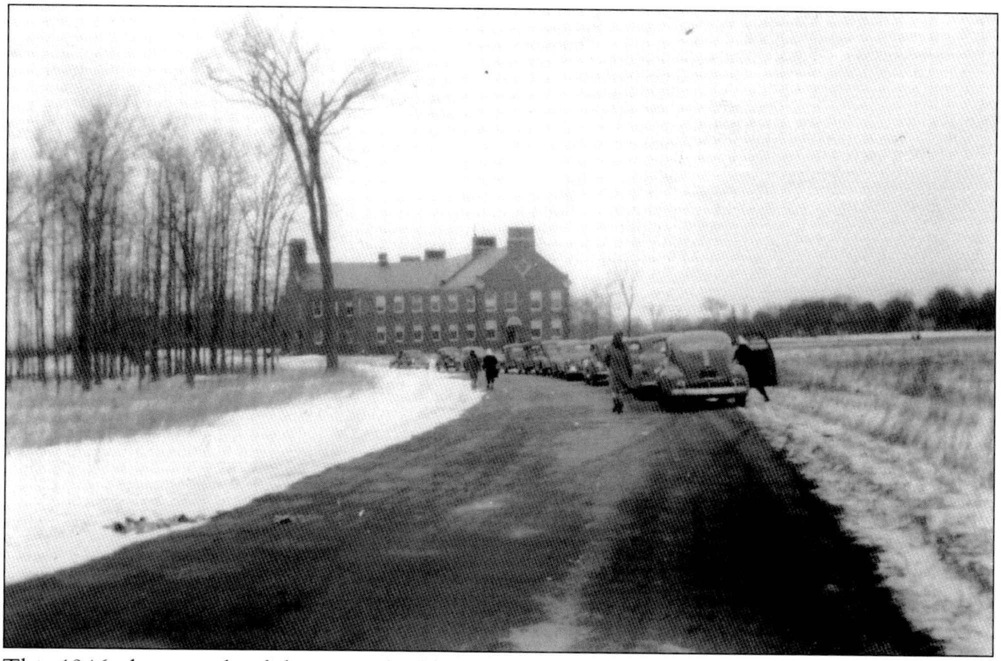

This 1946 photograph of the music building, or "old" Mason Hall, shows just how barren the land was before the vast expansion that happened over the next 25 years. Students came to this building for music classes and instruction, while their other classes were held at the main normal school building at the corner of Temple Street and Central Avenue.

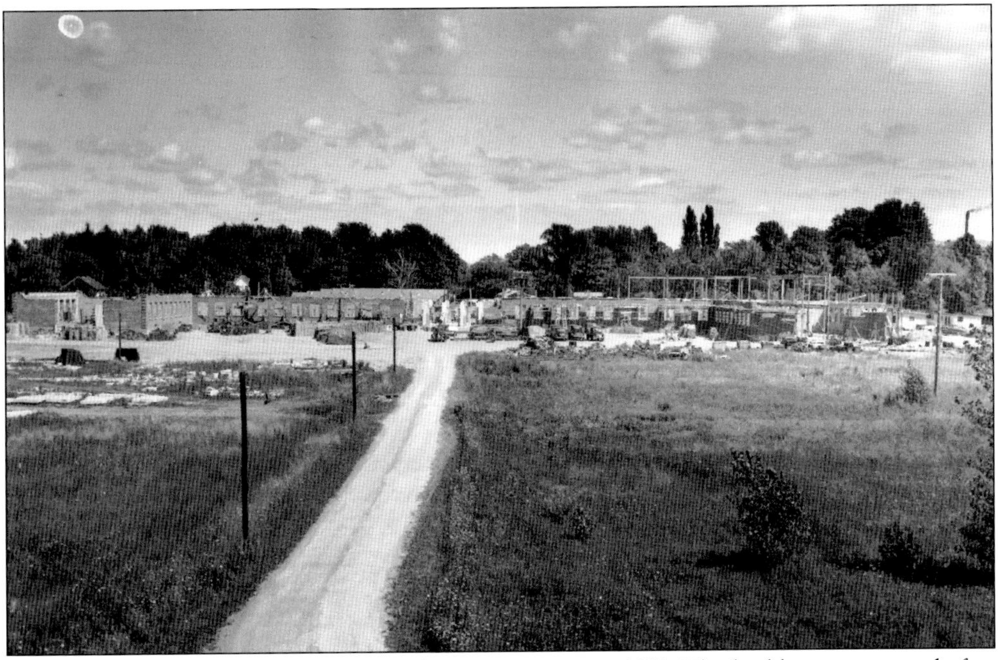

This photograph shows Fenton Hall under construction in 1951. The building was named after Gov. Reuben Eaton Fenton, who was born in Chautauqua County and served as governor of New York from 1865 to 1868. Fenton Hall was one of the next buildings to be built in this area after the original music building that is immediately behind it.

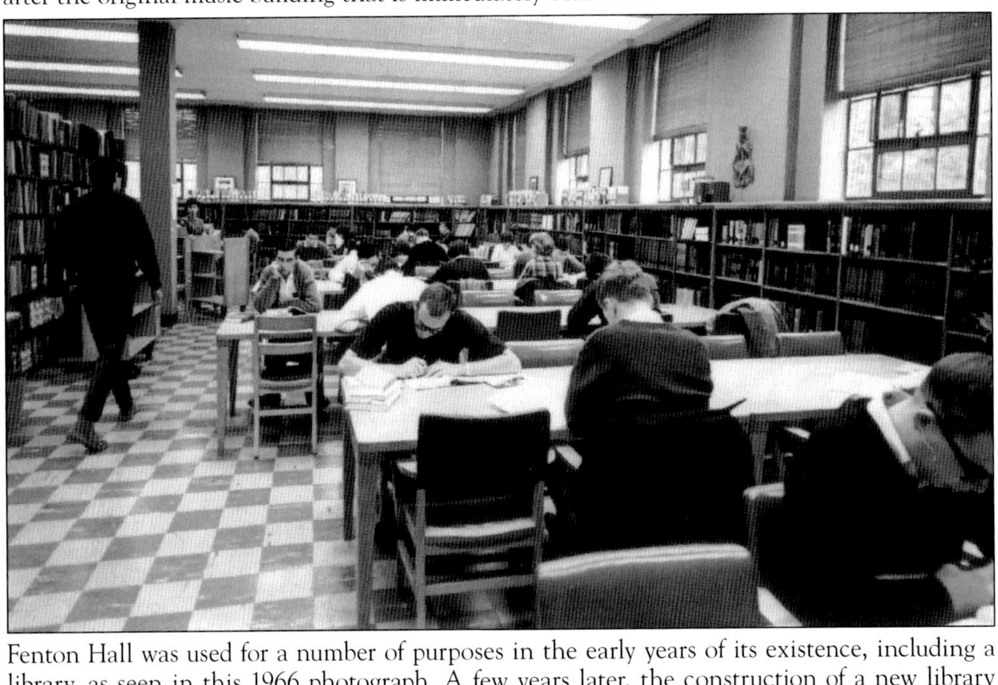

Fenton Hall was used for a number of purposes in the early years of its existence, including a library, as seen in this 1966 photograph. A few years later, the construction of a new library building allowed the space in Fenton Hall to be used for some of the things it houses today, including the president's office. The building is today also used as academic offices and classrooms for computer science, modern languages, English, and philosophy.

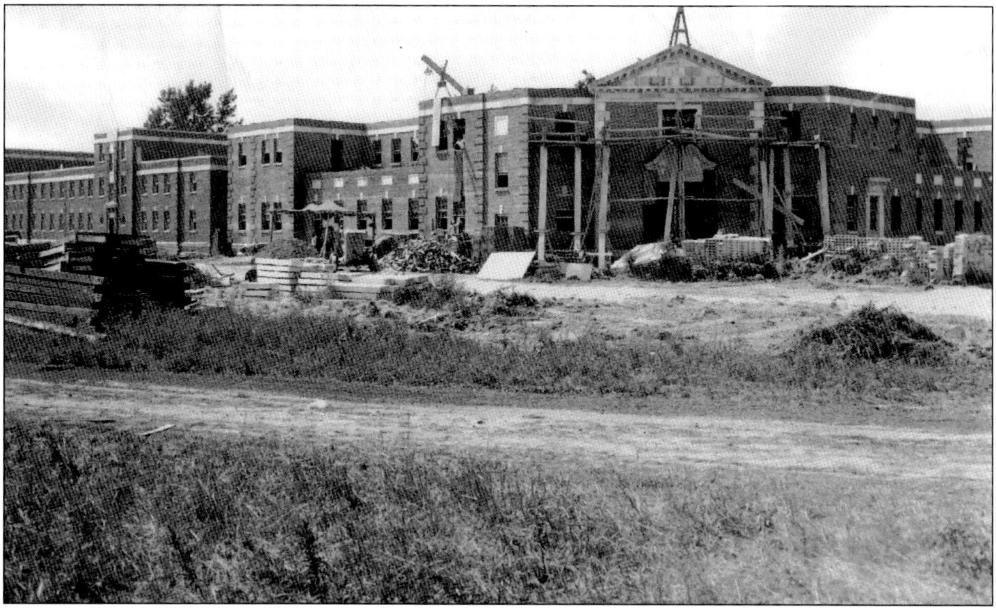

The second building to be built on the new SUNY Fredonia campus was Gregory Hall, seen here during construction in the late 1940s. Gregory Hall saw many different uses in its early years, just as Fenton Hall did in the same time period. Gregory Hall was originally used for housing, although it also served other purposes.

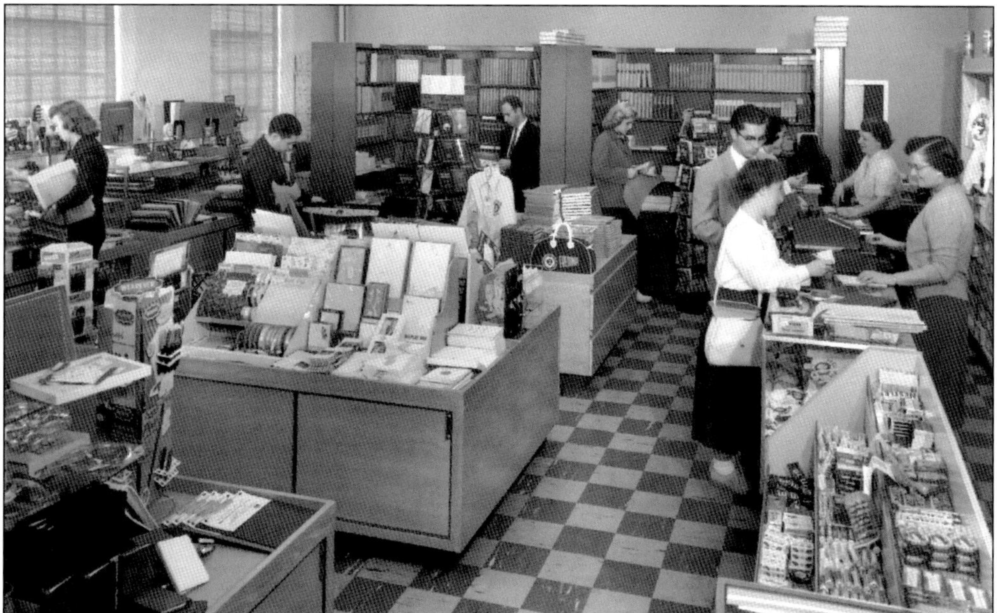

Gregory Hall became an important part of the campus in the early years, as evidenced by the busy scene in this picture showing the campus bookstore. The bookstore was housed in Gregory Hall for years while the campus grew, but it was a much different bookstore than the one currently housed in the campus center today. The Gregory Hall bookstore mainly sold books and items directly related to classes, however it did sell a few luxury items like the candy seen in the photograph.

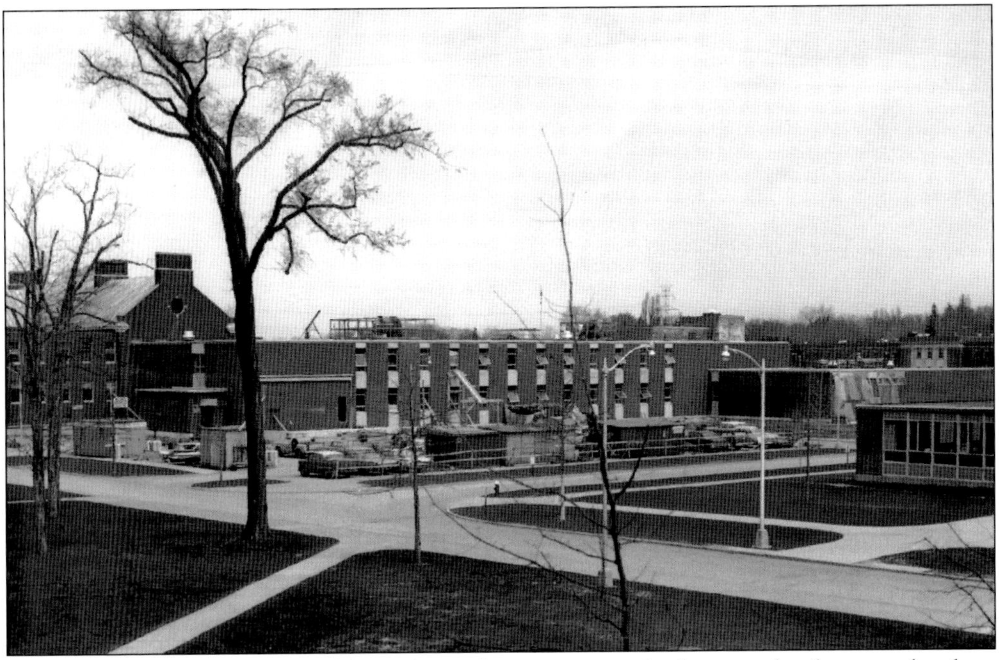

Jewett Hall was one of the buildings devoted to science with the growth of new technology during the period of its construction in the 1960s. This photograph shows the building during its last few months of construction in May 1963. Jewett Hall has served a number of purposes for the science department over the years, which currently includes biology and medical technology.

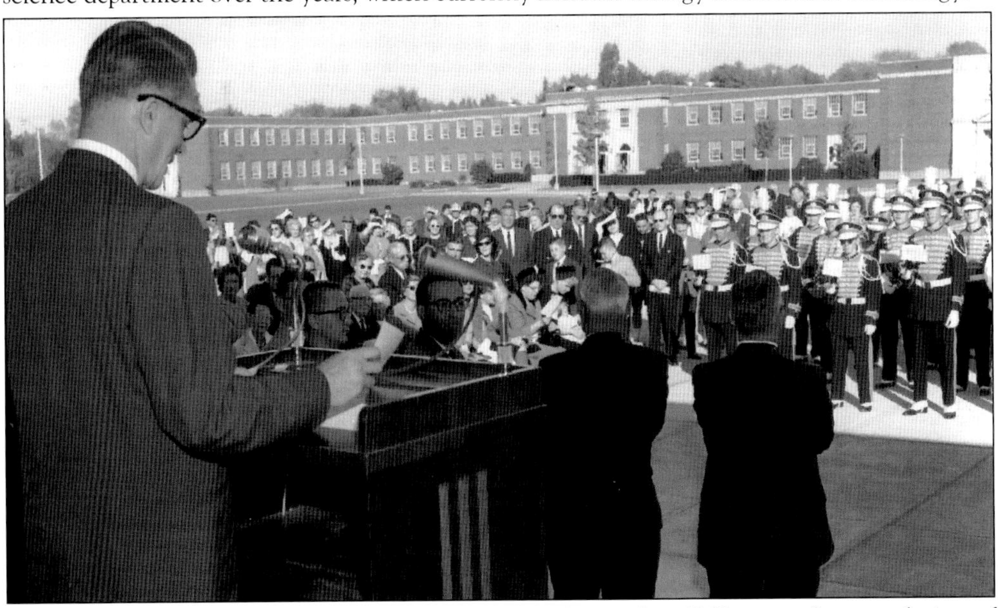

Jewett Hall was dedicated at a special ceremony in September 1963 upon the completion of construction for the fall semester that year. Dr. Harry Porter is pictured in this photograph as one of the many speakers at this ceremony. Porter was the president of SUNY Fredonia from 1953 to 1961 when he stepped down to accept the new position of provost of the SUNY system. Porter was very popular on campus before leaving for his new position. He was invited back to speak by his successor, Dr. Oscar E. Lanford.

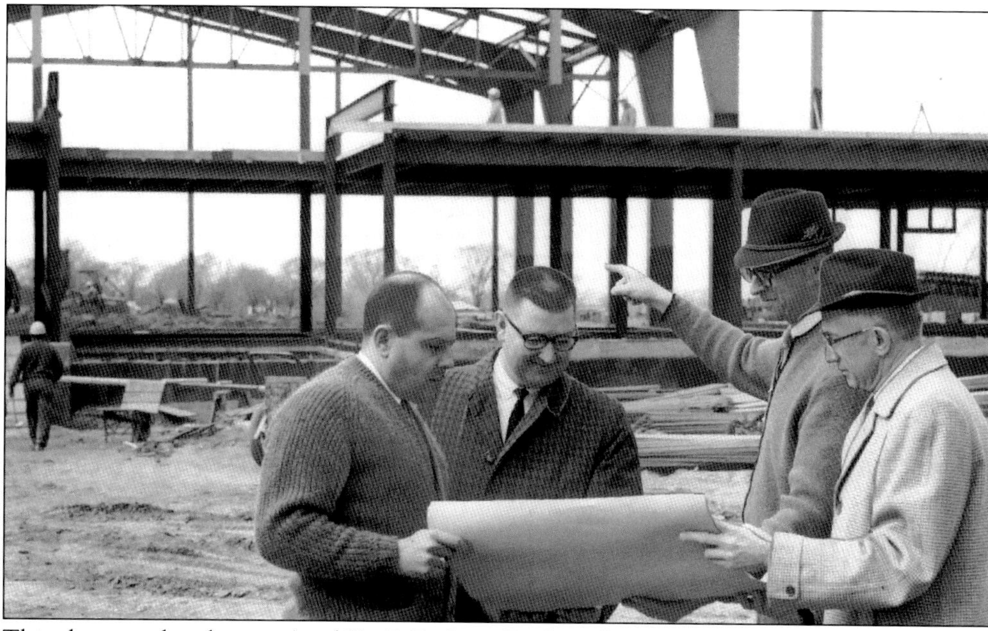

This photograph, taken on April 21, 1963, shows Dods Hall, which construction began on earlier that year. Dods Hall was built to house the new gymnasium and the rest of the athletic facilities, which included a four-lane bowling alley in the bottom level. Pictured from left to right are Pat Damore (soccer and basketball coach), Harold Hopkins (junior varsity basketball coach), William Ludwig (baseball and cross country coach), and Joseph Keyser (chairman of the health and physical education department).

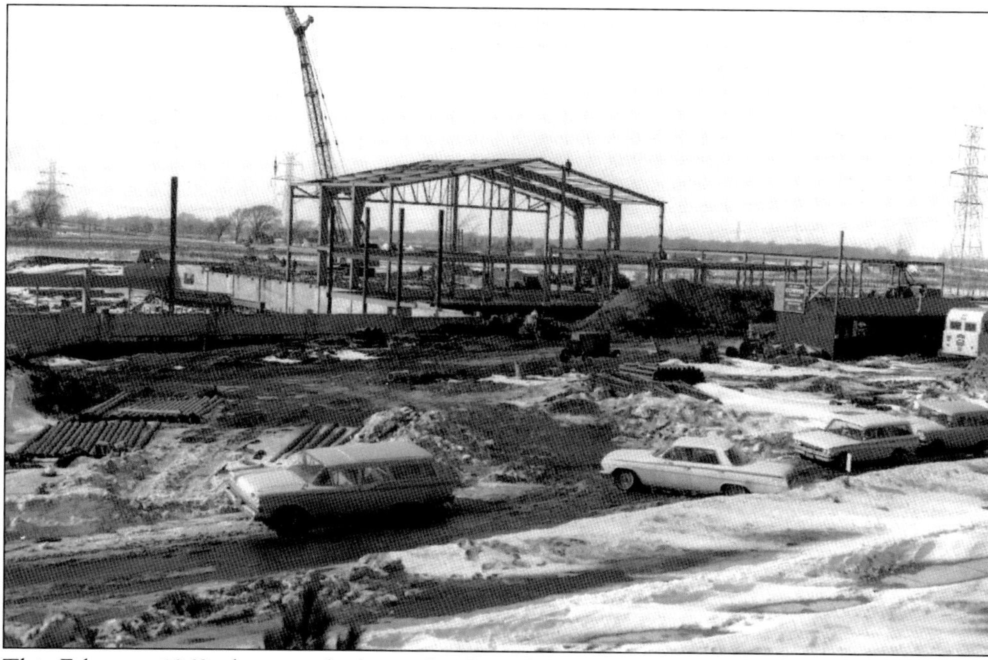

This February 1963 photograph shows the first phase of construction of the new Dods Hall. Today Dods Hall still houses the athletic facilities and has been joined by the new ice rink and swimming pool additions.

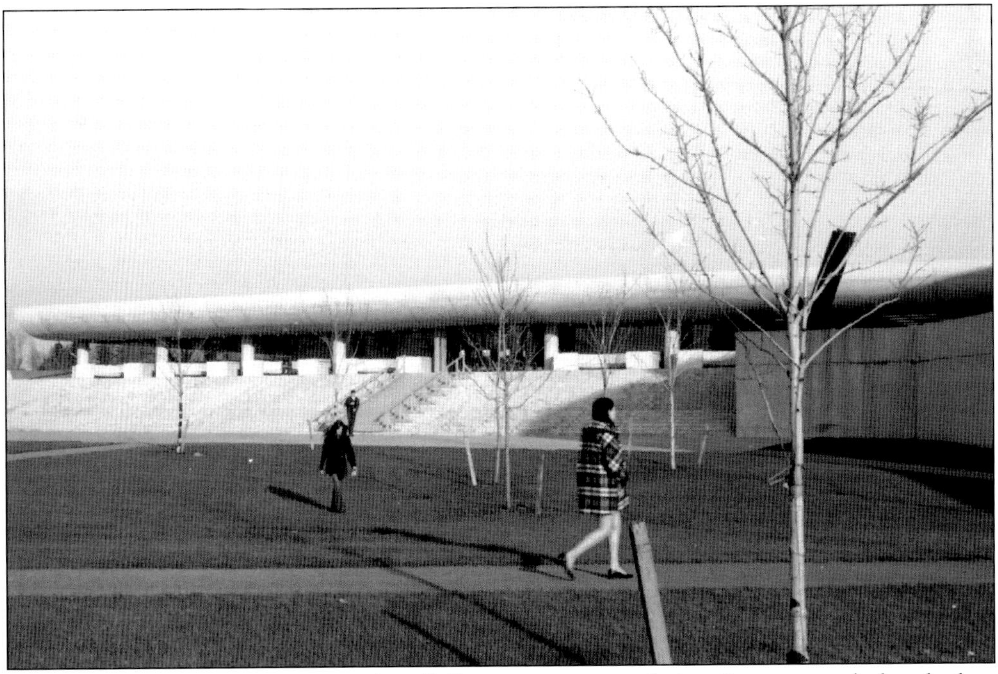

Here is the new library as it appeared in 1968, nearing its completion. It was named after the late Daniel A. Reed (1875–1959). Reed was a congressman from the Fredonia area for over 40 years. He was also chairman of the House Ways and Means Committee while in Congress. The library was designed by world-renowned architect I. M. Pei, who, with partner, Henry N. Cobb, designed the master plan for the modernized campus in 1968. The buildings that were designed by Pei as part of this plan include Maytum Hall, Williams Center, Daniel A. Reed Library, Michael C. Rockefeller Arts Center, McEwen Hall, and Houghton Hall.

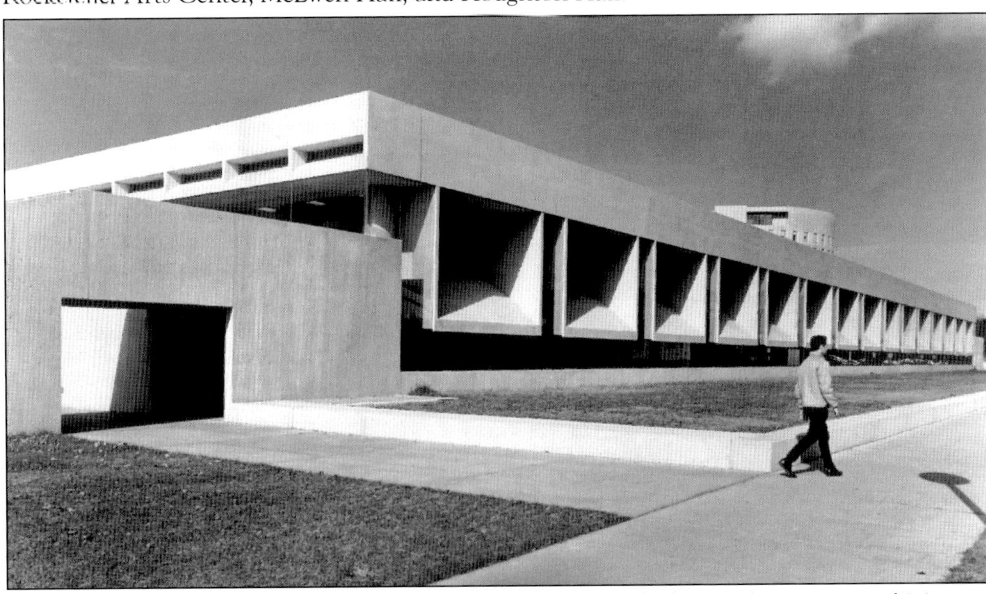

In 1968, the Daniel A. Reed Library neared completion, with the newly constructed Maytum Hall visible in the background. The library underwent another major renovation in 1992 with the addition of the atrium, which houses the archives where this photograph was found.

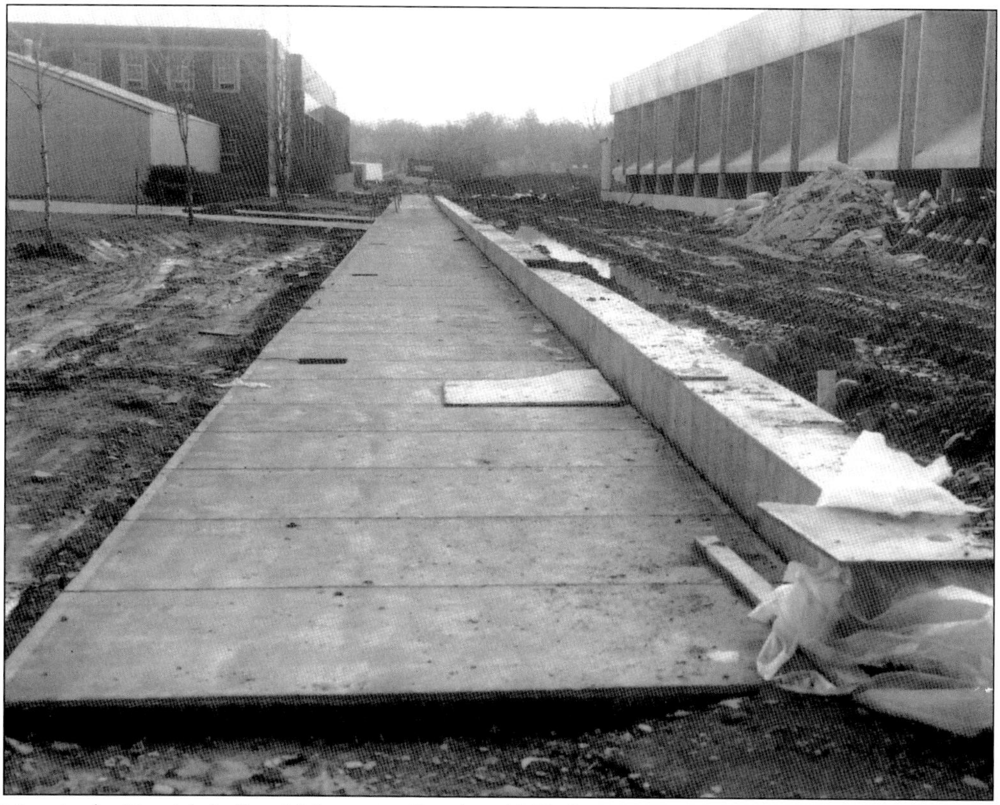

Here is the Daniel A. Reed Library in October 1967. Construction was complete in 1969. This is the sidewalk area between the library and Fenton Hall, shown at left.

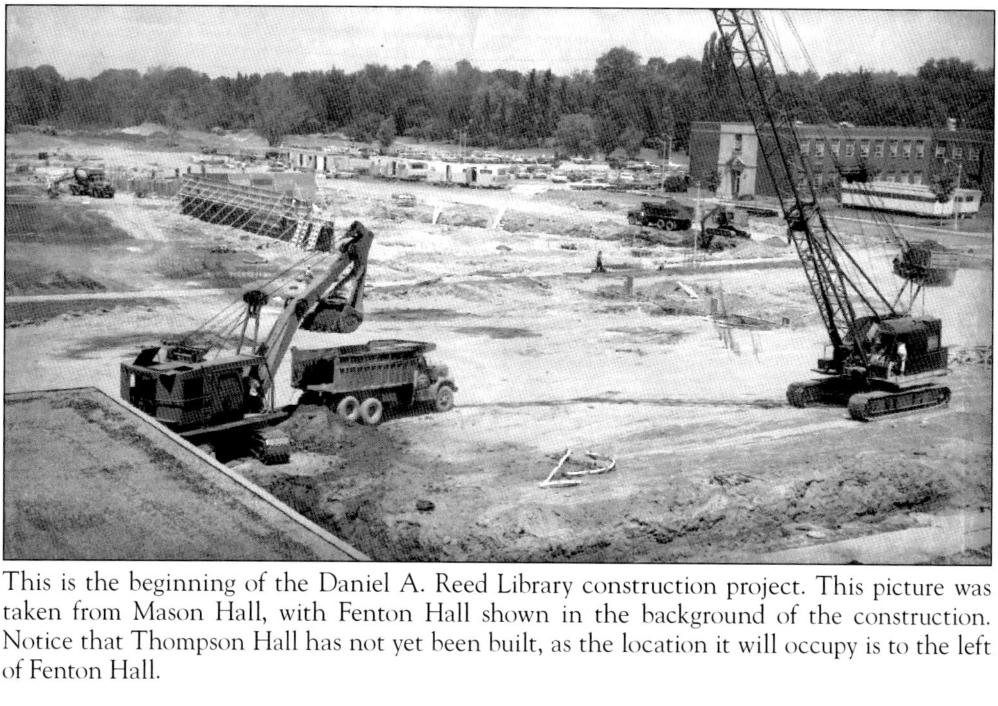

This is the beginning of the Daniel A. Reed Library construction project. This picture was taken from Mason Hall, with Fenton Hall shown in the background of the construction. Notice that Thompson Hall has not yet been built, as the location it will occupy is to the left of Fenton Hall.

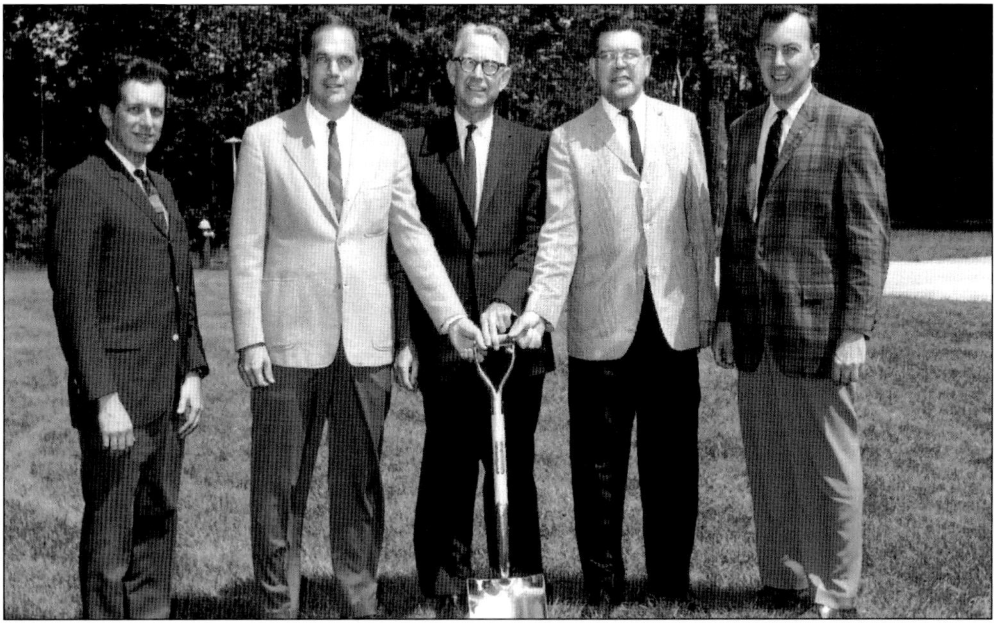

Shown in this photograph is the groundbreaking for the Michael C. Rockefeller Arts Center on June 20, 1966. Pictured from left to right are Robert Bates, Kirk Williams, Dr. Oscar E. Lanford (president), Dr. Robert Marvel, and Doug Carter. The center was named after the youngest son of New York governor Nelson A. Rockefeller, who disappeared in 1961 during an anthropological expedition in New Guinea.

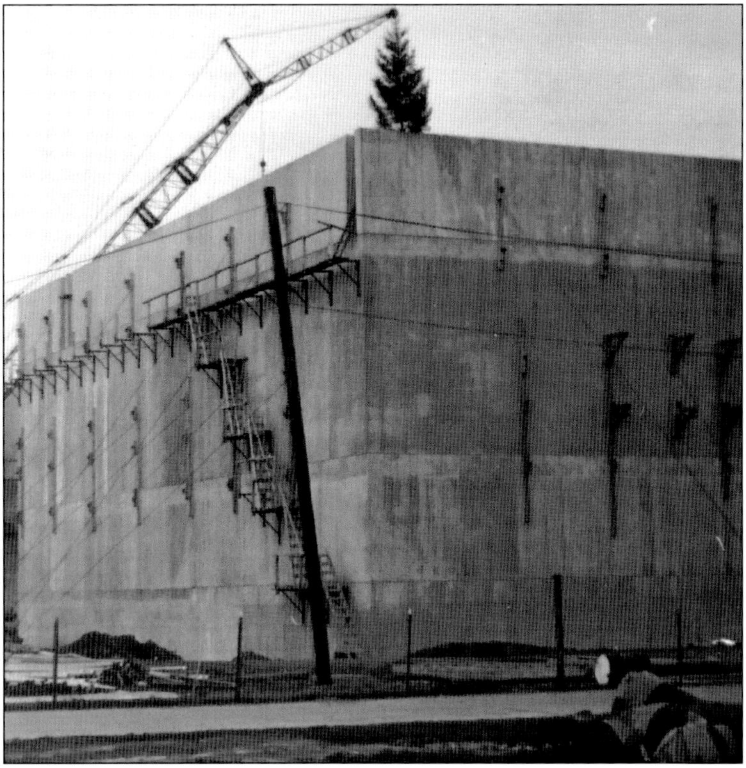

This December 1966 photograph shows great progress in the Rockefeller arts center in just six months of construction. This view of the project was taken from the area where Dods Hall and the Steele Hall Ice Rink are today.

Another picture shows the workmen in December 1966 as they progress on construction of the Rockefeller arts center. The center was designed by world-renowned architect I. M. Pei and features the 1,200-seat King Concert Hall and the smaller Marvel and Bartlett Theaters.

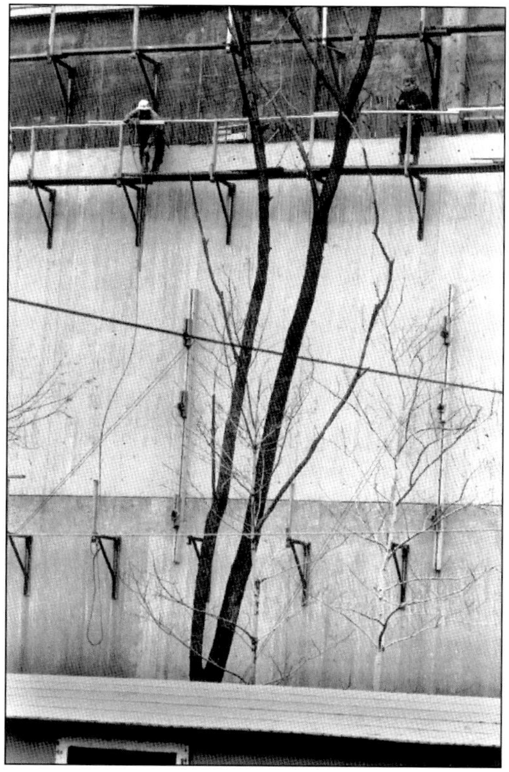

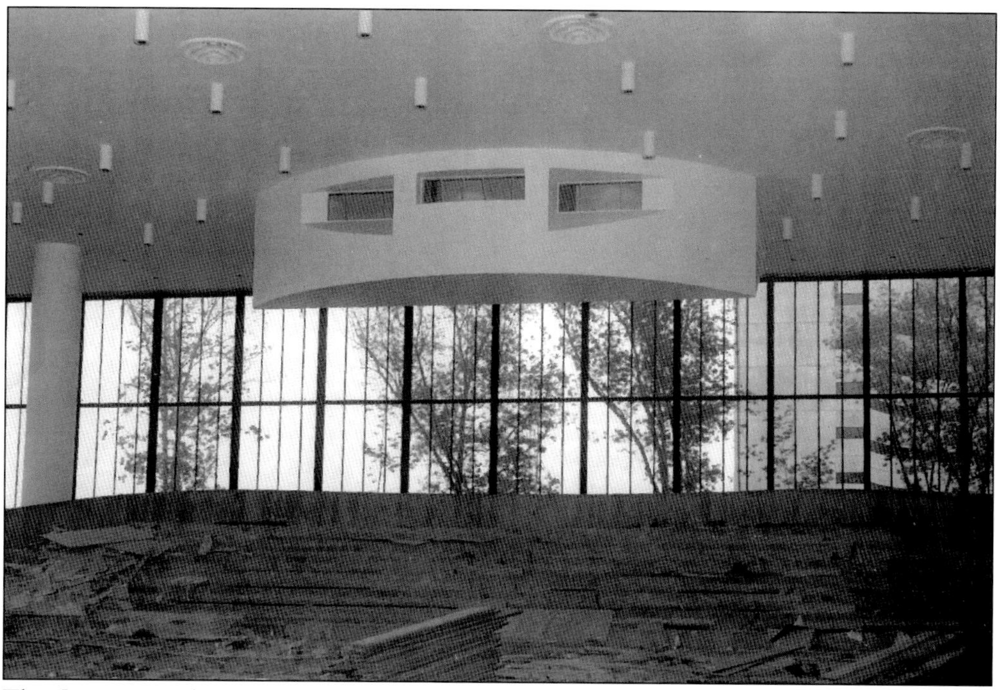

This June 1968 photograph shows work continuing inside the Rockefeller arts center. King Concert Hall is named after the SUNY Fredonia professor, violinist, and academic dean Harry A. King. The center was completed the following year.

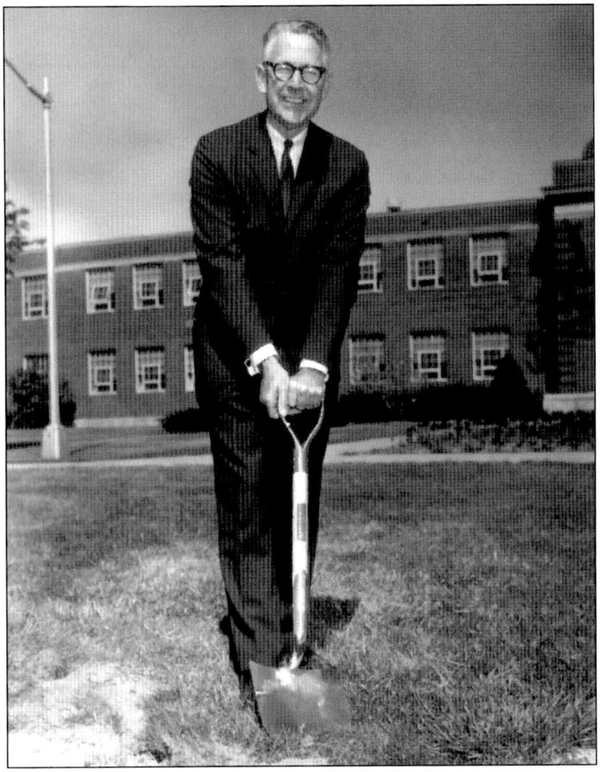

The groundbreaking ceremony in this photograph is for Maytum Hall, which was named after Arthur R. Maytum (1866–1953). He served as chairman of the board of visitors of the Fredonia Normal School and teachers college from 1928 to 1953. He also served as supervisor of the Town of Pomfret from 1931 to 1938. College president Dr. Oscar E. Lanford is shown here during the ceremony on May 31, 1966.

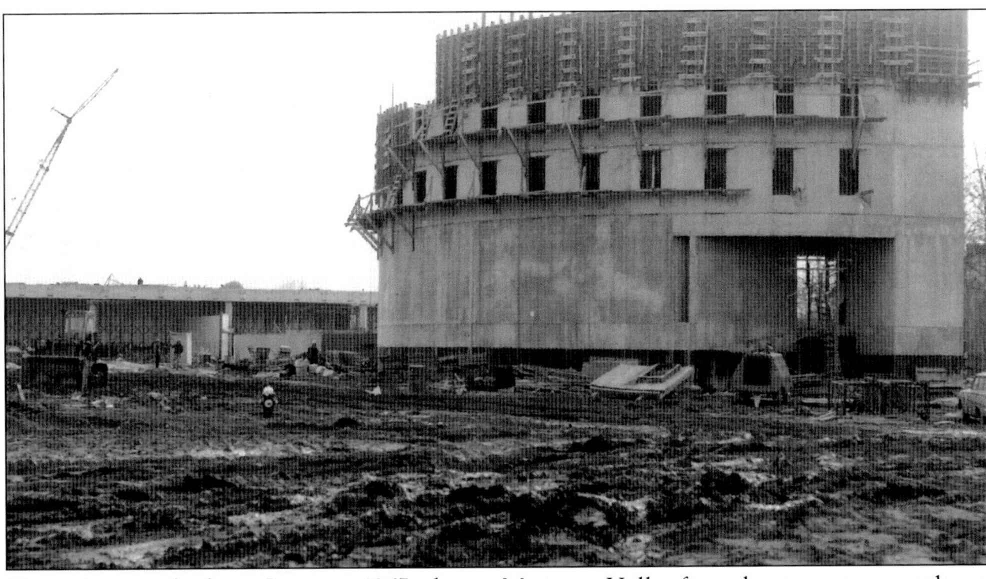

This photograph from January 1967 shows Maytum Hall after about seven months of construction. The unique design of the building was part of the master plan developed by I. M. Pei. Maytum Hall is one of the most recognizable buildings on the SUNY Fredonia campus today.

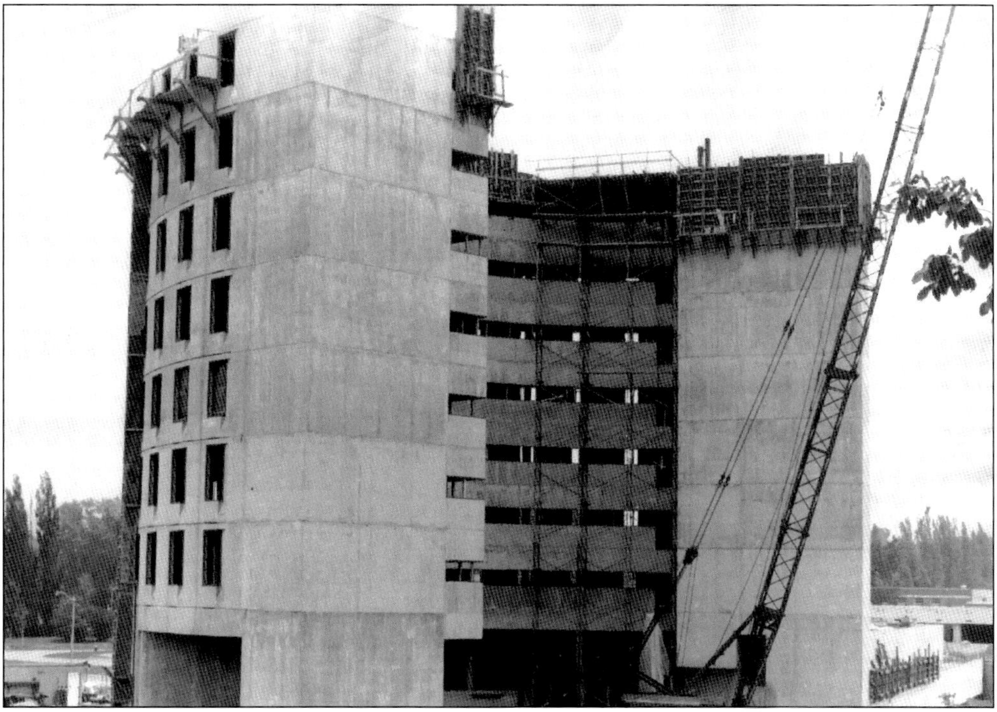

A great deal of work was accomplished in just six months, as seen in this July 1967 photograph of Maytum Hall. Today it is the home of the administrative offices and the office of the registrar.

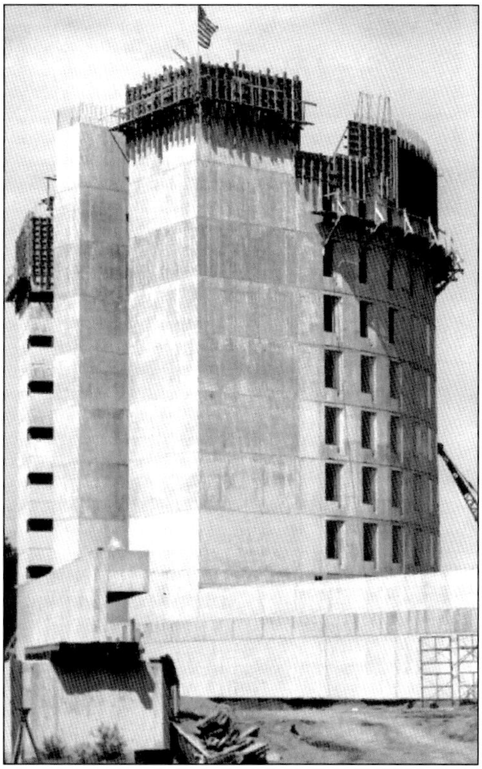

This unique photograph of Maytum Hall during the final phase of construction in September 1967 is a mystery. No one seems to know exactly why the American flag was placed at the top of the building during construction.

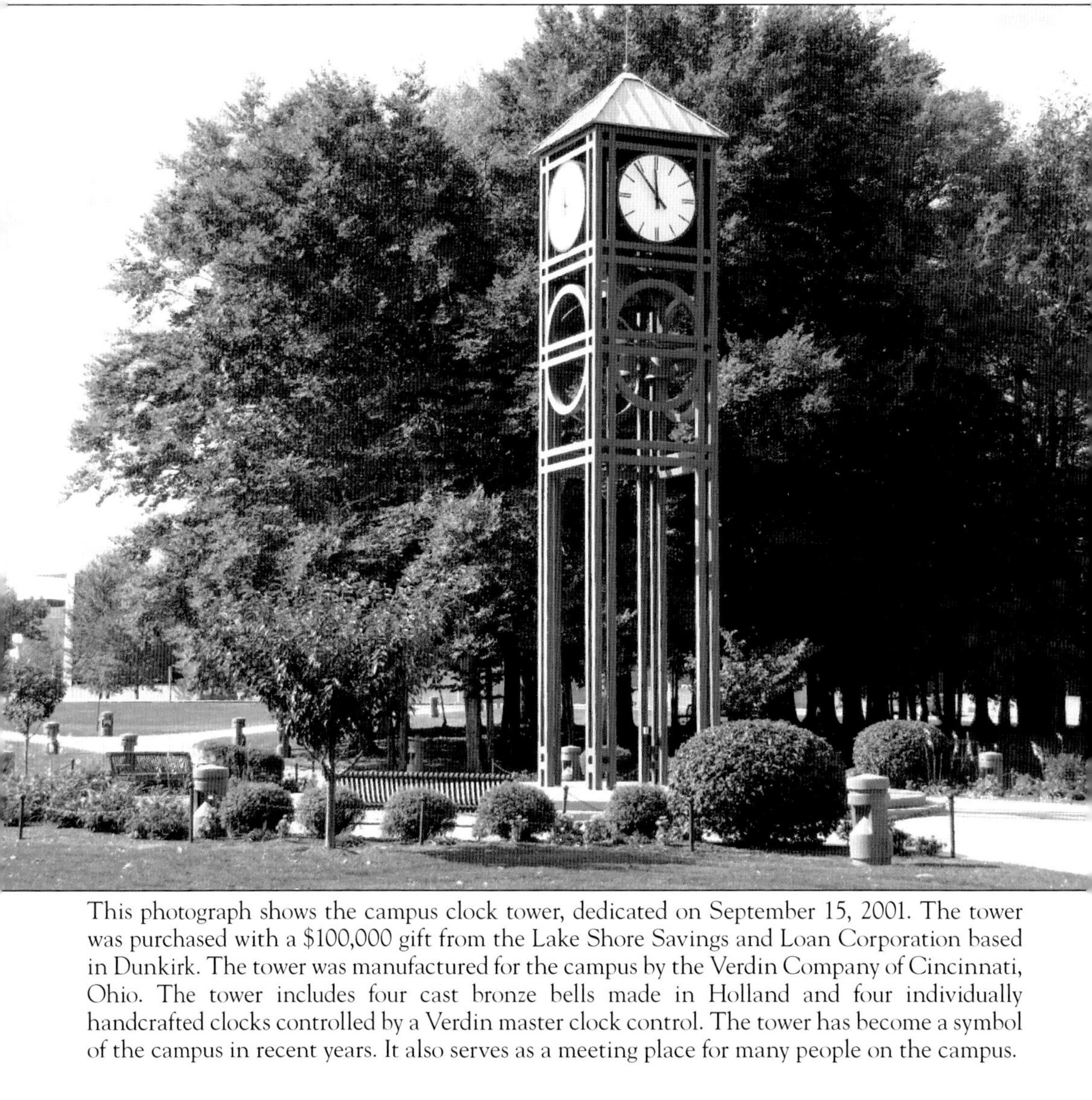

This photograph shows the campus clock tower, dedicated on September 15, 2001. The tower was purchased with a $100,000 gift from the Lake Shore Savings and Loan Corporation based in Dunkirk. The tower was manufactured for the campus by the Verdin Company of Cincinnati, Ohio. The tower includes four cast bronze bells made in Holland and four individually handcrafted clocks controlled by a Verdin master clock control. The tower has become a symbol of the campus in recent years. It also serves as a meeting place for many people on the campus.

Three

BUSINESSES

Many towns are founded with the hope that they will one day grow into vibrant communities that have everything a resident wants in a home. The success of any new town is usually determined by the success of the businesses within that town. Pomfret has been no exception to this belief, as it was with the growth of its economy due to many businesses that Pomfret has become what it is today. This chapter shows just a sampling of the businesses that have been a part of the town's growth. Some have become major corporations, while others have operated as family-run businesses. In each case, the community supported business growth and a better quality of life for the residents. This chapter was written in memory of the late Lou Nocek, an award-winning businessman from Pomfret, who helped shape the future of the business corridor on Route 60.

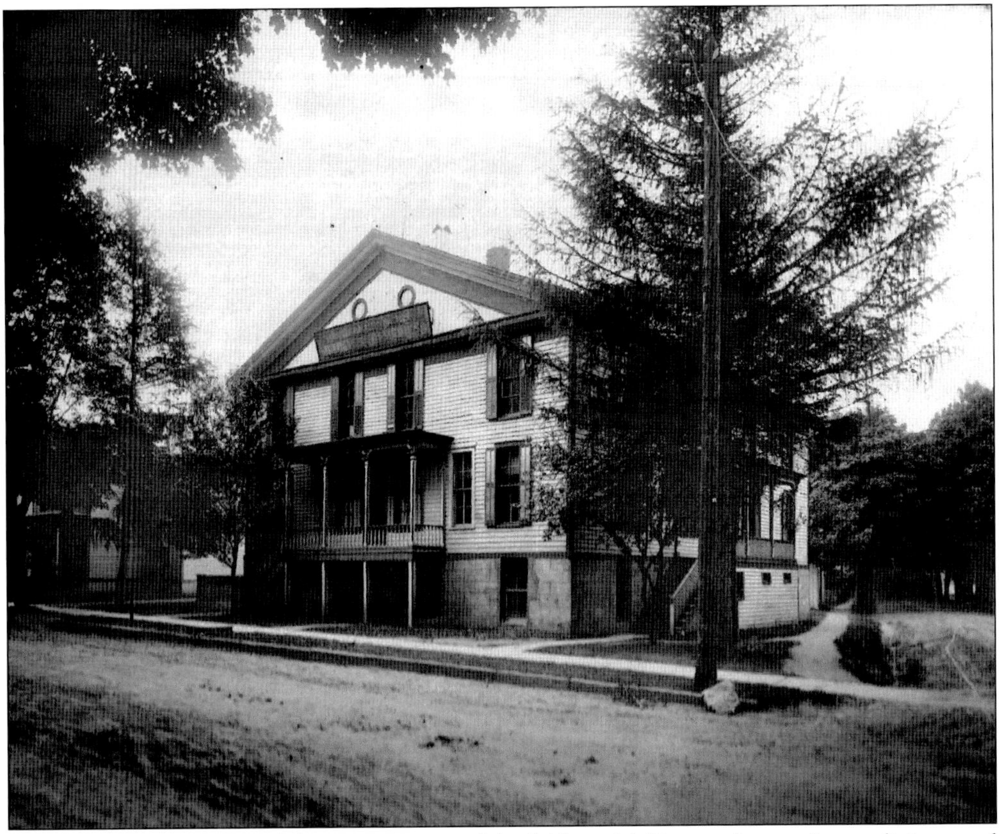

This photograph is one of the few existing of the Milton M. Fenner factory for medicines and tonics. The factory was located on Church Street near the Methodist church in this photograph from 1908. The factory produced Fenner's People's Remedies and Fenner's Golden Relief.

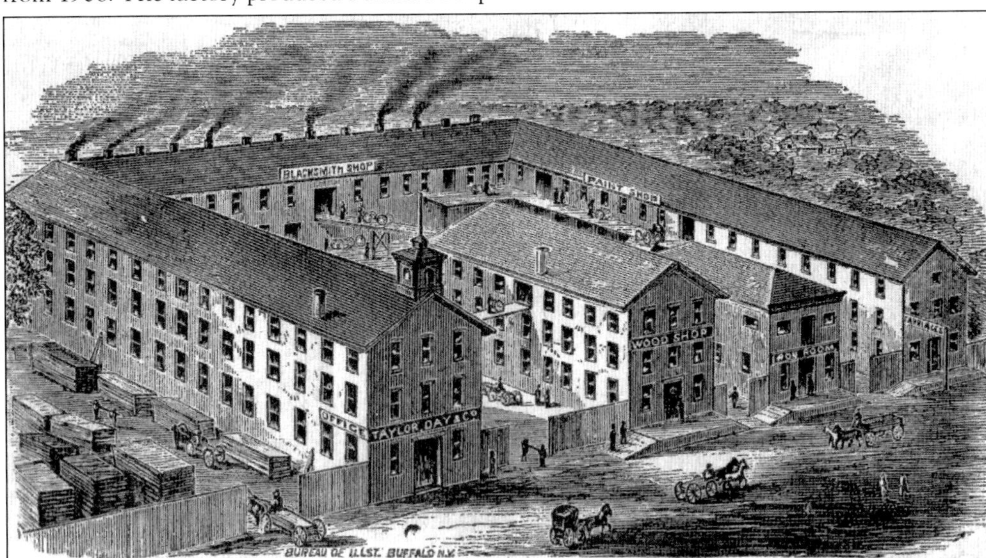

This is the Taylor and Day Company carriage works as seen in 1855. The business was located at 17–23 Center Street behind the old fire hall where the Hook and Ladder Deli is located today.

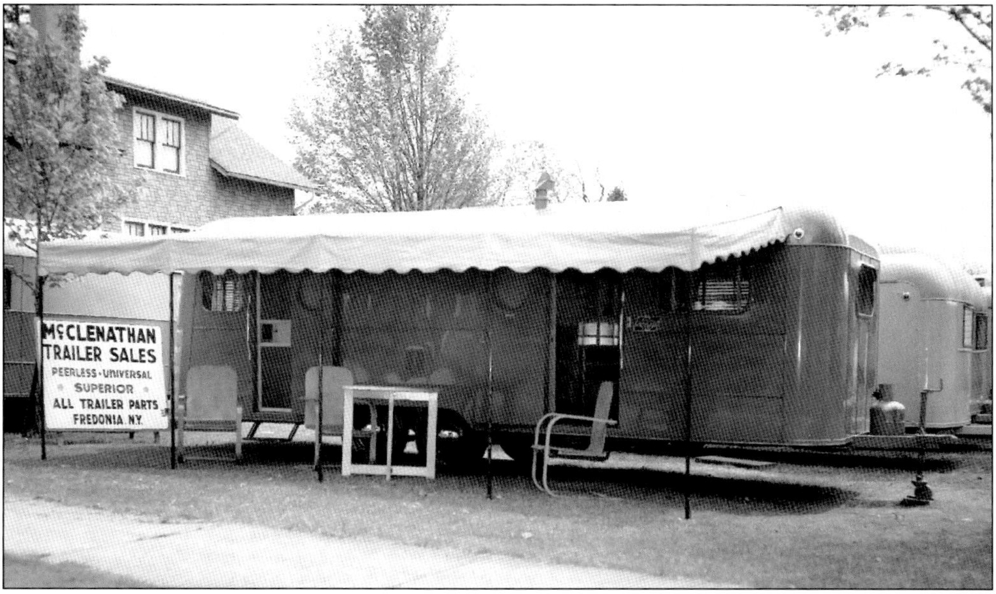

This photograph of McClenathan's Trailer Sales is the forerunner of what is today McClenathan's Mobile Home Park. Trailer sales was a blossoming new business in the 1930s, and its popularity spread even more in the next few decades as people gained more leisure time to travel.

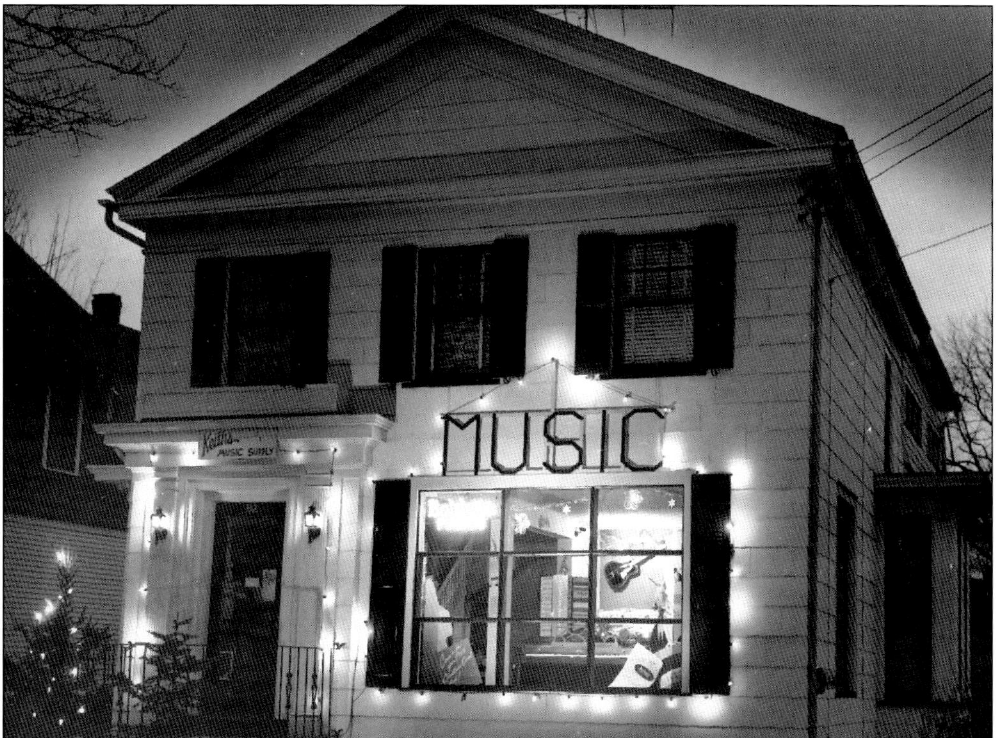

Music has always been a big part of Pomfret, especially during the normal school years and later at SUNY Fredonia. Keith's Music Store was just one of a number of small music shops that existed around Fredonia to cater to student musicians and residents.

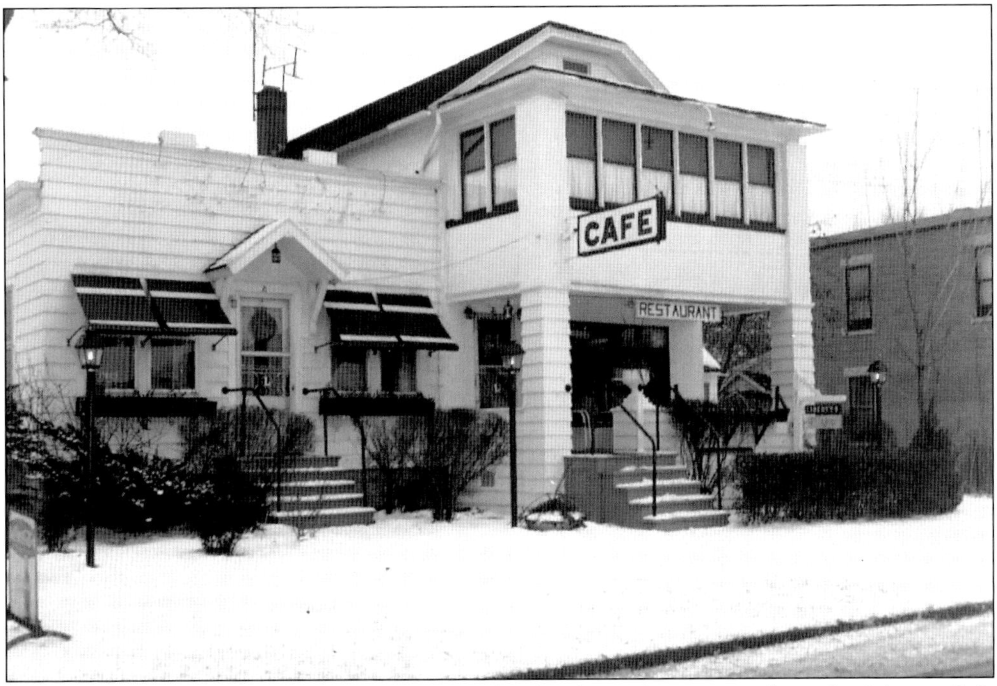

The Liberty Restaurant and Café is still around today, but is known simply as the Liberty Café at 21 Prospect Street. The little meeting place has still remained popular with many residents and is owned by Fredonia native Russ Leone.

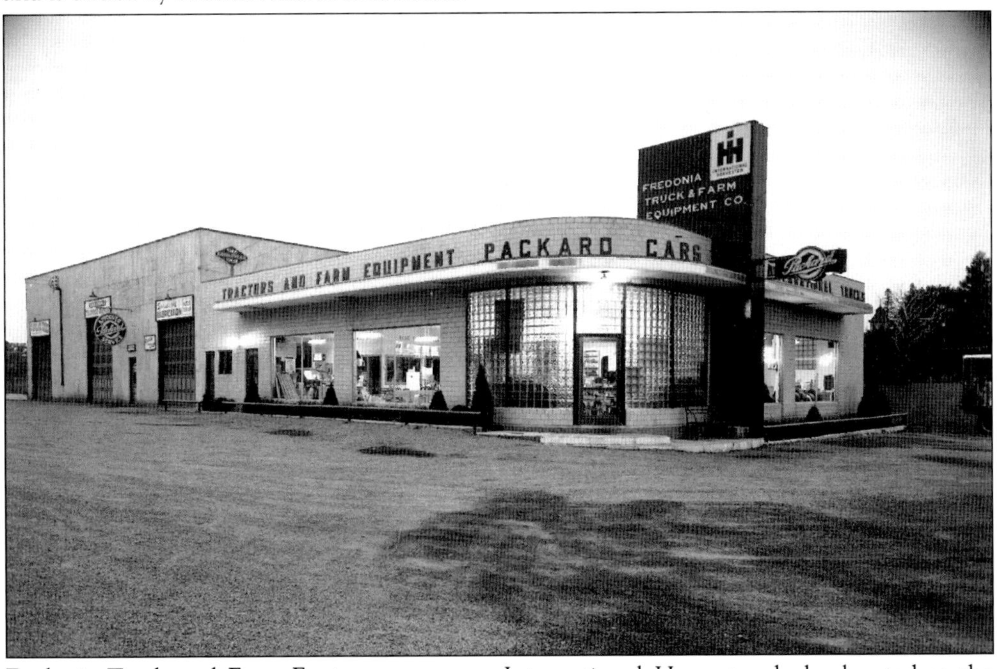

Fredonia Truck and Farm Equipment was an International Harvester dealer located at the corner of Route 60 and McCallister Road just outside the village. It has housed a number of businesses over the years, but currently is home to one of the town's most vibrant businesses, the Paper Factory.

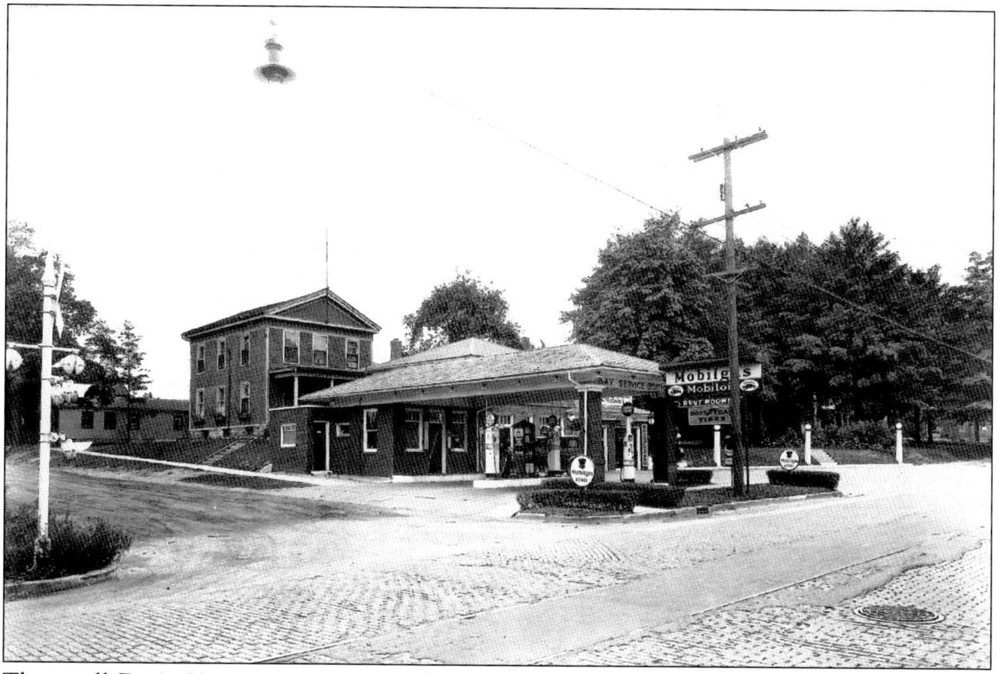

The small D. A. V. service station on the corner of Main and Prospect Streets got its name from the nearby line of the Dunkirk, Allegheny Valley and Pittsburgh Railroad (DAV&P). It was a very busy place in the 1930s and 1940s. The station is still in operation today as Pchelka's Wholesale Tires and Auto Parts. The station was typical of those from the time period, with full service including a very detailed cleaning of all the windows and a check of all lights and the horn. Attendants also checked the oil and other fluids upon request. This was definitely hometown service at its best.

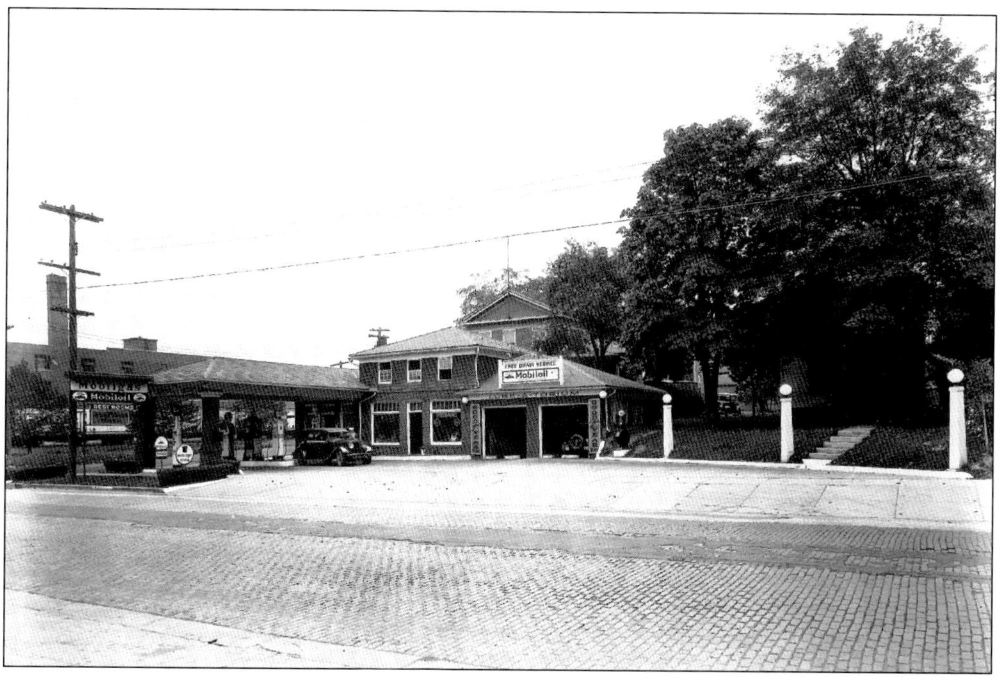

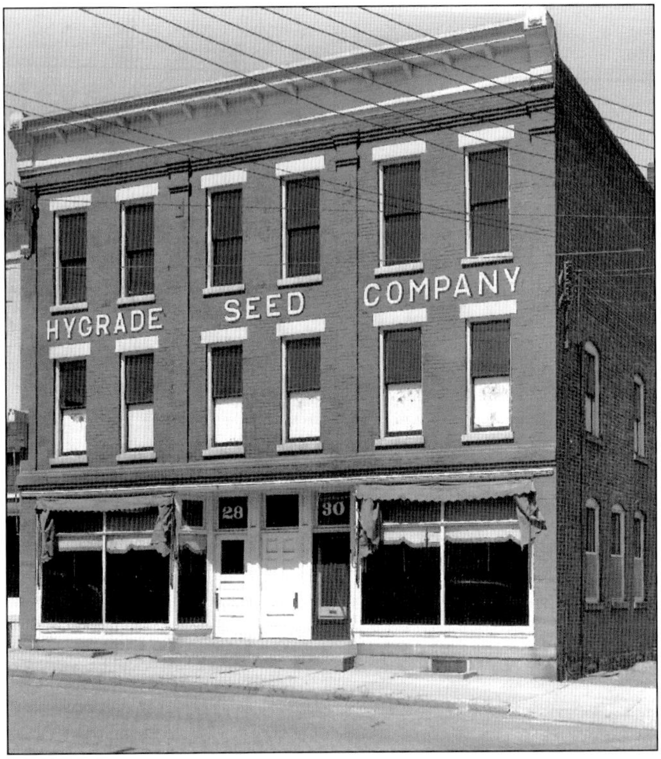

The early 20th century was dominated locally by a few types of businesses in Pomfret, but none was more important than the seed industry. This photograph shows the Hygrade Seed Company, located at 28–30 Water Street. Hygrade was just one of a number of seed companies in town. Hundreds of people worked at these seed companies, which contributed regularly to the community.

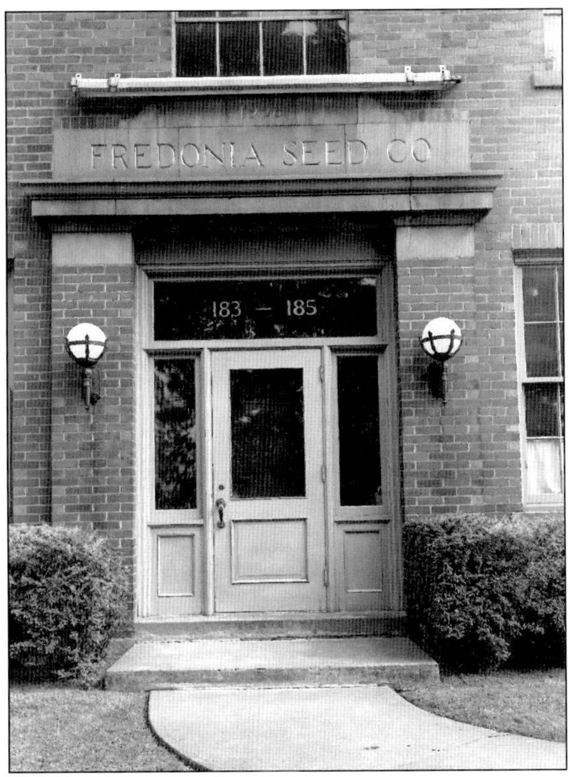

The Fredonia Seed Company was one of the most successful seed companies in the eastern United States during its heyday in the first half of the 20th century. Fredonia seed packets were shipped all over the world, making the area's name known as well. The company was sold in 1984, marking the end of an era in Fredonia. Today the building shown in this 1928 photograph is used for a number of different businesses and office space. It is located at 183–185 East Main Street.

The Card Seed Company was much smaller than the Fredonia Seed Company, but it was still part of the boom in the seed business locally that contributed to the area's growth. The building shown here also housed the J. H. McDonald liquor store.

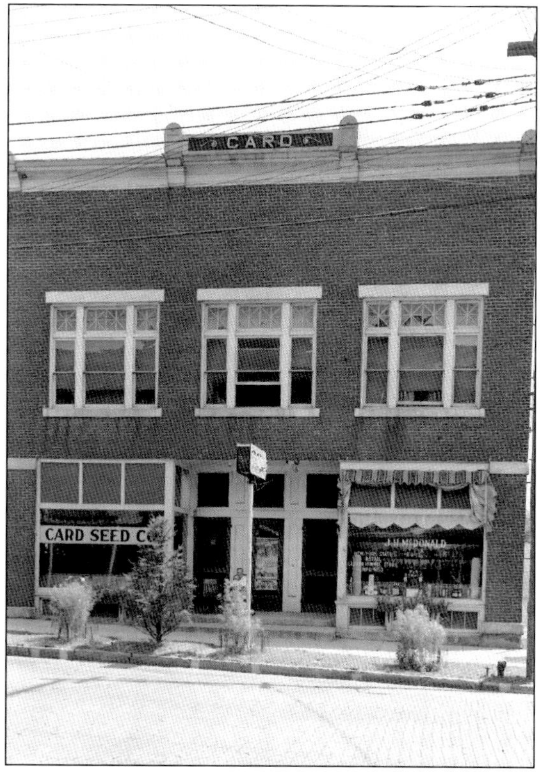

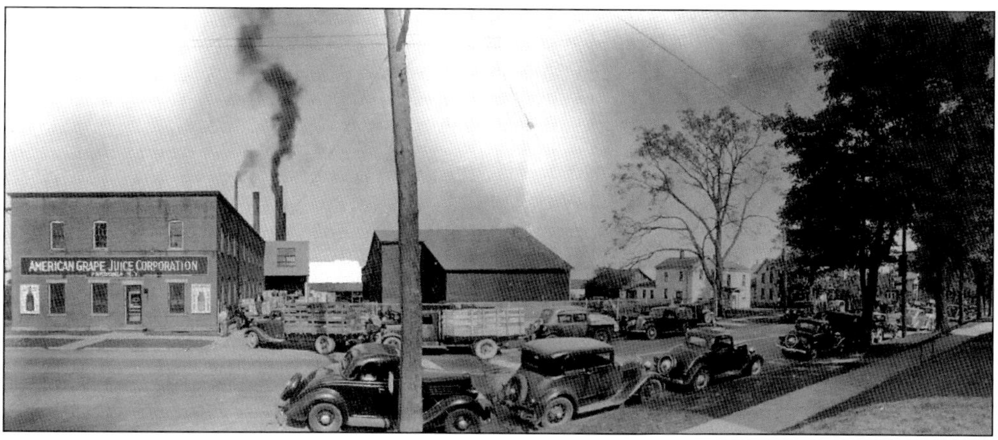

The American Grape Juice Corporation of Fredonia was an important employer in the area for many years. Many of the workers simply walked to work, so there was not much need for a parking lot. Those workers that did drive to work simply parked on the street near the plant as seen in this photograph. Today this type of food-processing industry remains a major employer of the town's residents in the form of Carriage House and Cliffstar Corporations.

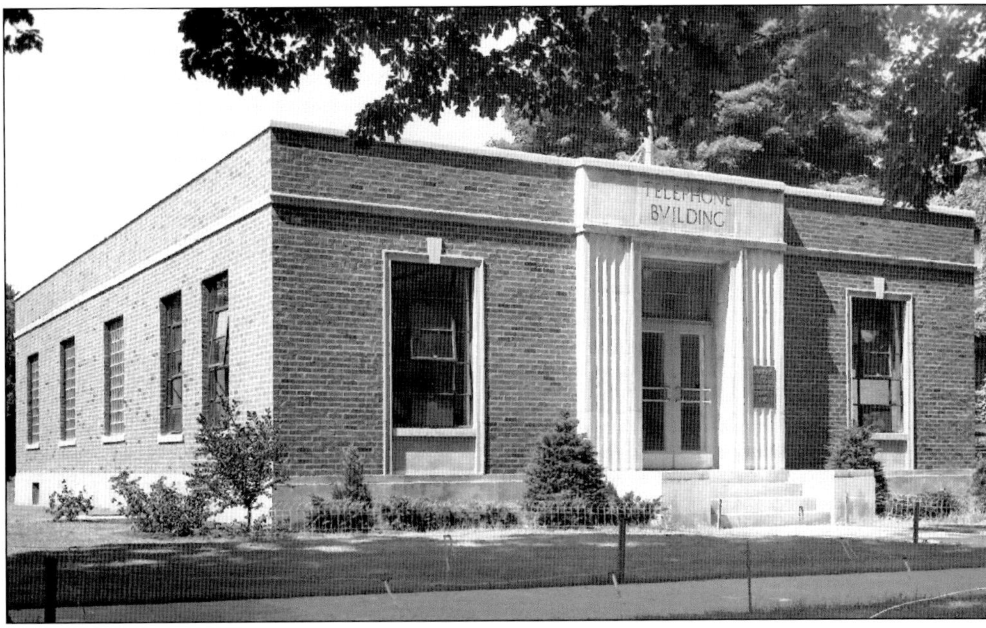

The Dunkirk and Fredonia Telephone Company may have had a modest beginning, but it has surely become a vital part of the community in Pomfret. The company has transformed under the leadership of the Maytum family into a regional communications giant, providing not only phone service, but also Internet services and security systems. The company's main building, shown here, was built in 1946 and is located at 40 Temple Street.

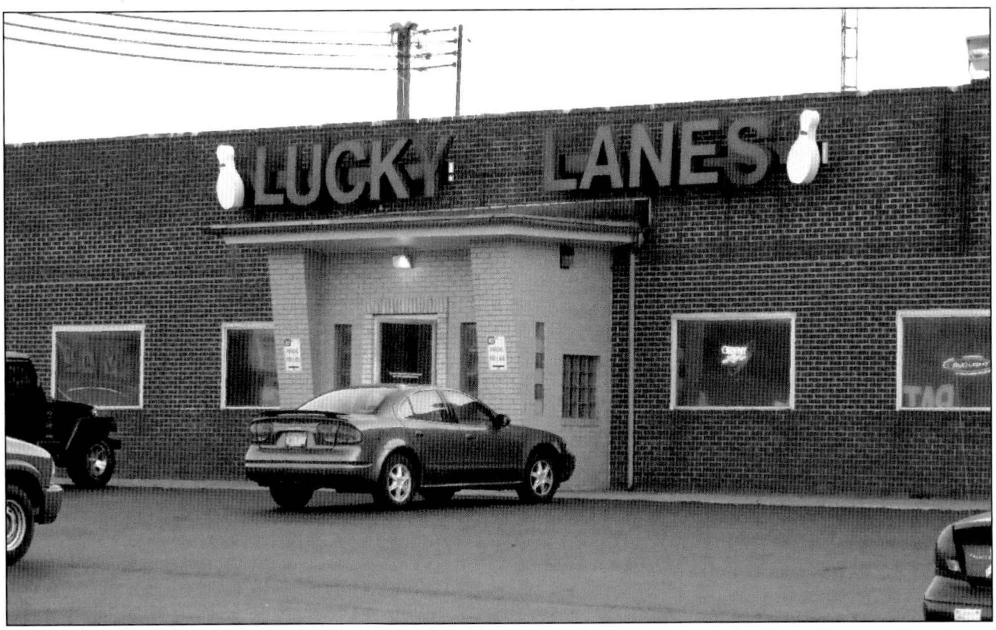

One of the most popular entertainment businesses in the town over the last 50 years has been Lucky Lanes, located on Bennett Road just inside the village line. The original name of the bowling center was Modern Lanes when it was opened in the 1960s by the late Lou Nocek. Today Lucky Lanes continues as a 40-lane bowling center operated by Nocek's son Paul and his mother, Nancy.

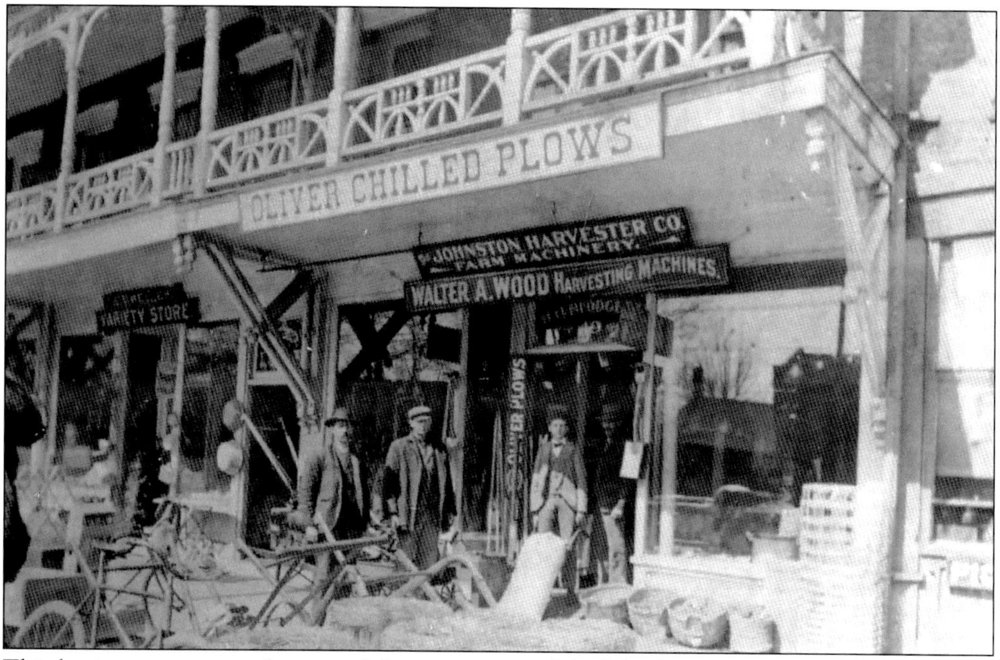

This business appears to be one of the most successful of the late 19th century. The Johnston Harvester Company farm machinery featured Oliver chilled plows and Walter A. Wood harvesting machines. Located at 49 Main Street, this business must have been vital to many farmers in the town due to the high number of family farms that were part of Pomfret.

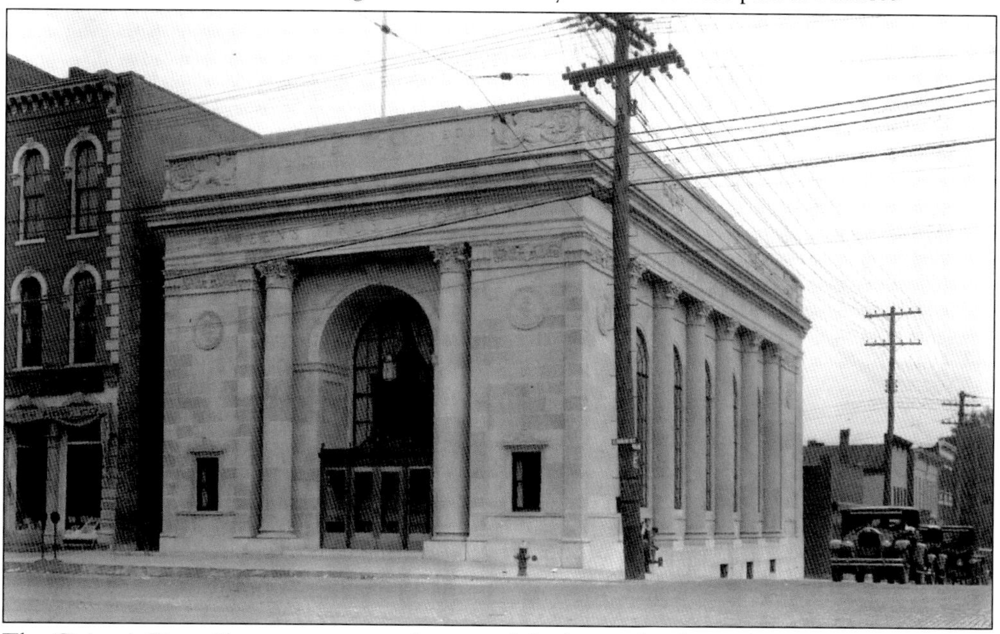

The Citizen's Trust Company came to be one of the largest banks in the area in the first part of the 20th century. The building shown in this photograph is easily recognizable today at the middle of the village of Fredonia. The building was built in 1929, but the company was founded in 1906. Today the building continues to be a bank and is the home of the local branch of M&T Bank.

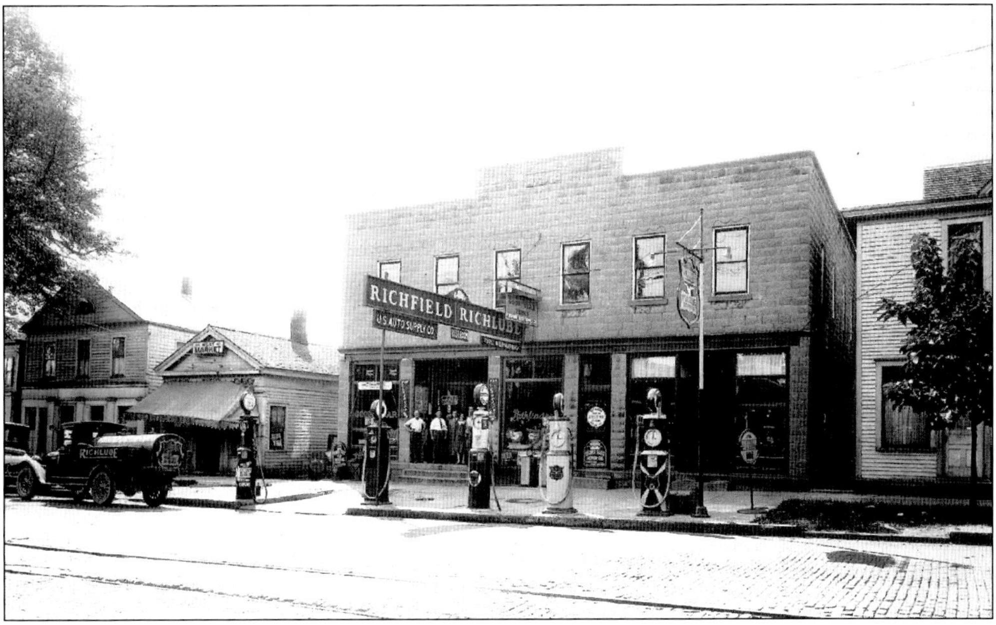

The Richfield Richlube and U.S. Auto Supply was located in the Baron Building on West Main Street just west of Forest Place. A number of these small service stations opened up in the village with the growth of the automobile. Today this area of Main Street looks similar to the way it looks in this 1920s photograph, as most of the buildings have changed very little over the years.

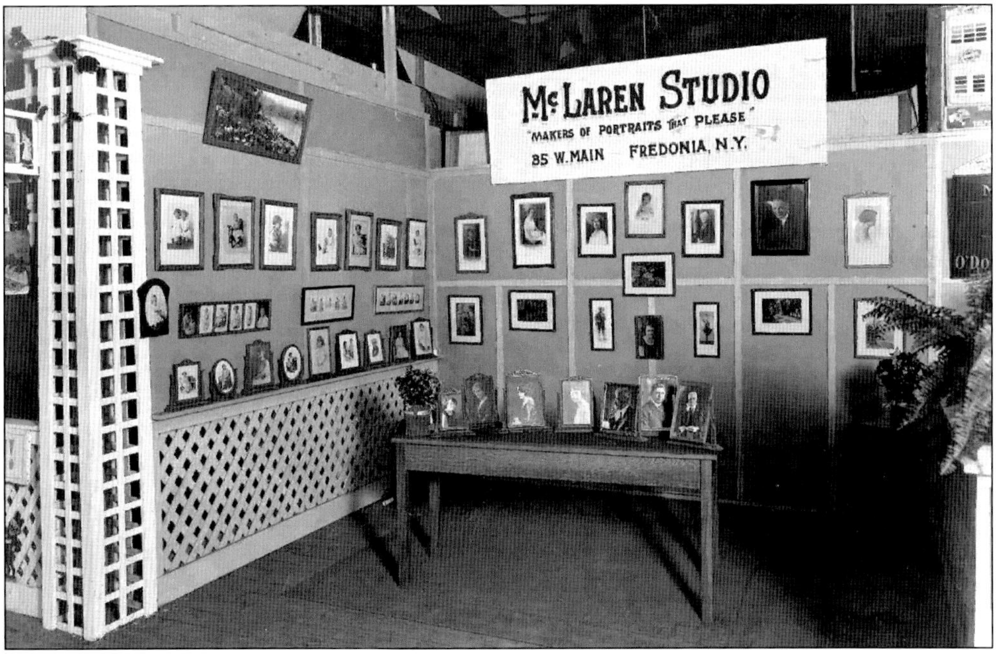

The McClaren Studio was one of the finest photography studios in the area during the first half of the 20th century. The studio, located at 35 West Main Street, opened in 1918 and continued for the next three decades. The McClarens took many of the photographs seen in this book. The photographs that remained in the family collection were given to the Darwin R. Barker Museum, where they have been housed ever since.

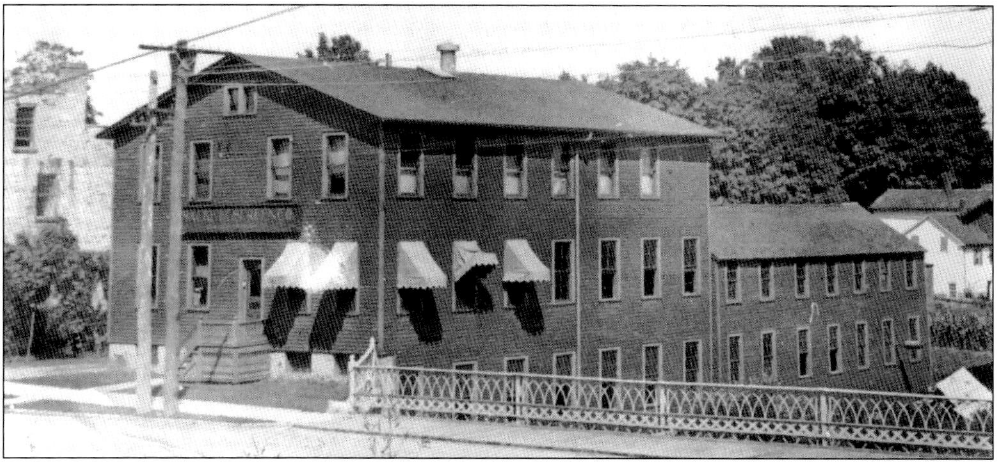

This photograph is of the Sackett Screen Company, which was located at the southeast end of West Main Street near the bridge. This specialized company was extremely successful for many years as a manufacturer of coal chutes and coal screens. As the need for its type of product dwindled, so did the business.

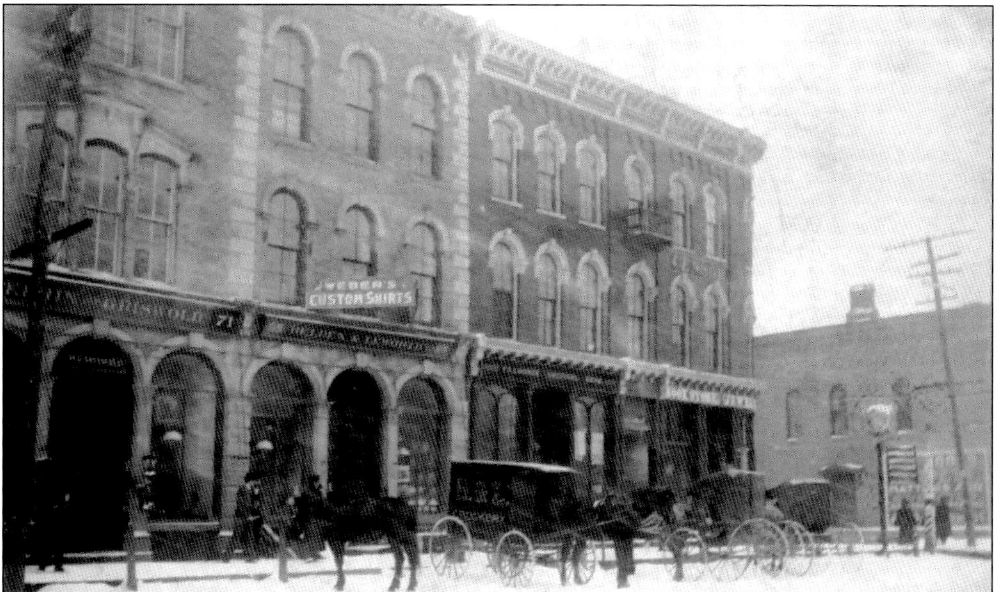

In this 1890 photograph, there are a number of businesses seen near the corner of Main and Water Streets at the center of the village. It shows the current site of M&T Bank and the adjacent offices of the Fredonia Chamber of Commerce and Festivals Fredonia.

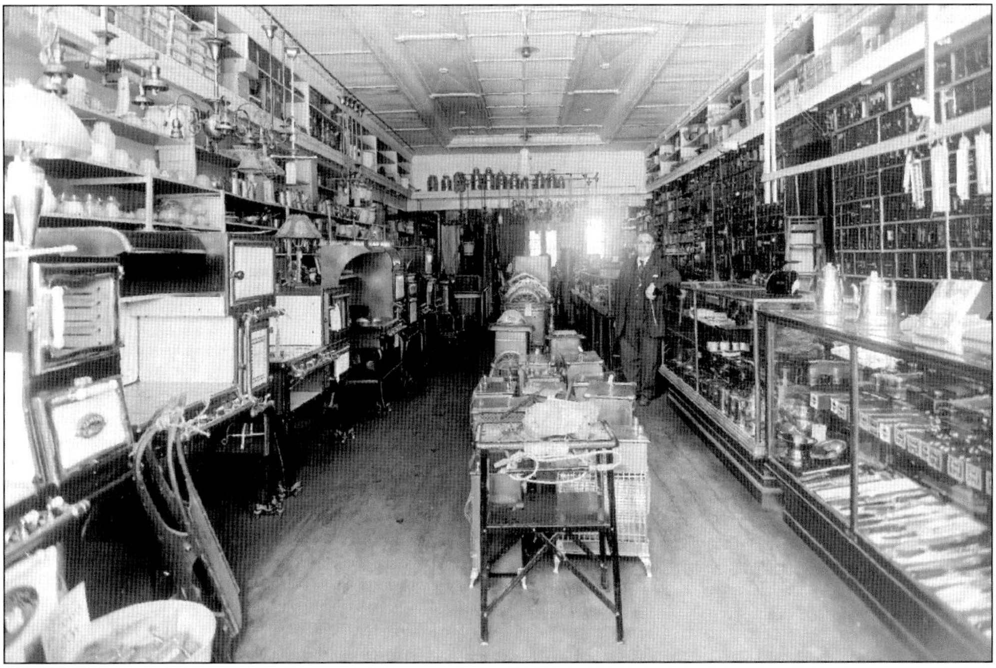

Life in a village late in the 19th century revolved around small businesses that catered to the needs of the community. Seen here is the Fredonia Hardware Store on East Main Street, operated by C. D. Sessions and D. L. Adams in the 1890s. The store was one of the busiest places in the village during this time period.

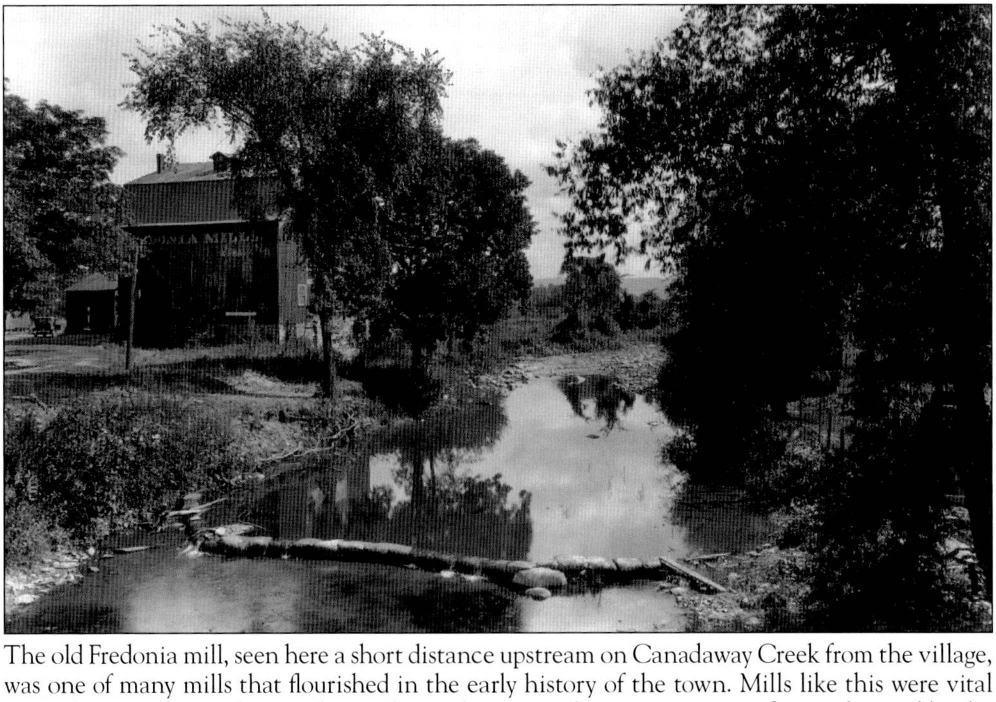

The old Fredonia mill, seen here a short distance upstream on Canadaway Creek from the village, was one of many mills that flourished in the early history of the town. Mills like this were vital to residents, as it gave them a place to bring their crops for processing into flour to be used by the family or sold. This photograph was taken in the 1920s when the mill was no longer operating.

Four

Around Town

This chapter is devoted to some of the special places in the town of Pomfret. Many of the photographs found in this chapter are rare and have not been seen by residents in the town. They are interesting to view because they represent places that longtime residents may have never seen or may not have seen in many years.

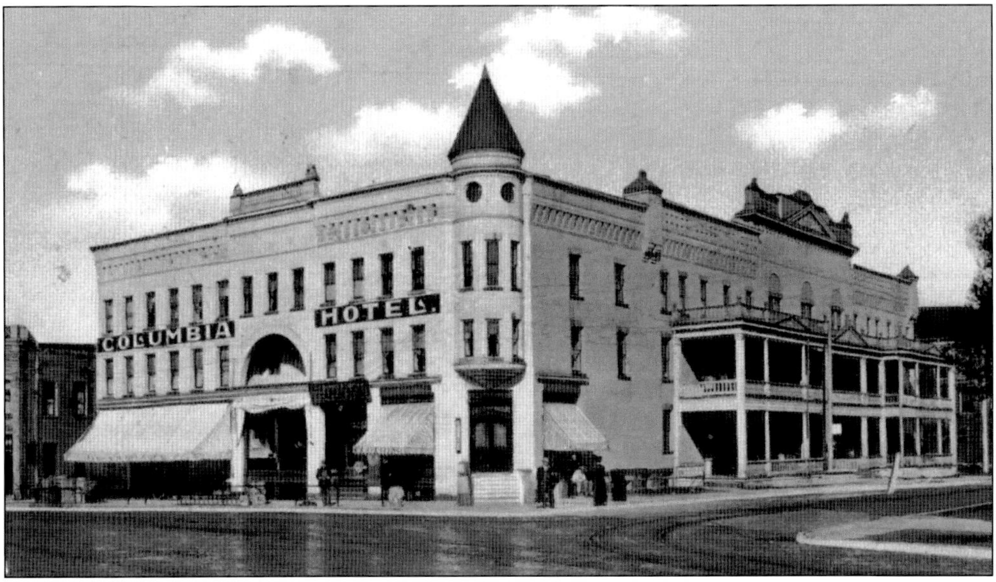

This is the Columbia Hotel as it appeared around 1900. The Columbia was the last in a series of hotels that occupied the present location of the Russo building. The hotel was destroyed by fire and rebuilt as a business and office center. It was a beautiful facility, with a guest list that often included visitors from all over the country.

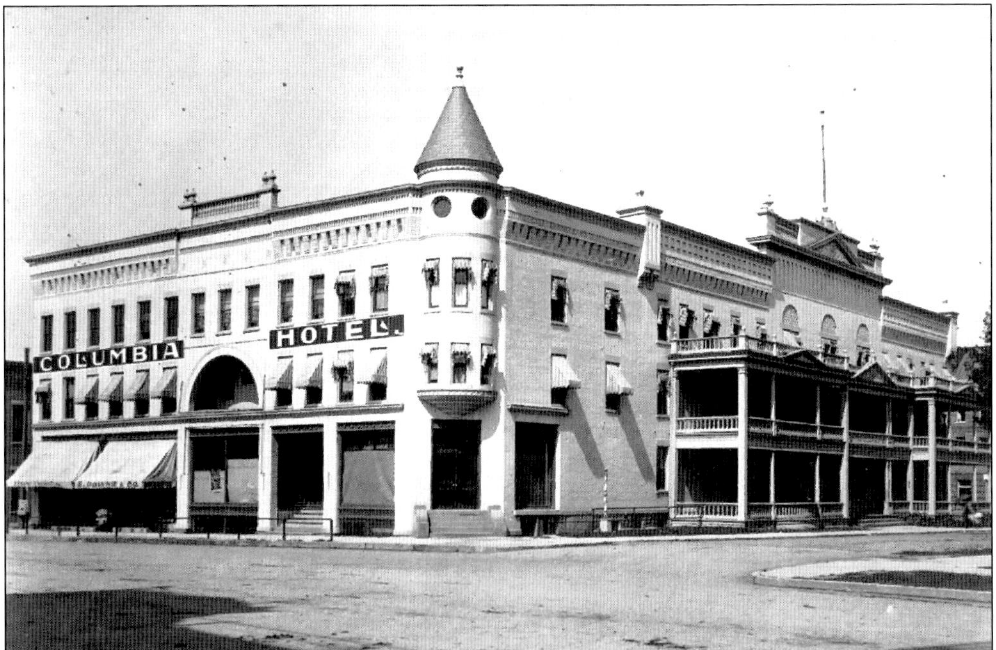

Here is another view of the Columbia Hotel, which housed a full-size dining room and a number of small shops where guests could purchase whatever they might need for their stay. The covered porch area was a favorite area to relax and look out upon Lafayette Park.

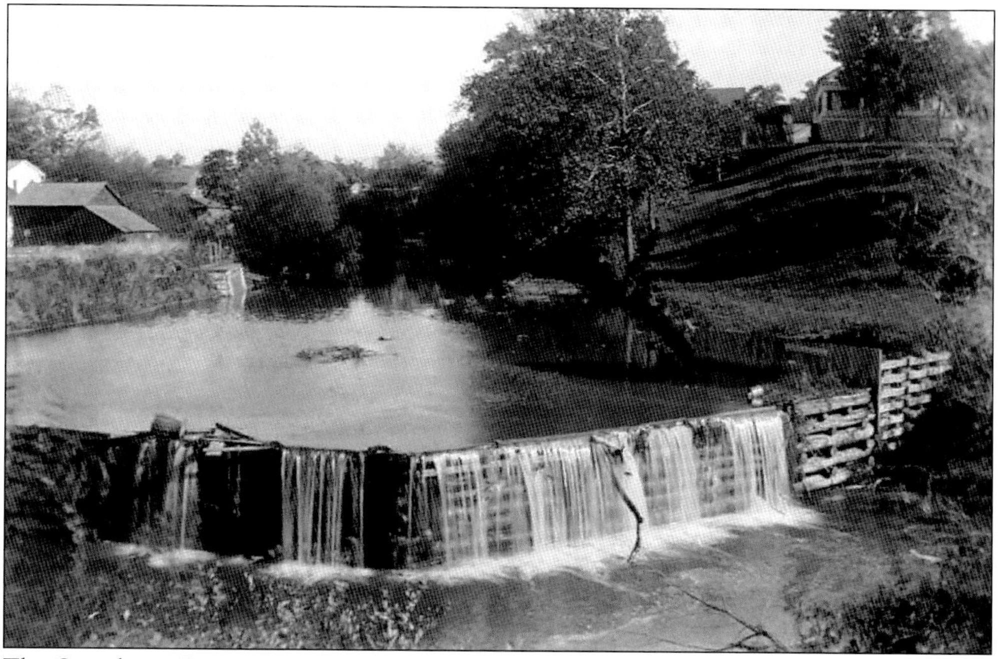

The Canadaway Dam is an example of how the creek was relied on by residents for a number of needs. The dam was used as a method of controlling the creek in order to use the water for different needs. The dam has been gone for many years, but there are still remnants of these old uses that can be seen along the length of the creek today.

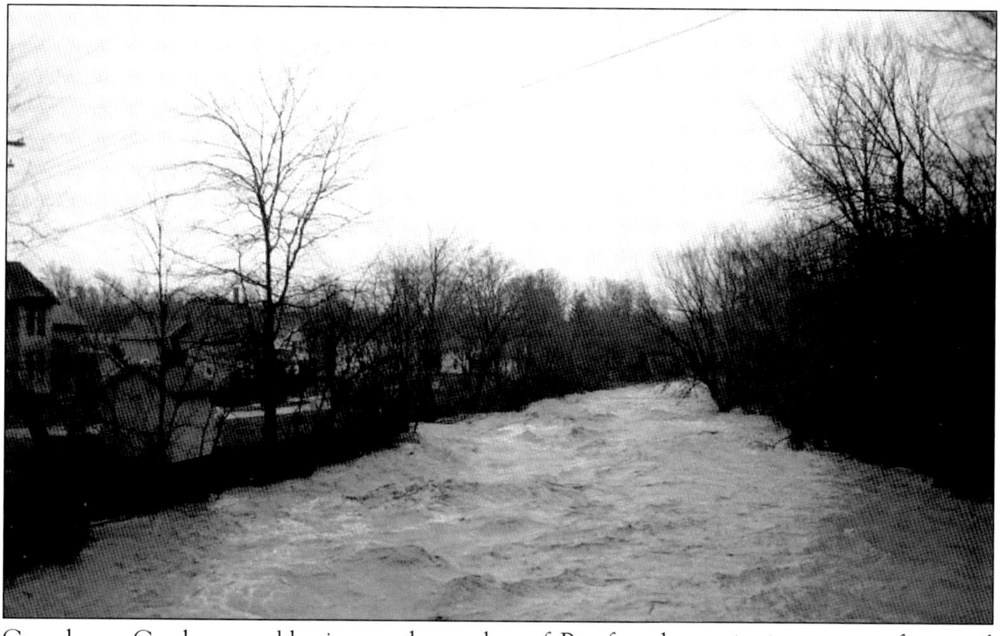

Canadaway Creek was a blessing to the settlers of Pomfret due to its importance for travel and the economy. On a number of occasions, the creek has overflowed its banks, causing great hardship. This photograph from a high-water period in 1934 shows just how much the size of the creek can increase. The bridge over Water Street has been seriously damaged a number of times, which has resulted in major construction projects to protect against further flooding.

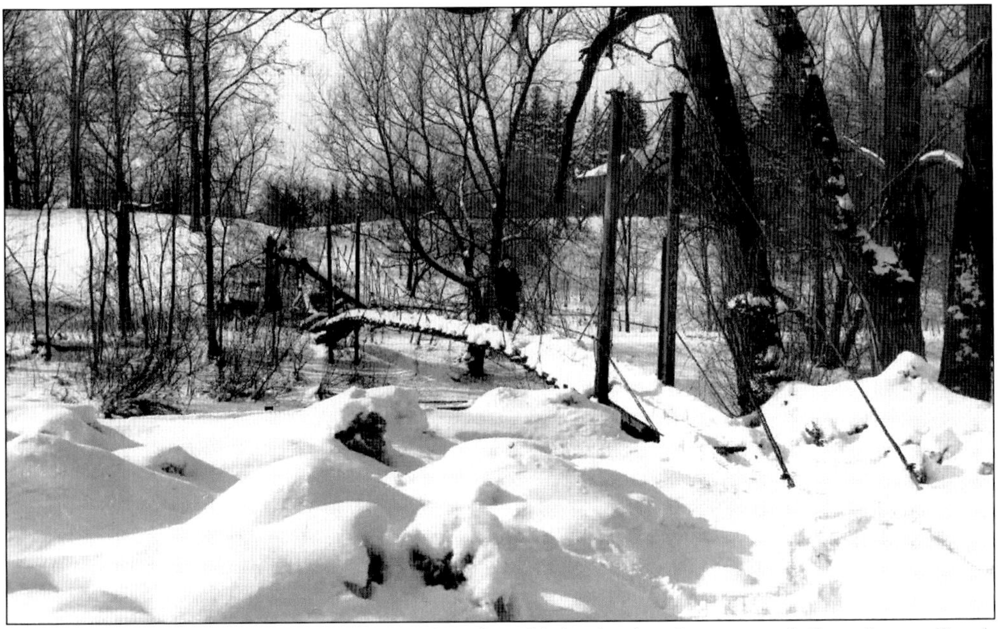

Many older residents of the town remember the old footbridge that crossed Canadaway Creek not far from where the Risley Street bridge is today. This photograph shows the bridge as it was starting to deteriorate and the No Trespassing sign that was placed there in an effort to keep people off the bridge, fearing collapse. Eventually the bridge was torn down, as it became so poor that it was falling down anyway.

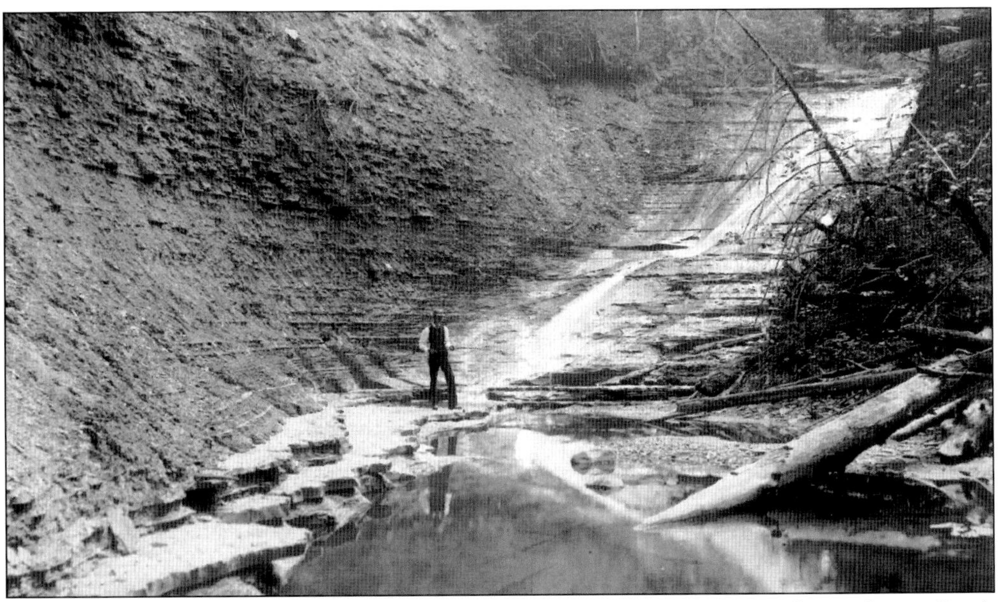

This view of one of the falls at an unidentified location on the upper part of Canadaway Creek was taken around 1895. There were a number of falls on the creek 100 years ago, but over time, many have disappeared due to erosion and construction projects that have changed the flow of the creek.

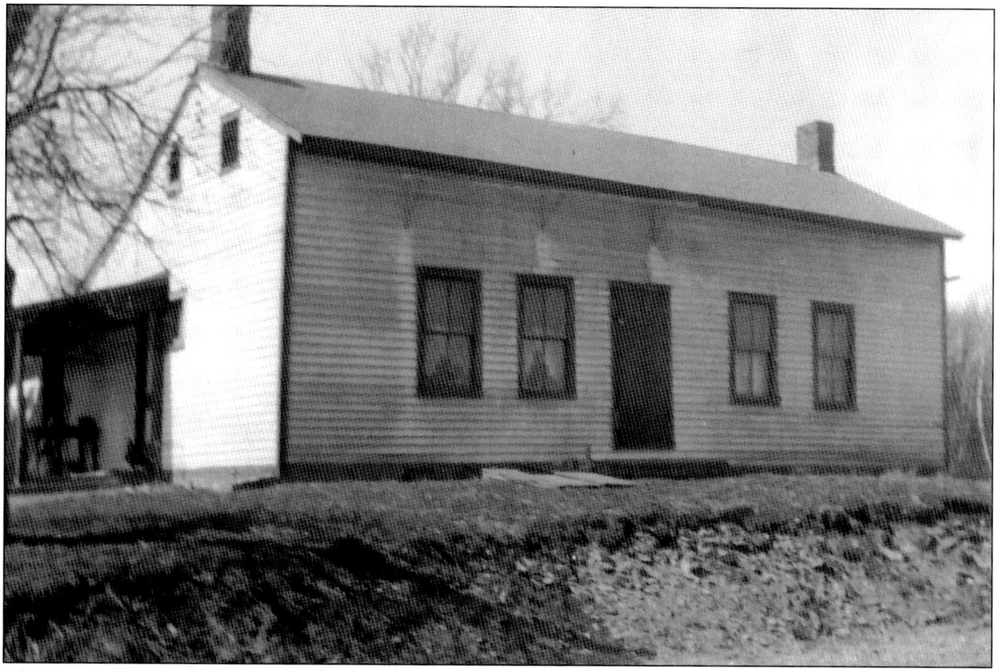

This early Laona house was the home of Hiram and Sarah (Sprague) Hinckley, who lived in Laona for years after marrying in 1838. A number of early homes in Laona still exist, but many have been renovated extensively, making it difficult to tell which may be from the early period.

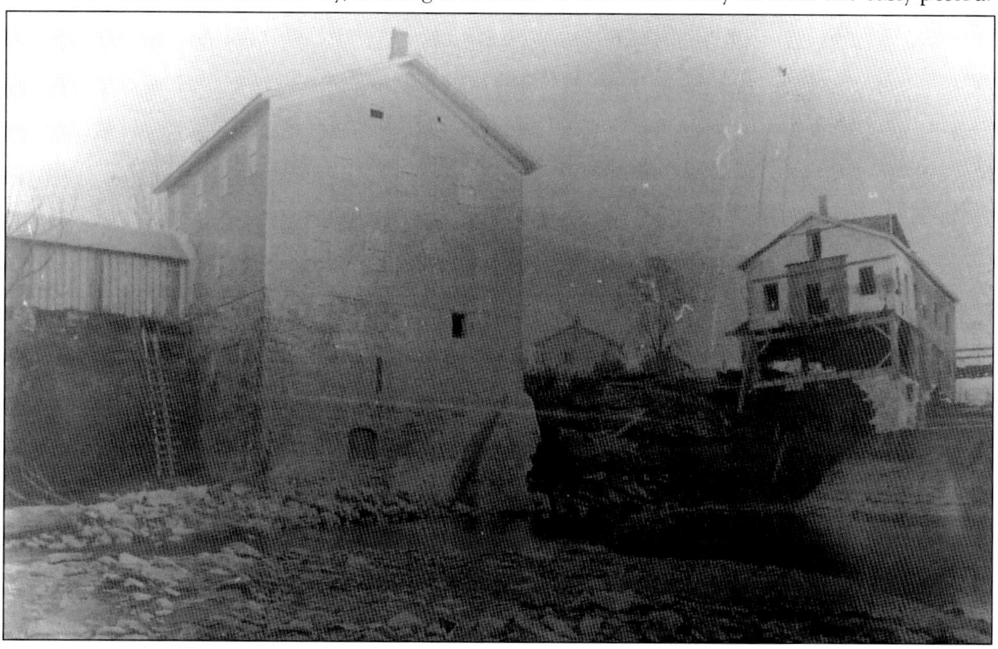

Laona was a bustling community during the majority of the 19th century, with a number of prominent businesses and citizens. This photograph shows one of the major industries in Laona, the gristmill built by Thomas and Hezekiah Bull in 1810. Laona's position just upstream from Fredonia on the Canadaway Creek made it an important trade center on the waterway. The creek also supplied waterpower for businesses like this gristmill, just like in Fredonia.

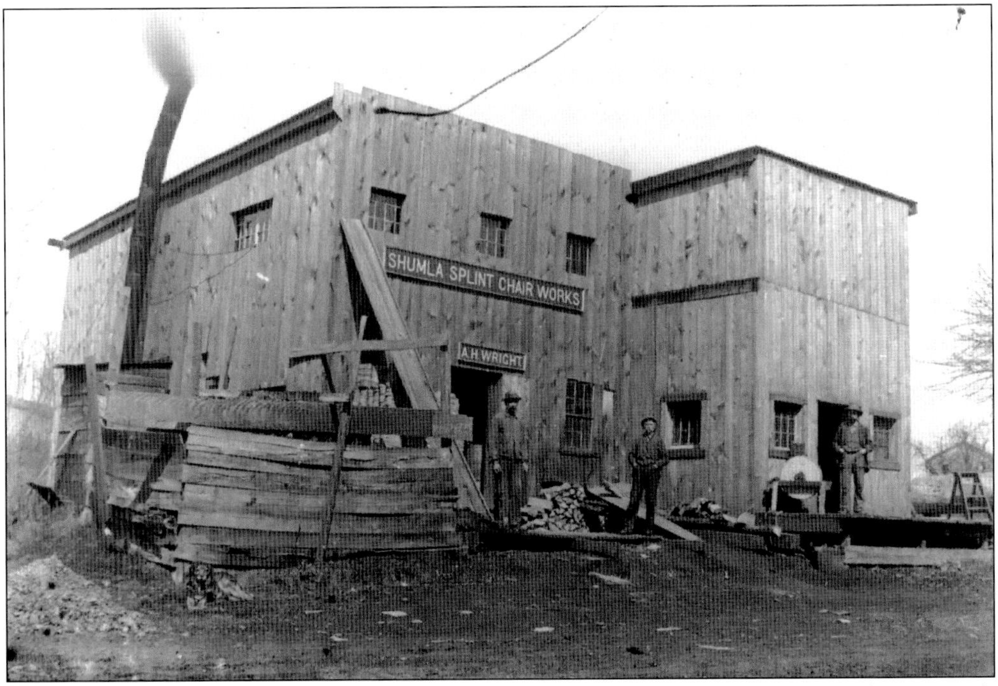

The area known as Shumla is just south of Laona along Canadaway Creek heading towards Cassadaga. Shumla was another area that benefited from its location along the creek during the 19th century. Shown here is the Shumla Splint Chair Works, which was owned and operated by A. H. Wright.

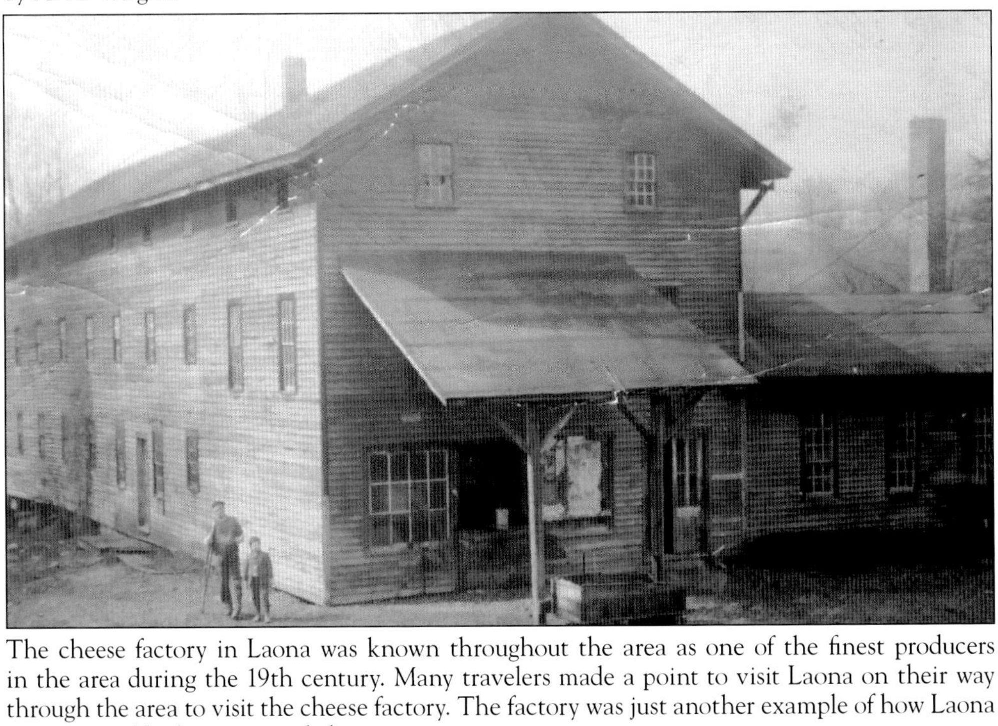
The cheese factory in Laona was known throughout the area as one of the finest producers in the area during the 19th century. Many travelers made a point to visit Laona on their way through the area to visit the cheese factory. The factory was just another example of how Laona grew so quickly during its early history.

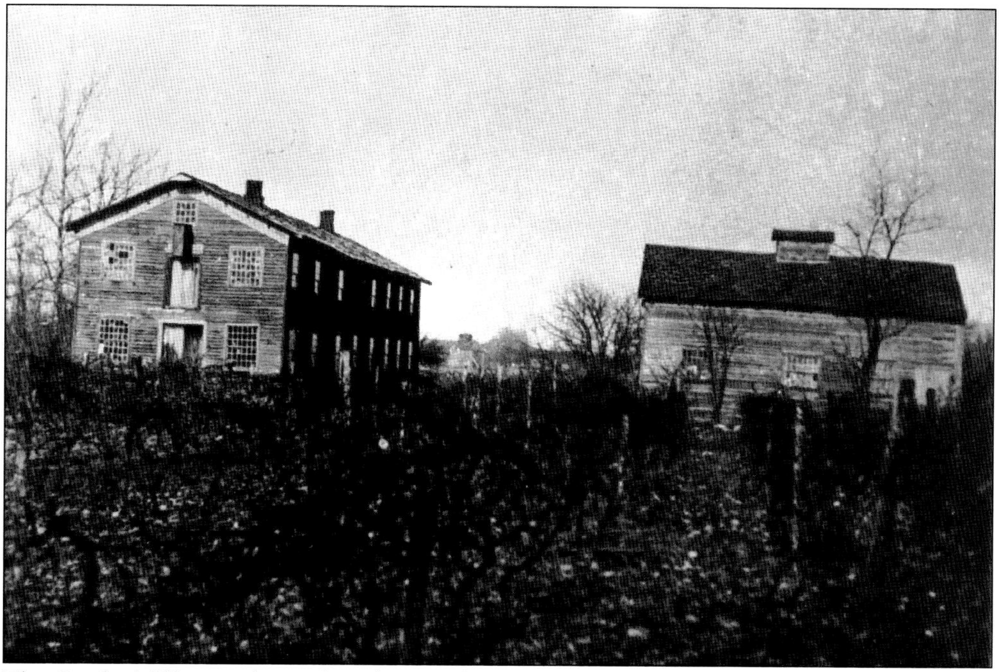

The Crosby Mills were located in the area known as Cordova, which was located in the area near where the intersection of Matteson Street and Brigham Road is today. This photograph was taken in 1909, shortly before the mills were torn down.

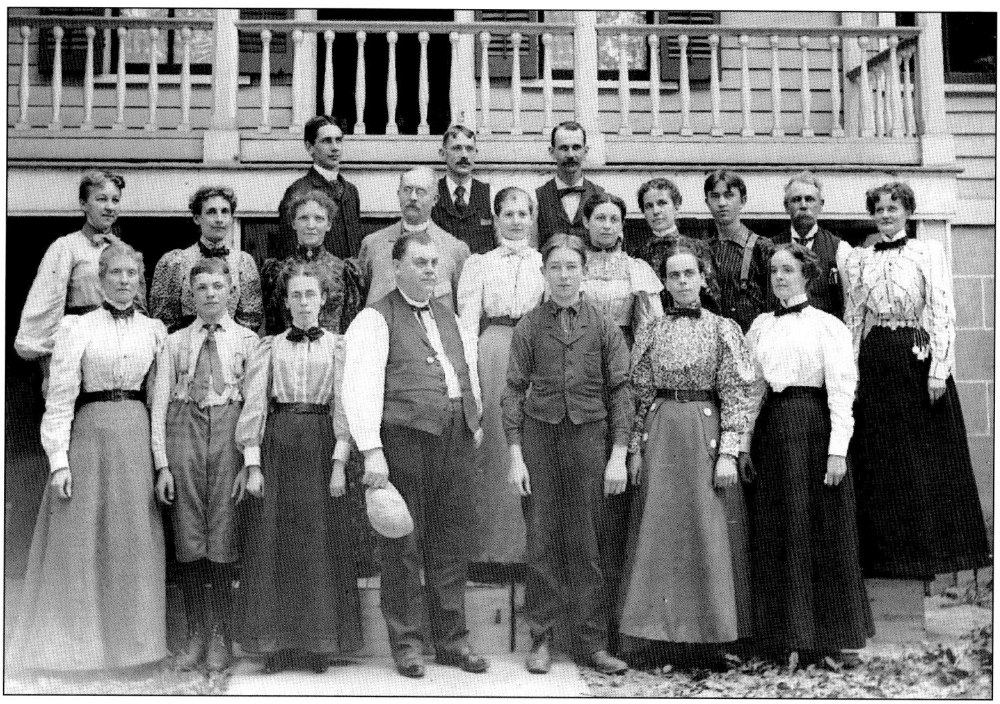

Dr. Milton M. Fenner was responsible for one of the most successful businesses in Fredonia during the 19th century, the Fenner Medicine Factory. Here workers are seen outside the factory posing with Fenner (man holding the cap). See page 17 for more information about Fenner.

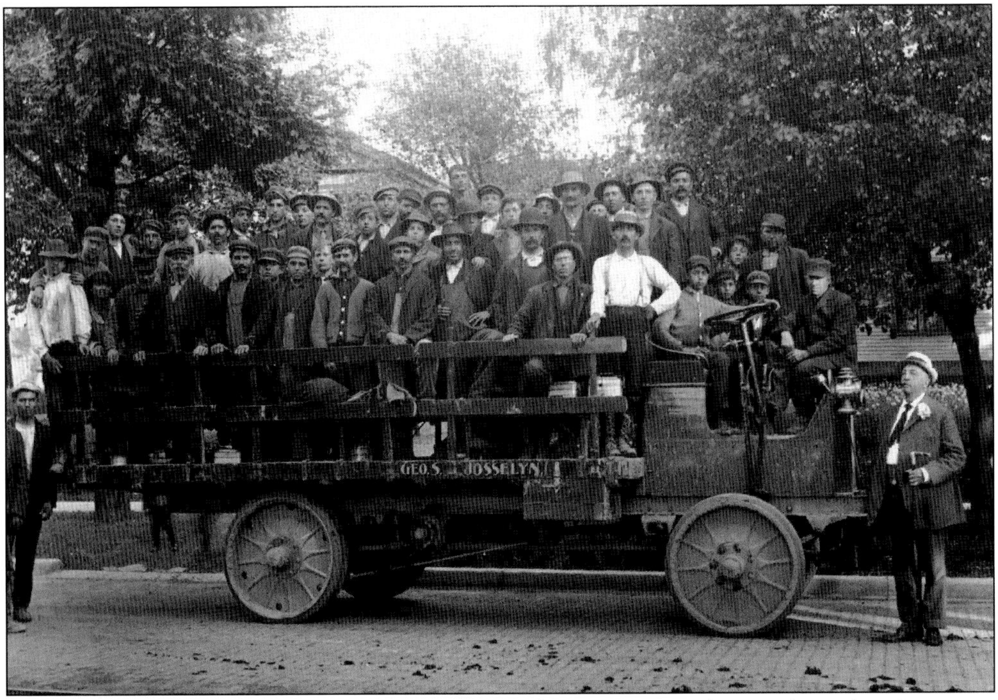

Seen in this photograph is the new George S. Josselyn Nursery truck near the railroad crossing on Main Street in 1919. Notable men in the photograph include driver Charles R. Barker and Albert Phillips on the dashboard.

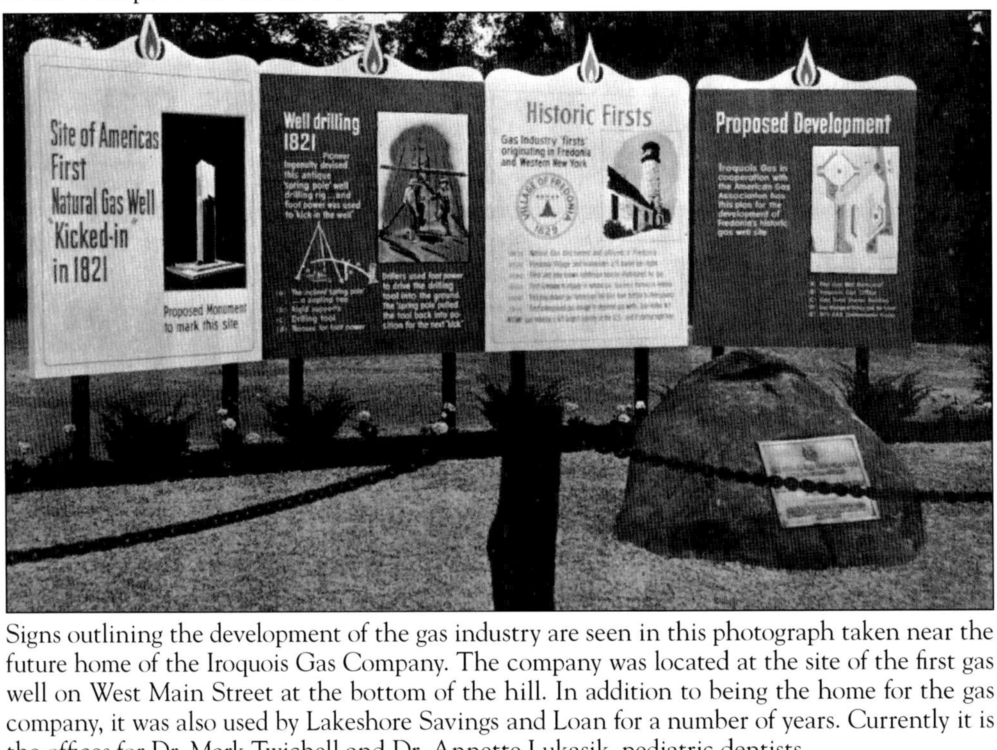

Signs outlining the development of the gas industry are seen in this photograph taken near the future home of the Iroquois Gas Company. The company was located at the site of the first gas well on West Main Street at the bottom of the hill. In addition to being the home for the gas company, it was also used by Lakeshore Savings and Loan for a number of years. Currently it is the offices for Dr. Mark Twichell and Dr. Annette Lukasik, pediatric dentists.

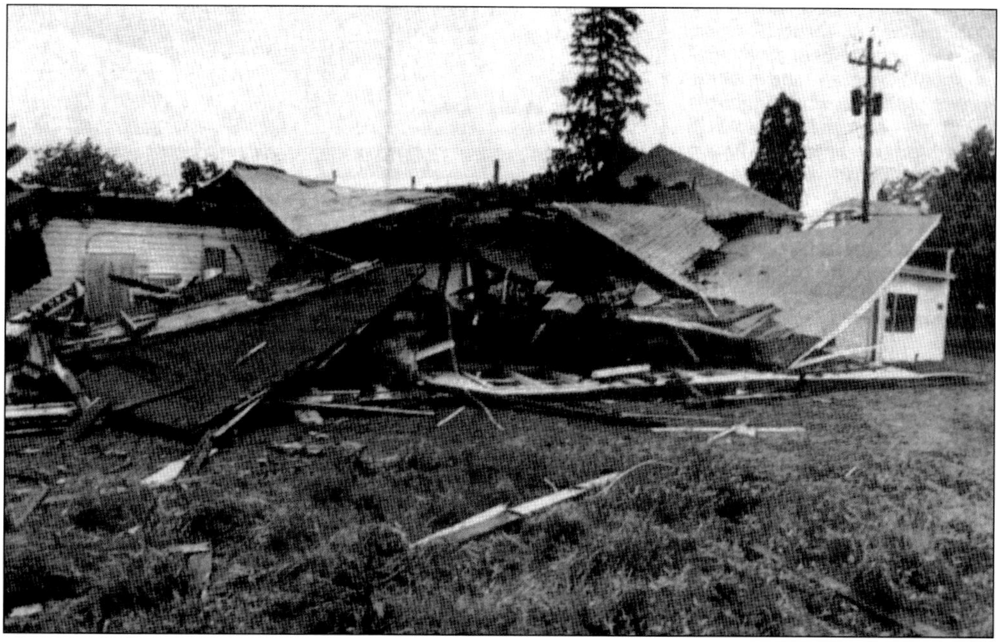

The area is known for its wild weather during the winter, but on July 12, 1992, a summer tornado touched down in Fredonia and caused millions of dollars in damage. This photograph shows the Foster Nursery on Orchard Street the day after the storm.

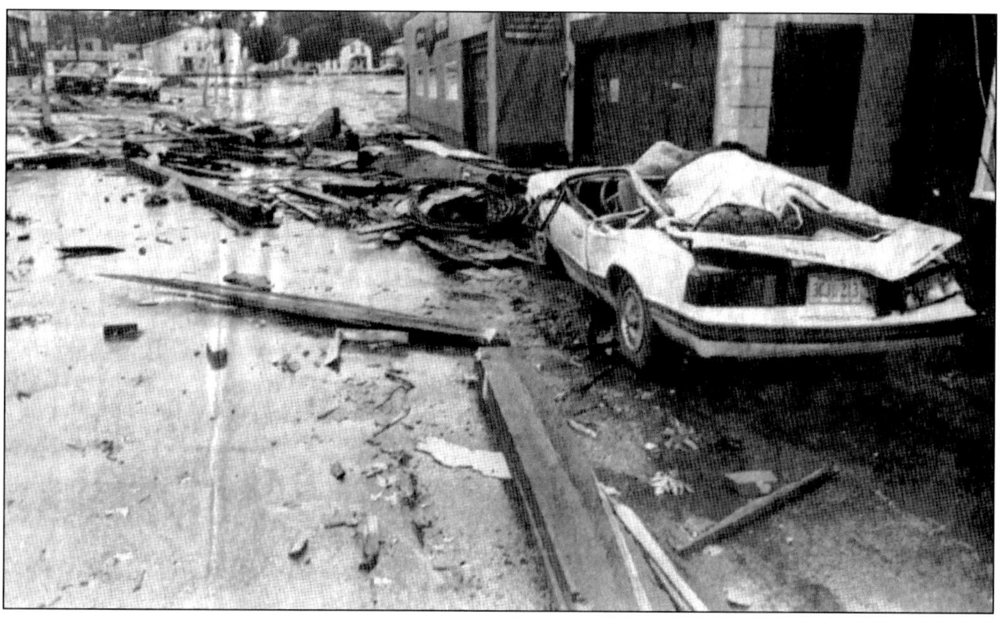

Another view of the damage from the 1992 tornado is seen here in this July 13, 1992, photograph. The East Main Street parking lot saw a great deal of damage during the storm, with cost estimates between $2 million to $3 million.

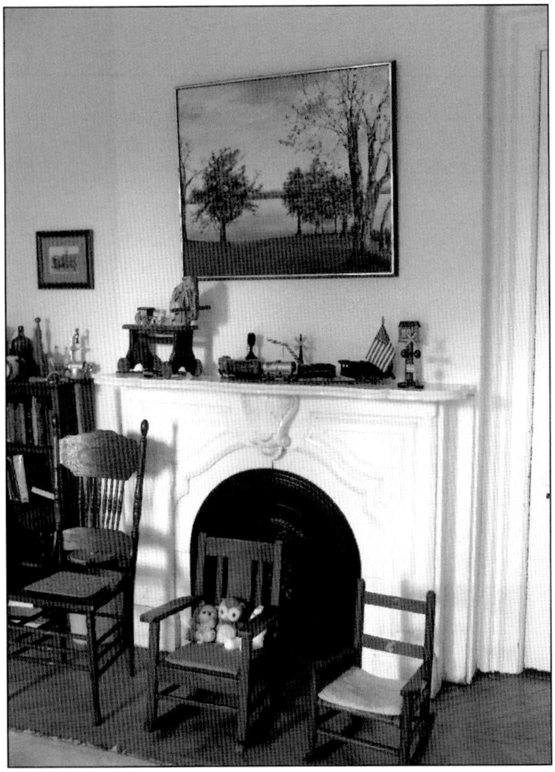

This is the first of many images of one of the area's most noteworthy residences, the Brookside Manor Bed and Breakfast. The manor was originally built in 1875 at a cost of around $5,500. It was built by local tannery owner Horace White for his personal residence. The design of the home was by Maj. Enoch A. Curtis, who is discussed on page 28. This photograph shows the mantle in the front sitting room, which faces Route 83. The manor is currently owned and operated by Andrea Andrews and Dale Mirth.

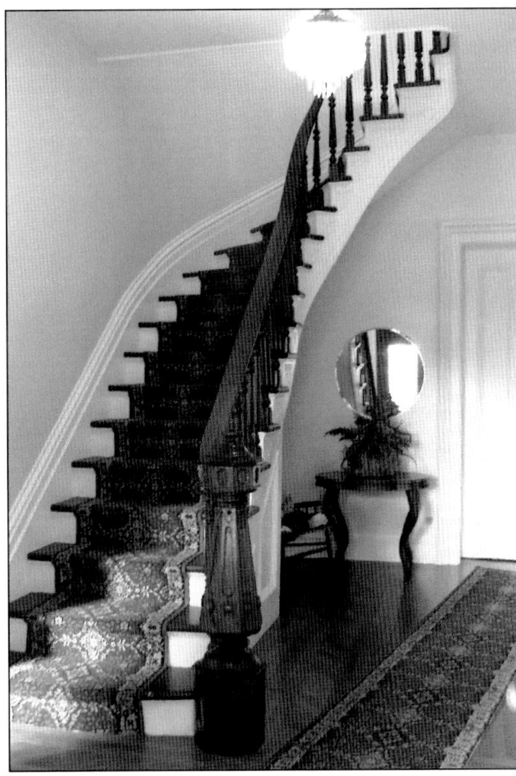

One of the most beautiful features of Brookside Manor Bed and Breakfast is the entrance. The spiral staircase seen here is a favorite feature of many guests. The manor is located a short distance up Route 83 from its intersection with Route 60. The original owner's tannery business was located just around the corner off Route 60.

The front entrance to Brookside Manor Bed and Breakfast faces Route 83 on the south side of the building. The house has more than 6,200 square feet of living space, while the grounds include over five acres of land.

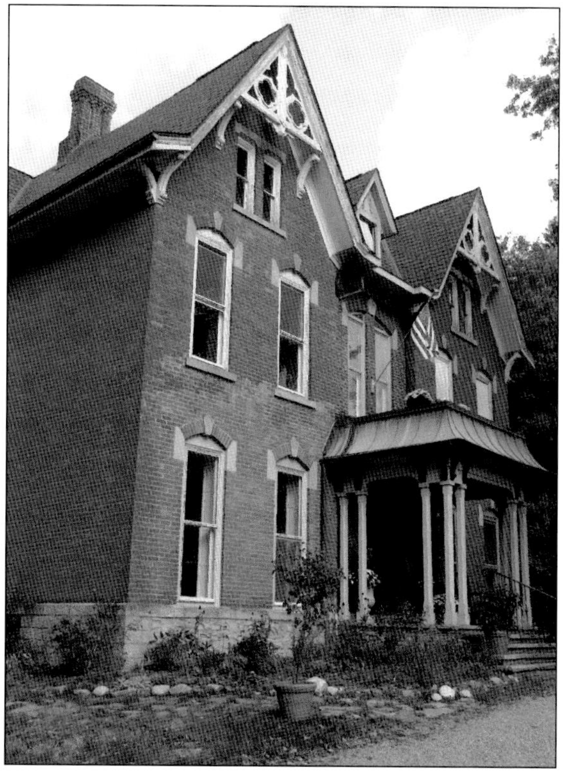

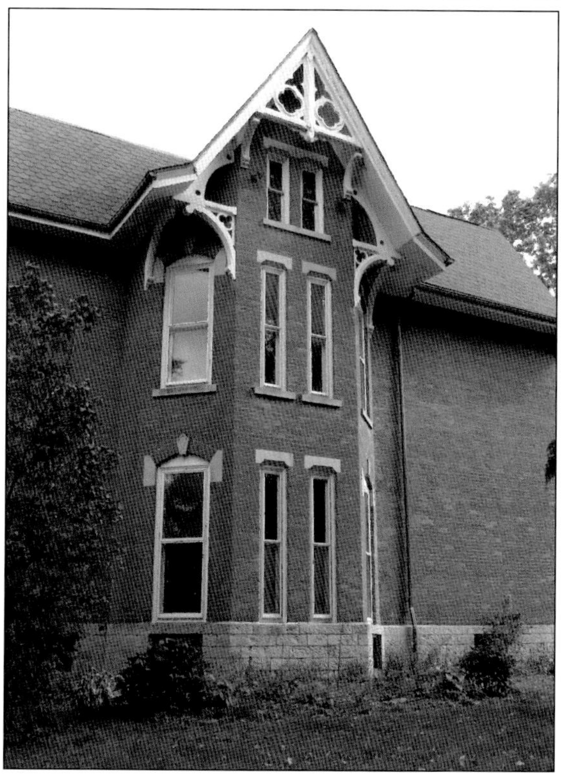

This side of the Brookside Manor Bed and Breakfast faces Route 60, which is only a few hundred yards away. The style of architecture is Victorian Gothic, with a number of updates done to the design by Curtis. White was very involved in the design process, giving feedback to Curtis as he carefully planned the home for his client.

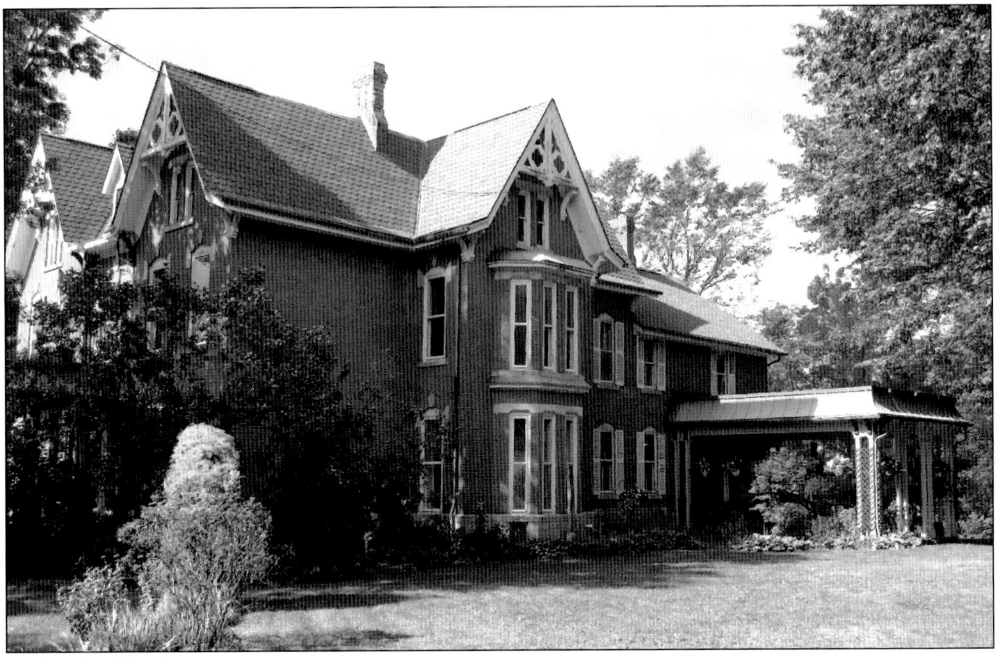

This view of Brookside Manor Bed and Breakfast shows the side of the home that faces up the hill along Route 83. Horace White owned the local tannery in Laona with his partners, Henry Bumpus and Lyvenus Ellis. The smokestack for the factory was 150 feet high in 1859, when it was listed as the highest in the United States.

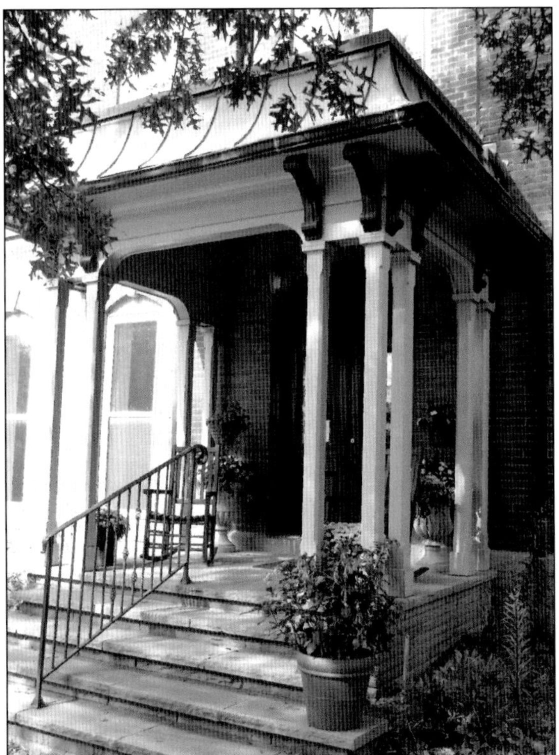

The porch of the Brookside Manor Bed and Breakfast has been updated a number of times since the manor was built. Compare this photograph with the one on the following page, and a great difference in its style will be noticeable. The photographs were taken more than 100 years apart.

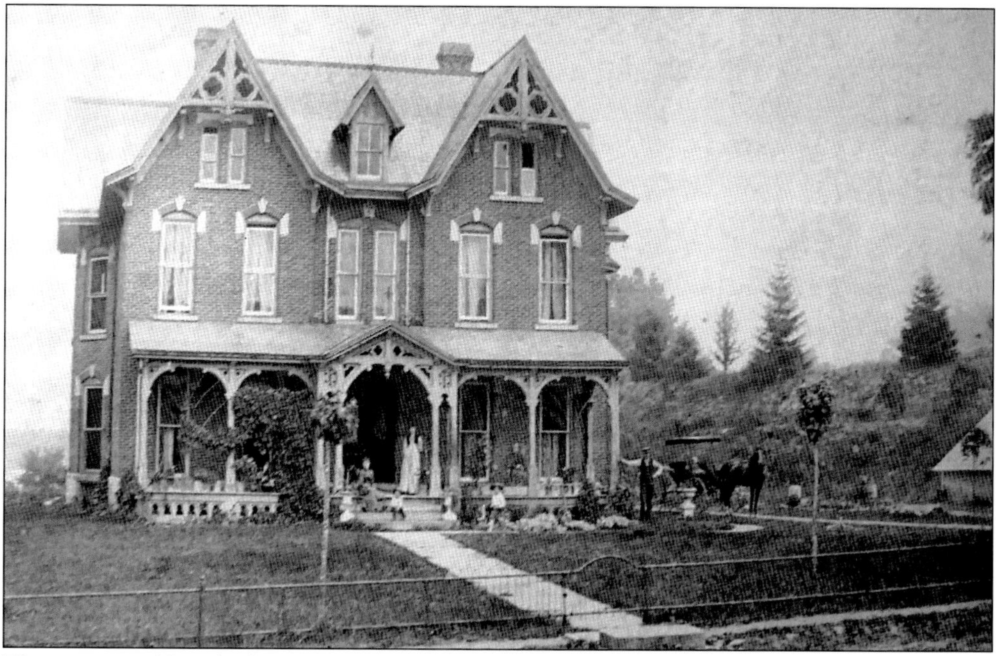

This picture of Brookside Manor Bed and Breakfast was taken in 1896. Of special note is how small the trees are in this photograph compared to the trees seen on the preceding pages. In this photograph, the trees that are nothing more than saplings are huge today. The grounds of the manor look much different today than do the original designs by Enoch A. Curtis and Horace White.

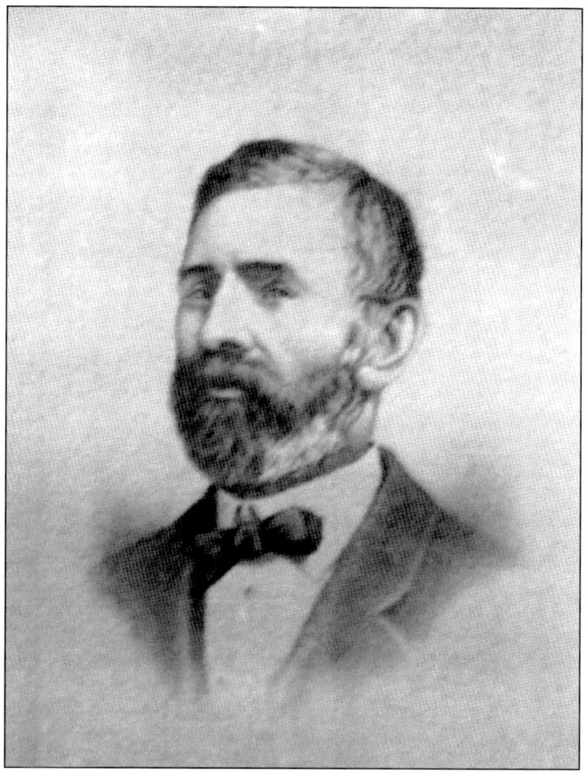

This is a photograph of White from around the time that he lived in what eventually became Brookside Manor Bed and Breakfast.

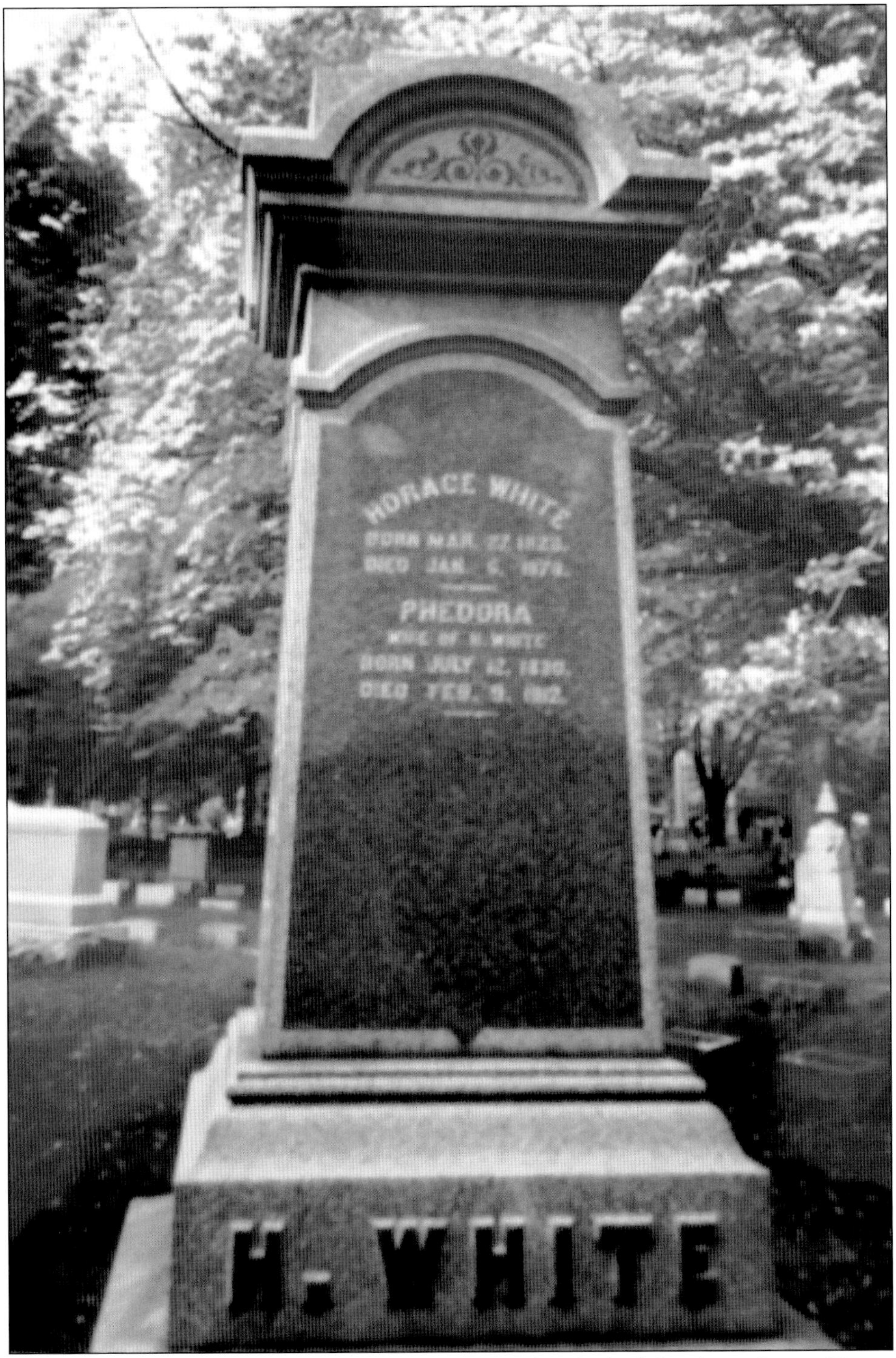

Horace White was a wealthy man in the 19th century when he built his dream home. His grave is located in Forest Hill Cemetery, where he is buried with his wife, Phedora White. White died only a few years after his home was completed, so he did not have much time to enjoy his wonderful manor.

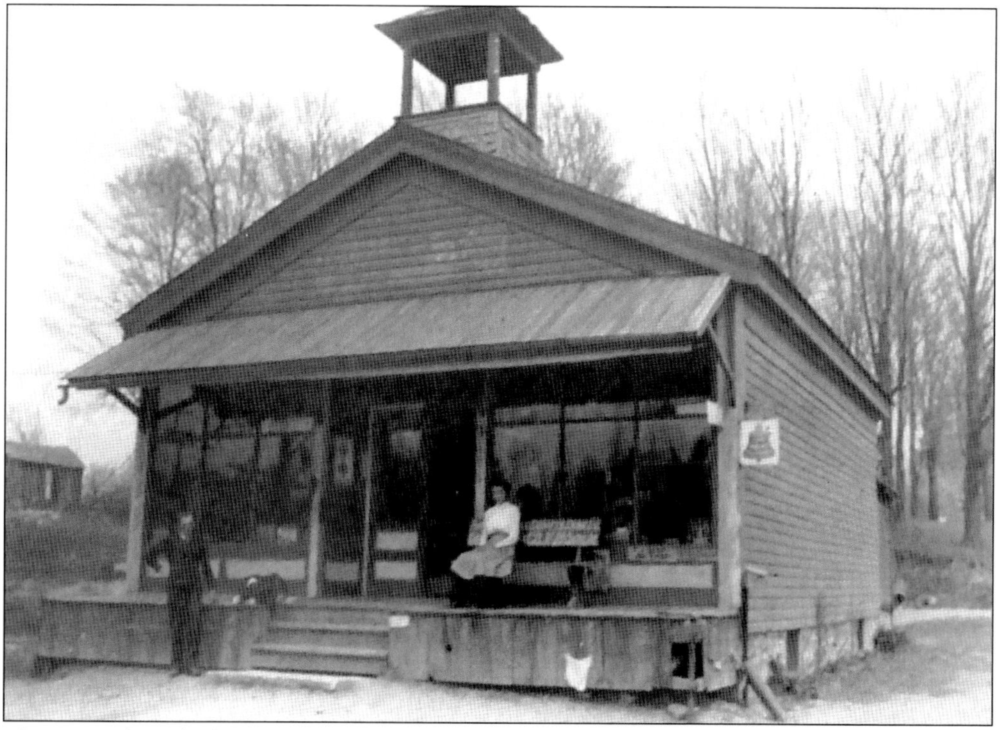

The year after Phedora died, her home was sold to Charles F. Thies. The store seen in this photograph was the general merchandise store he owned near the home on Route 60. The home remained in the Thies family for over 50 years.

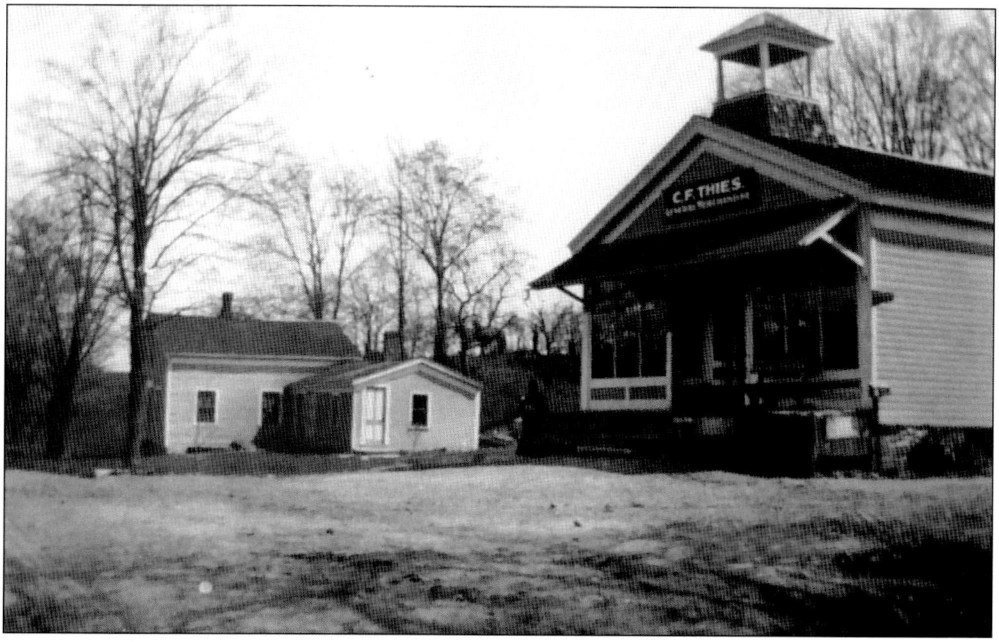

Here is another view of the store as it appeared in the 1930s. The store was a popular stop in the Laona area during this time period. The store was also the target of thieves that broke into the store a few years after this photograph was taken.

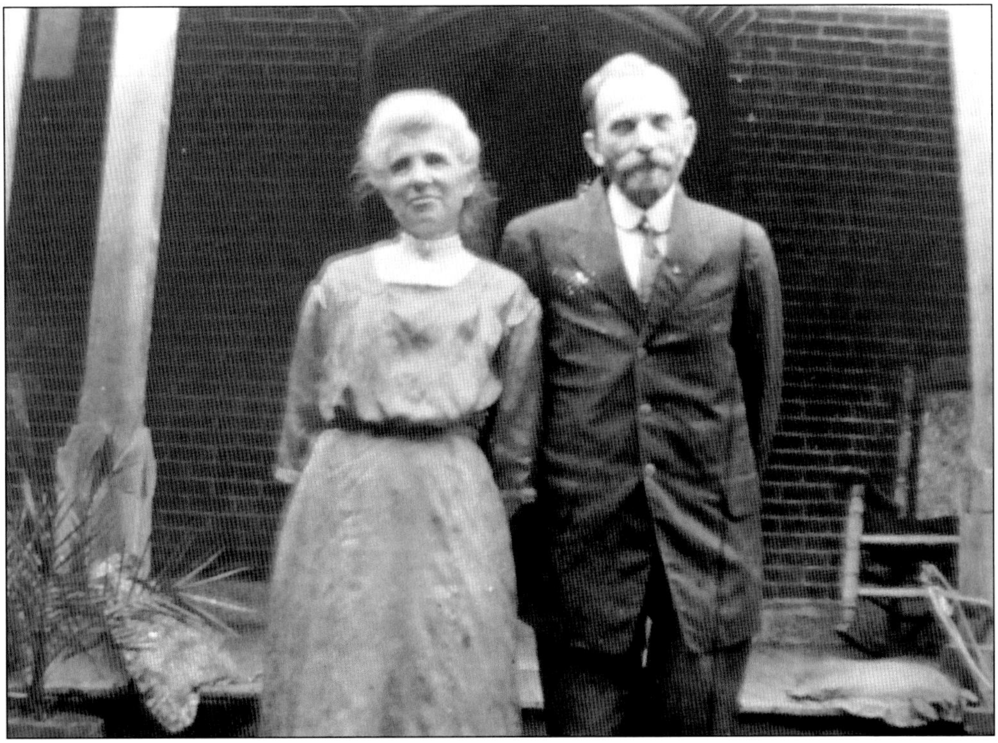

This photograph shows Charles F. Thies with his wife, Elsie. During their stay in the home that became Brookside Manor Bed and Breakfast, a number of changes were made to the original design by Enoch A. Curtis. However, the basic Victorian Gothic style still remains, despite the many small changes.

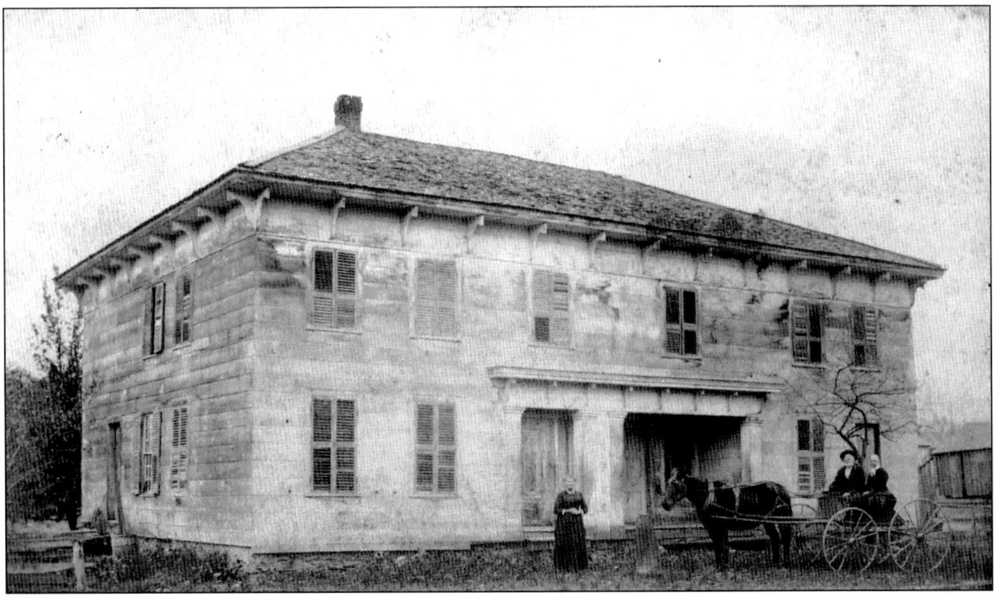

The Laona area featured a number of businesses, which included the hotel seen in this 1870s photograph. Few photographs remain from this era in Laona's history, which is intertwined with its neighbor Fredonia.

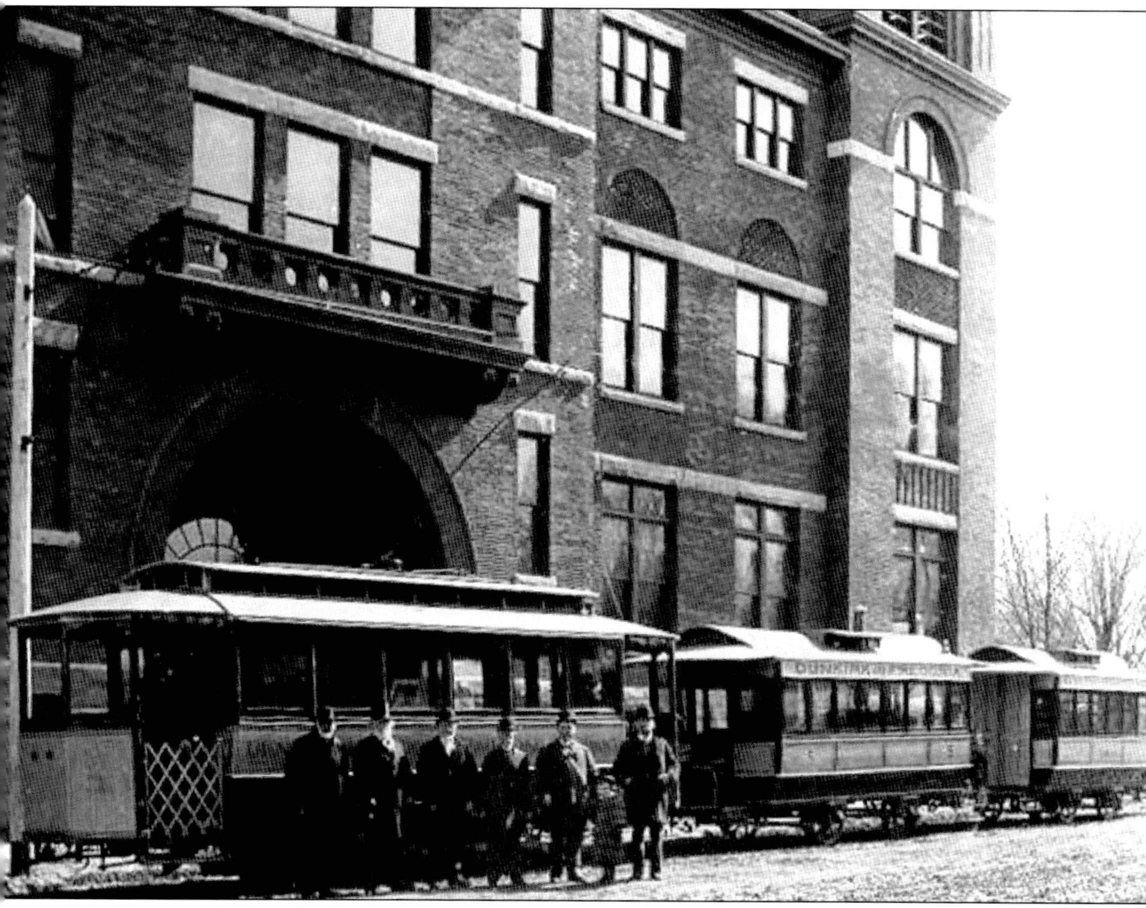

The Fredonia Village Hall groundbreaking took place on June 11, 1890, at its present location opposite Barker Commons between Temple and Day Streets. The village acquired the site in 1869 after the Fredonia Academy had closed on the site two years earlier. The academy had been replaced by the Fredonia Normal School at a new location further down Temple Street. The old academy building was not well suited as a village hall, so after some years, residents approved the plans for a new village hall to be designed by Enoch A. Curtis. This picture from 1895 was taken on Temple Street only a few years after the building was finished. Today the building still serves as the village hall and the home of the 1891 Fredonia Opera House. The Fredonia Police Department is also located in the building, making it one of the busiest buildings in town.

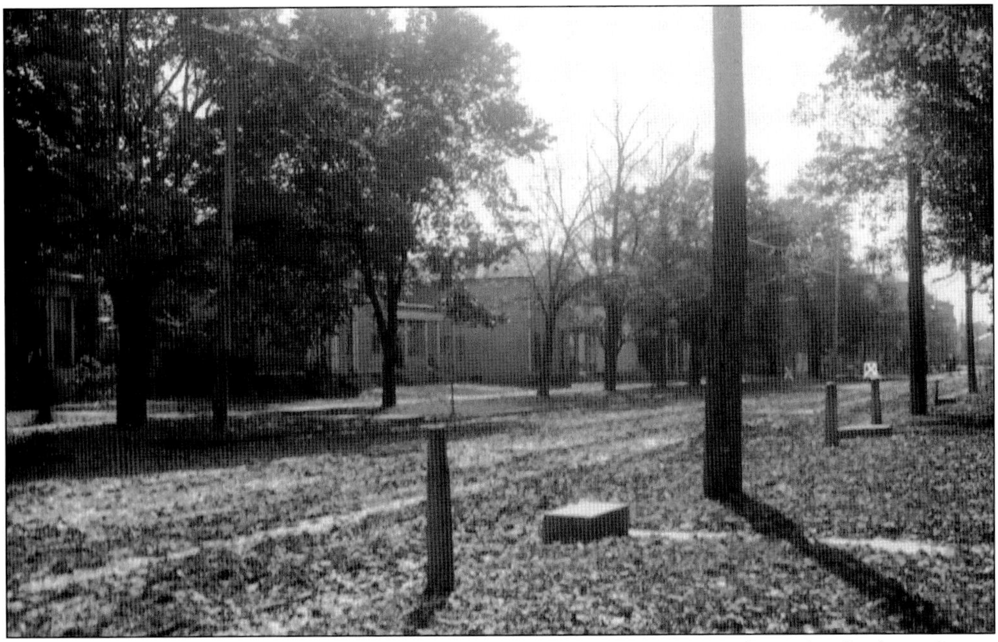

This picture of East Main Street was taken on October 21, 1907, near where the Cushing Street intersection is today. On the very left side of the picture is the home of Judge S. Ray Fairbanks. This street underwent a major renovation two years later.

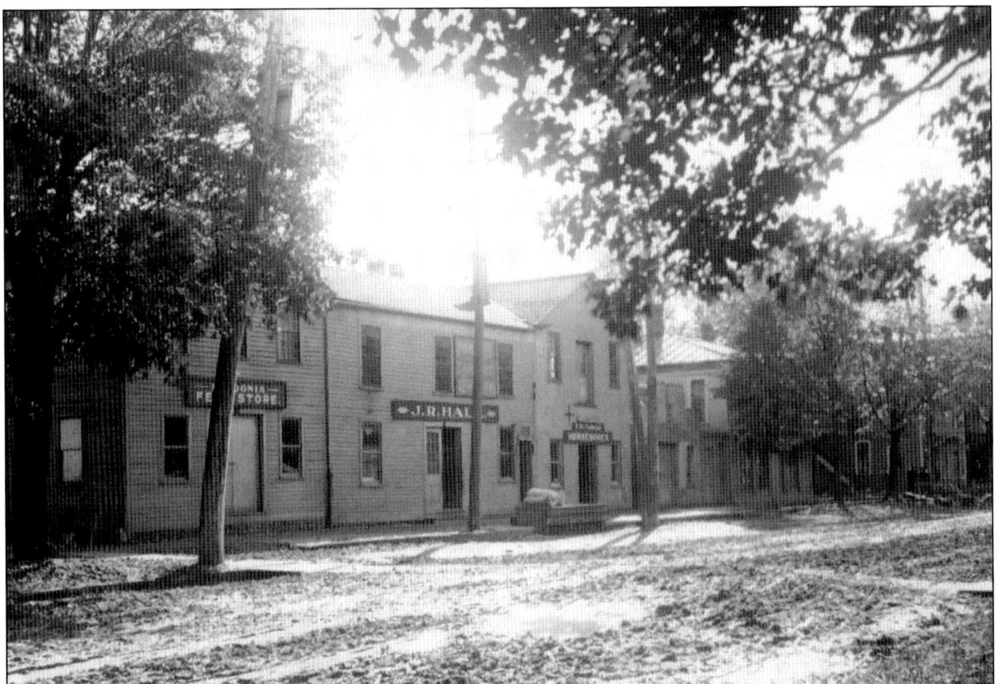

West Main Street looked much different on October 21, 1907, than it does today. This photograph was taken just east of Canadaway Creek, where a number of small businesses like the ones shown flourished for the first 100 years of the town. Many of the buildings shown still stand as they did then, although they have been renovated.

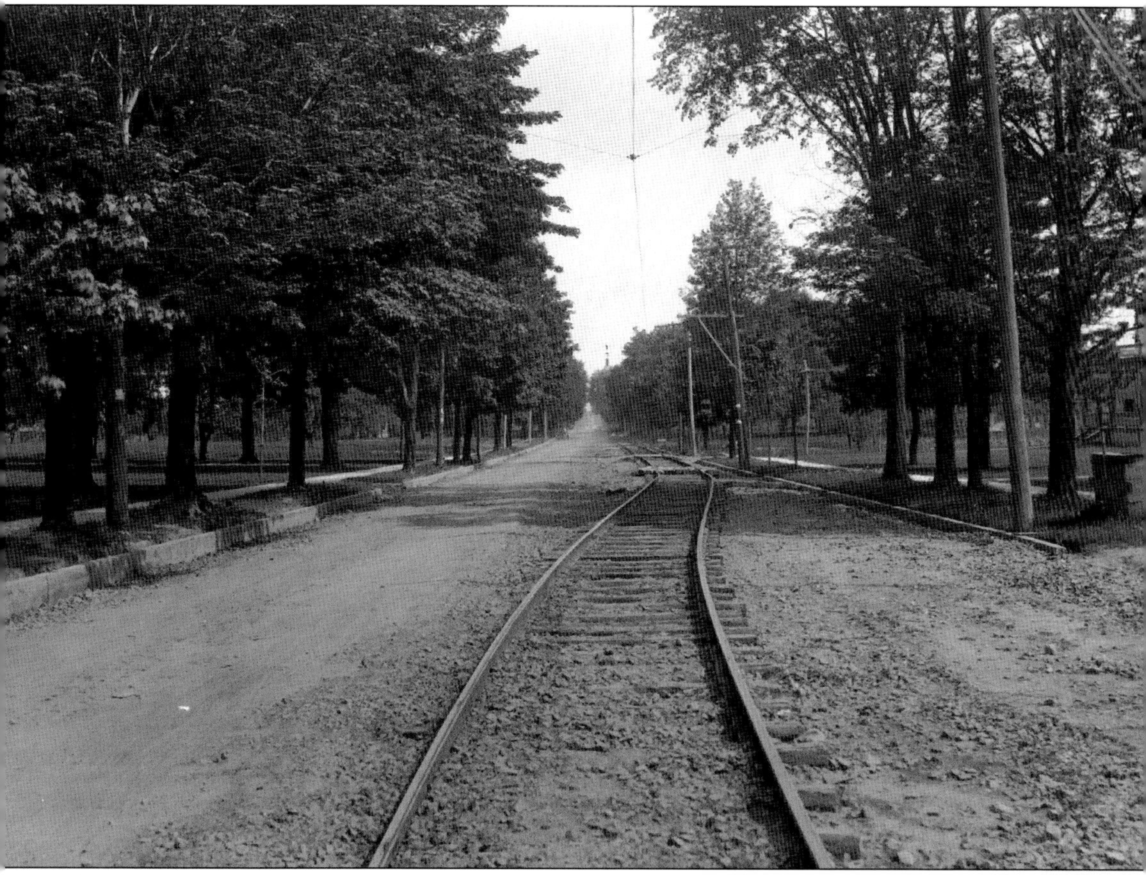

This is the beginning of a major road construction project that included nearly all the streets within the village in 1909. Local newspapers reported that it disrupted traffic for the entire summer that year. This photograph shows Central Avenue on June 3, 1909. Note the trolley line running up the street. Some of the vacant land seen in the distance was purchased about 20 years later by the normal school. This land formed the beginning of SUNY Fredonia.

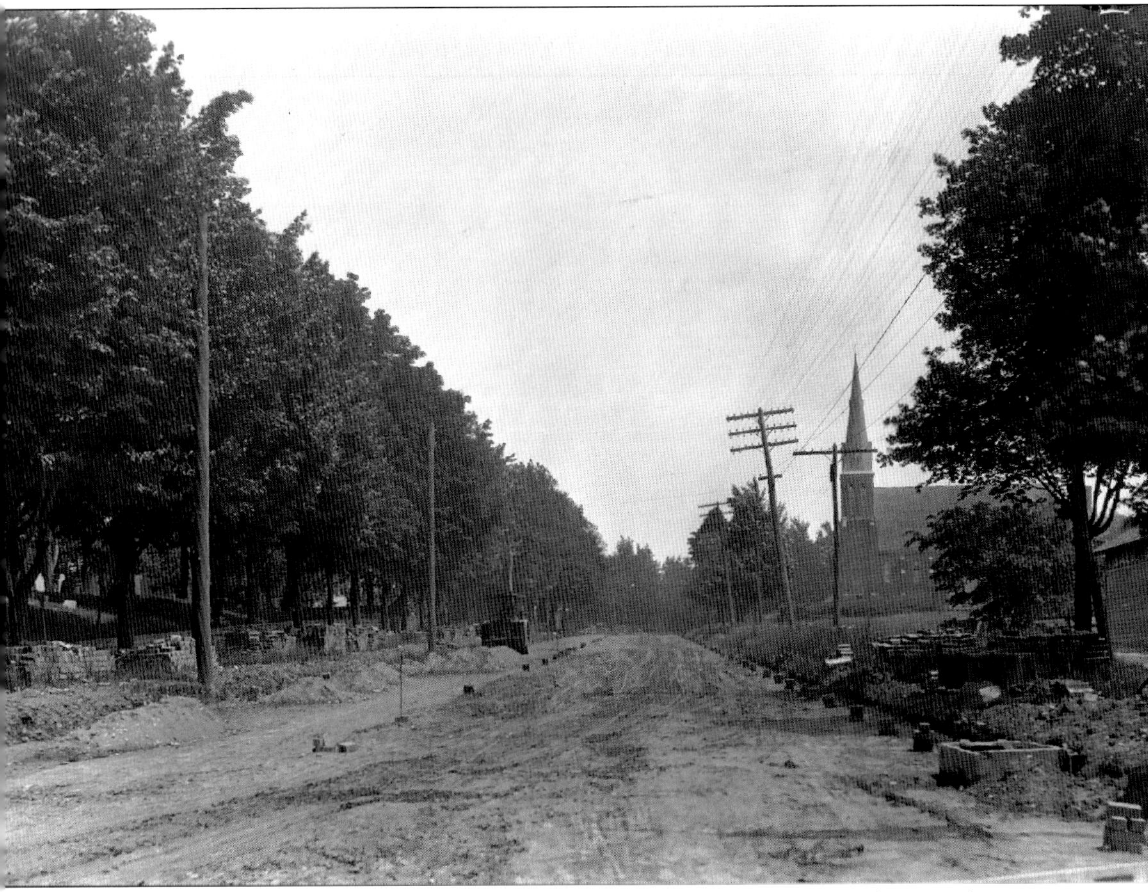

The road construction project was a major undertaking in the summer of 1909. This picture from June 11 shows East Main Street in front of the Pioneer Cemetery (left). St. Joseph's Church is seen in the distance on the right side of the street. Also notice in this photograph that the small houses presently on the right side of the street before the church have not yet been built.

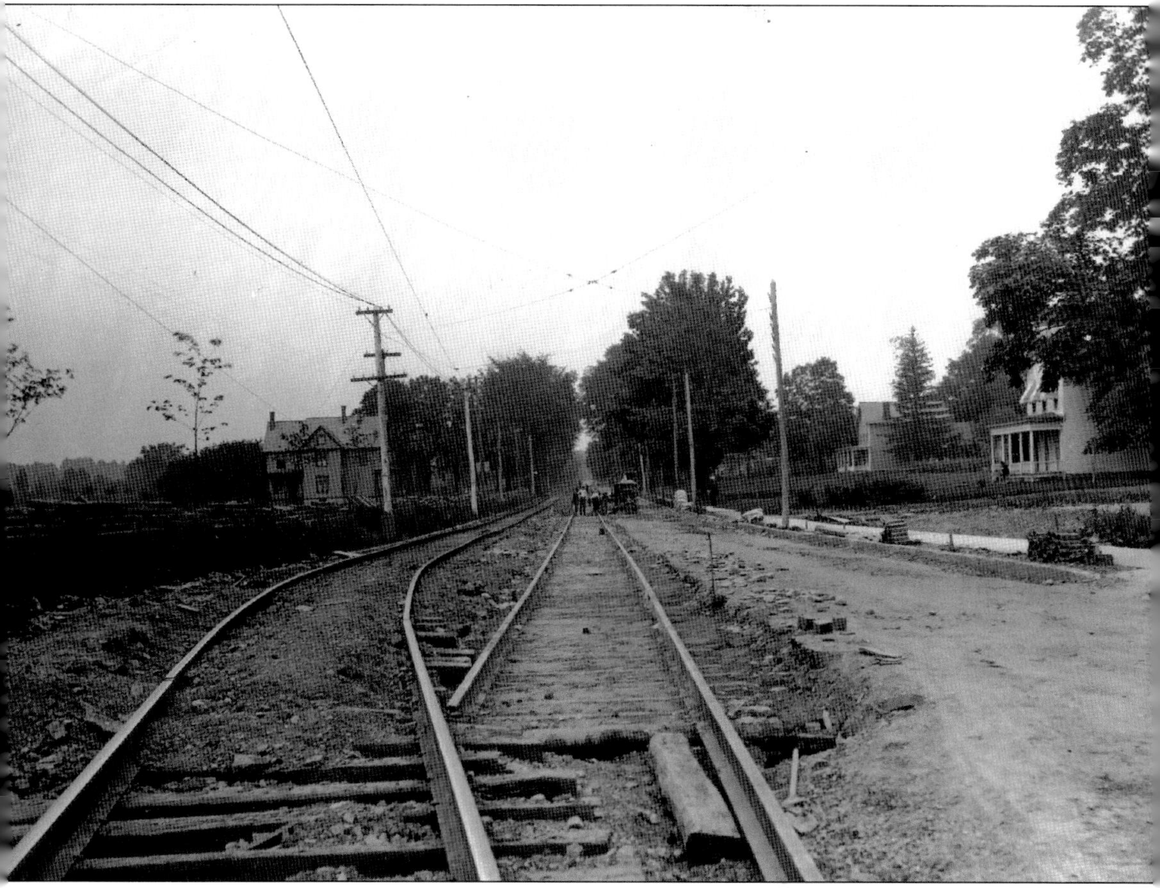

Central Avenue was a busy place during the construction project in 1909, as seen in this June 17 photograph. The view is looking back towards Fredonia from the Dunkirk city line, near where the D&F Plaza is located today on the left. Since the time this photograph was taken, this portion of Central Avenue has gone through a tremendous transformation with the expansion of the university campus and the addition of various stores and homes. The items stacked on the right side are the old clay tiles used for drainage. Many people that have dug for driveways have often found pieces of these tiles broken in the soil. They were simply laid end to end to give the water a natural path to drain from an area under the soil.

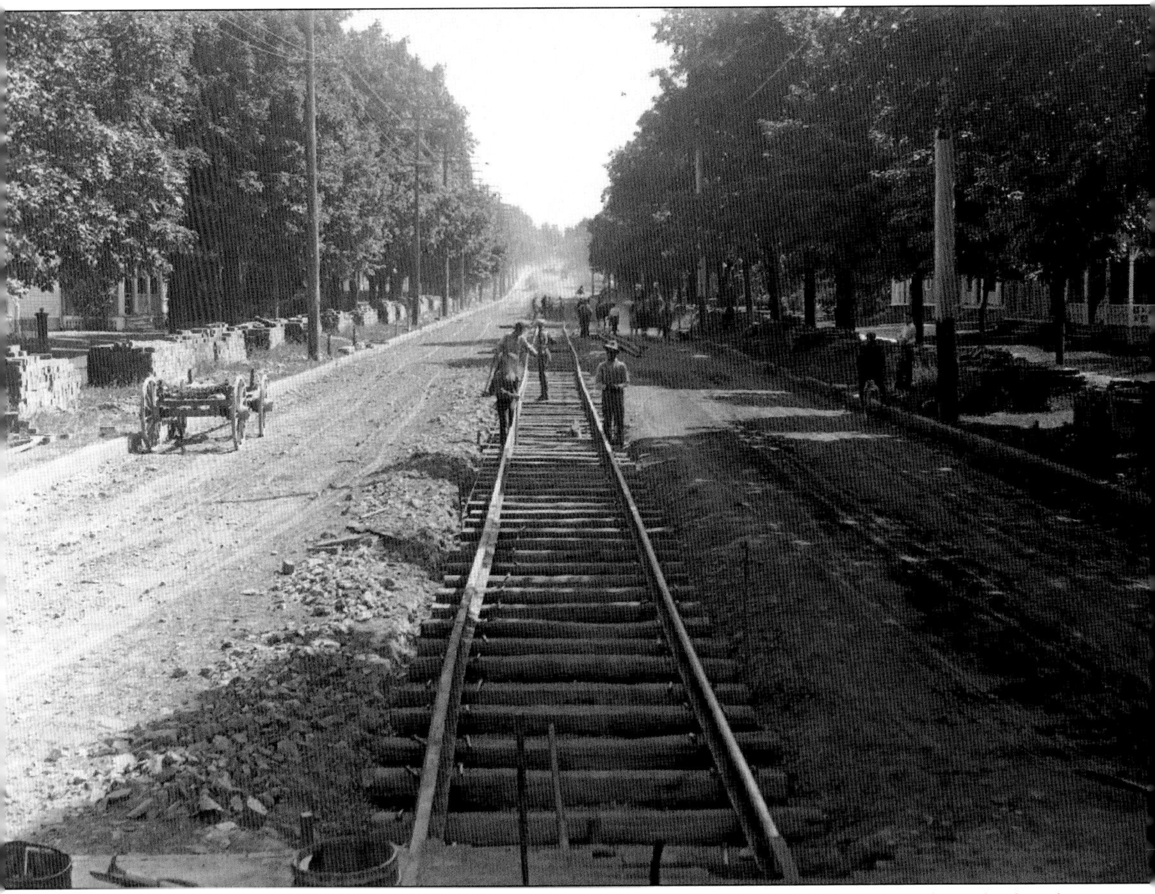

On June 30, 1909, East Main Street was completed up to the railroad line and ready for the bricks to be laid. The stacks of bricks along the sides of the street were placed to make it easier to get materials as the men worked. The materials were brought in by horse-drawn wagon. Many streets throughout the area still have the old brick, which many residents have said looks more appealing than the standard blacktop paving of today.

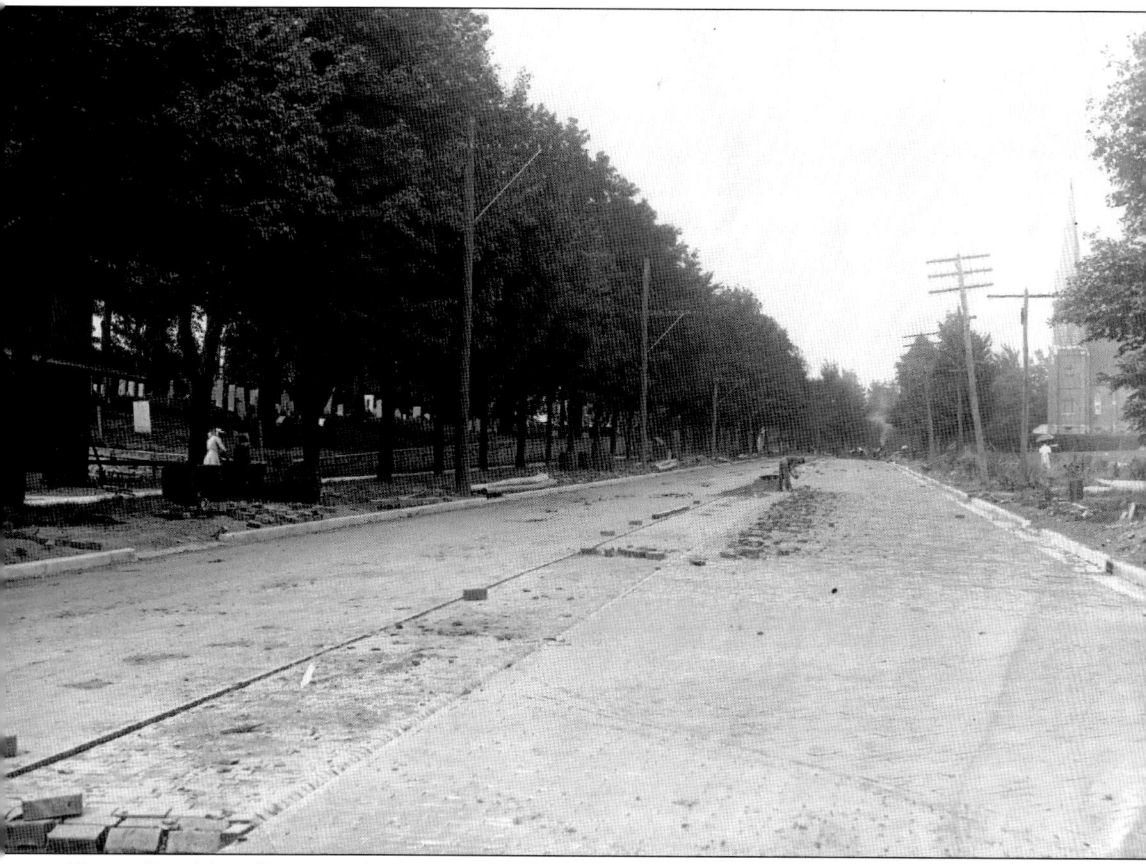

Here is East Main Street on August 2, 1909, as the project nears completion. The last few bricks are being added, with the broken bricks (or imperfect ones) being left on the street for collection afterwards. This is essentially from the same vantage point as the photograph on page 86, with Pioneer Cemetery on the left. Of special interest is the fact that the workers needed to work around the trolley line, seen in the center of the street. This made the project much more difficult than if the trolley line was not present.

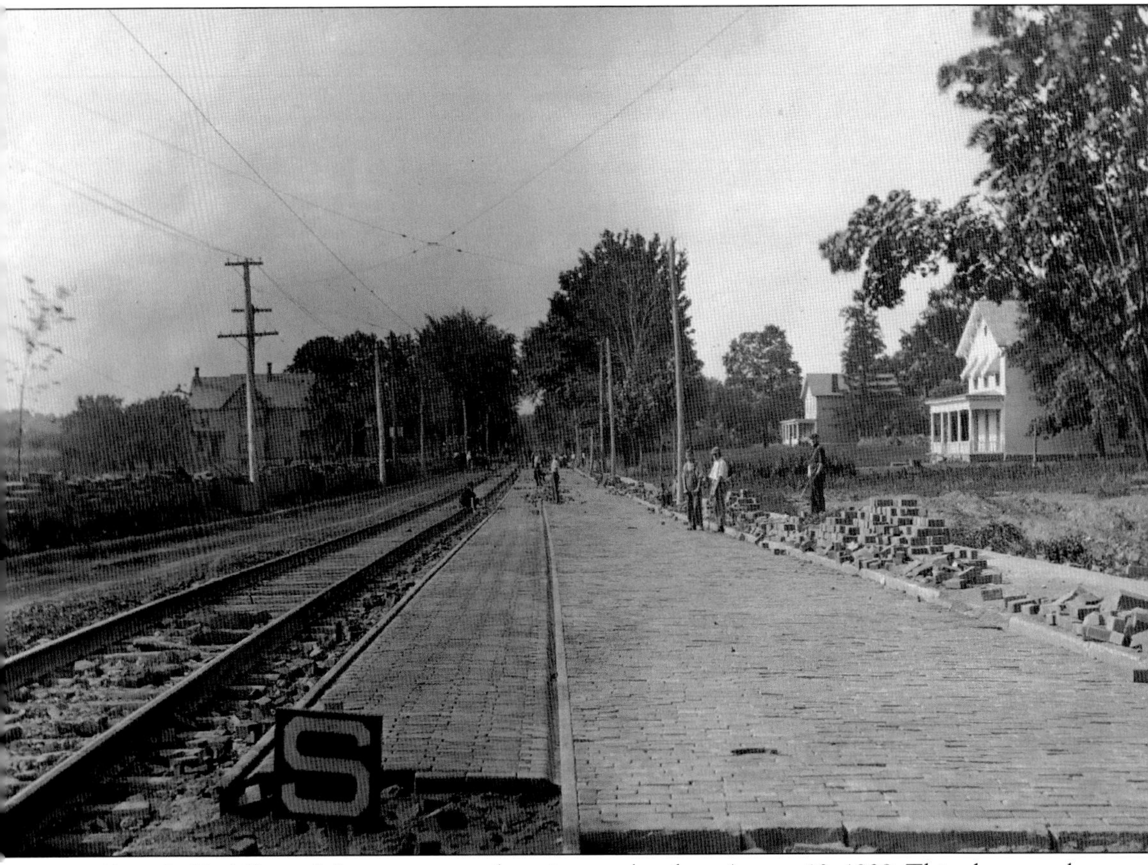

About half of Central Avenue as seen here is completed on August 10, 1909. This photograph was taken from the Dunkirk city line looking towards Fredonia. About halfway down the street on the right is where the entrance to the SUNY Fredonia campus was added about another 60 years later. This area was even more difficult than the other streets with trolley lines because Central Avenue had a double trolley line for a portion of the street. This took extra time to complete, as workers had to meticulously place all the bricks in between the two lines.

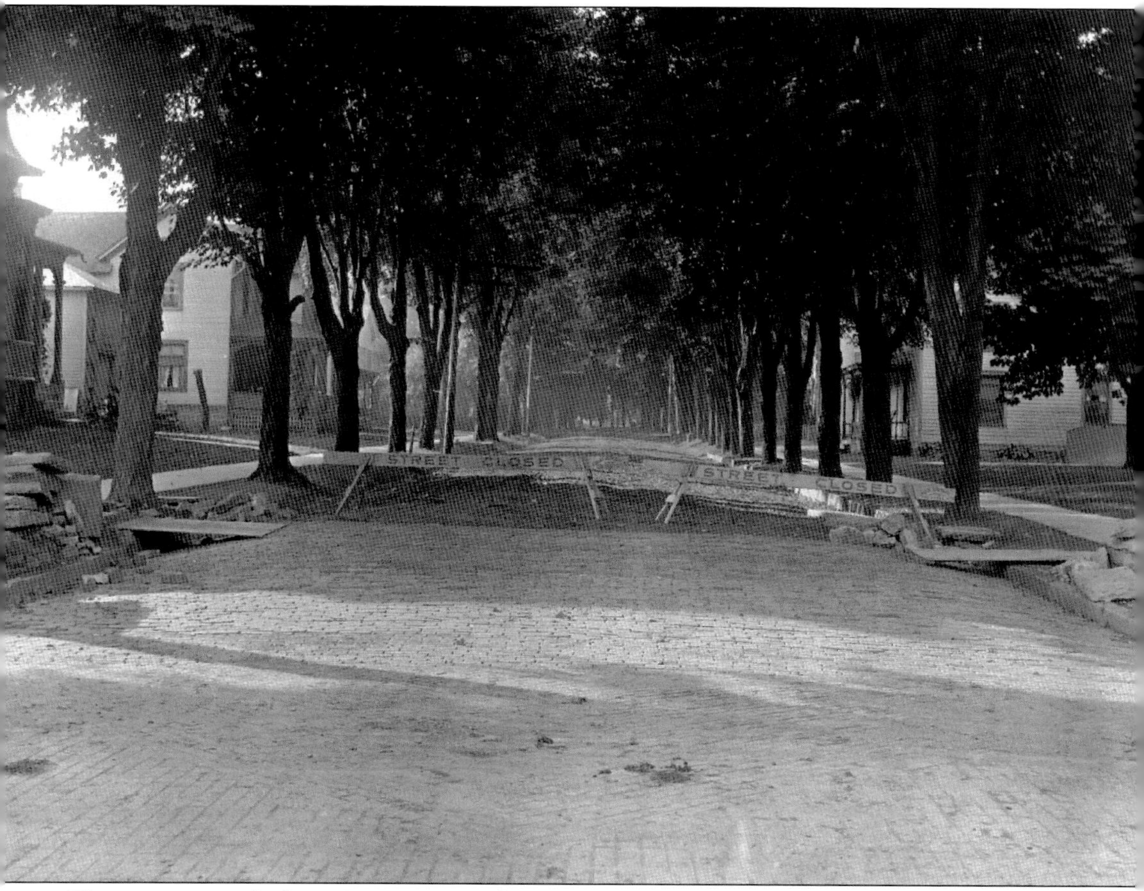

The entrance to Cushing Street was nearly completed on August 10, 1909. On the side of the street are large pieces of concrete that had been taken out to prepare for the bricks and the installation of the new curb. Cushing Street looked very similar at this time to what it looks like today, with many of the old houses still present. Many of the trees lining the street have been removed over the years to make way for power lines, driveways, and other construction projects. Some trees were also removed when they died.

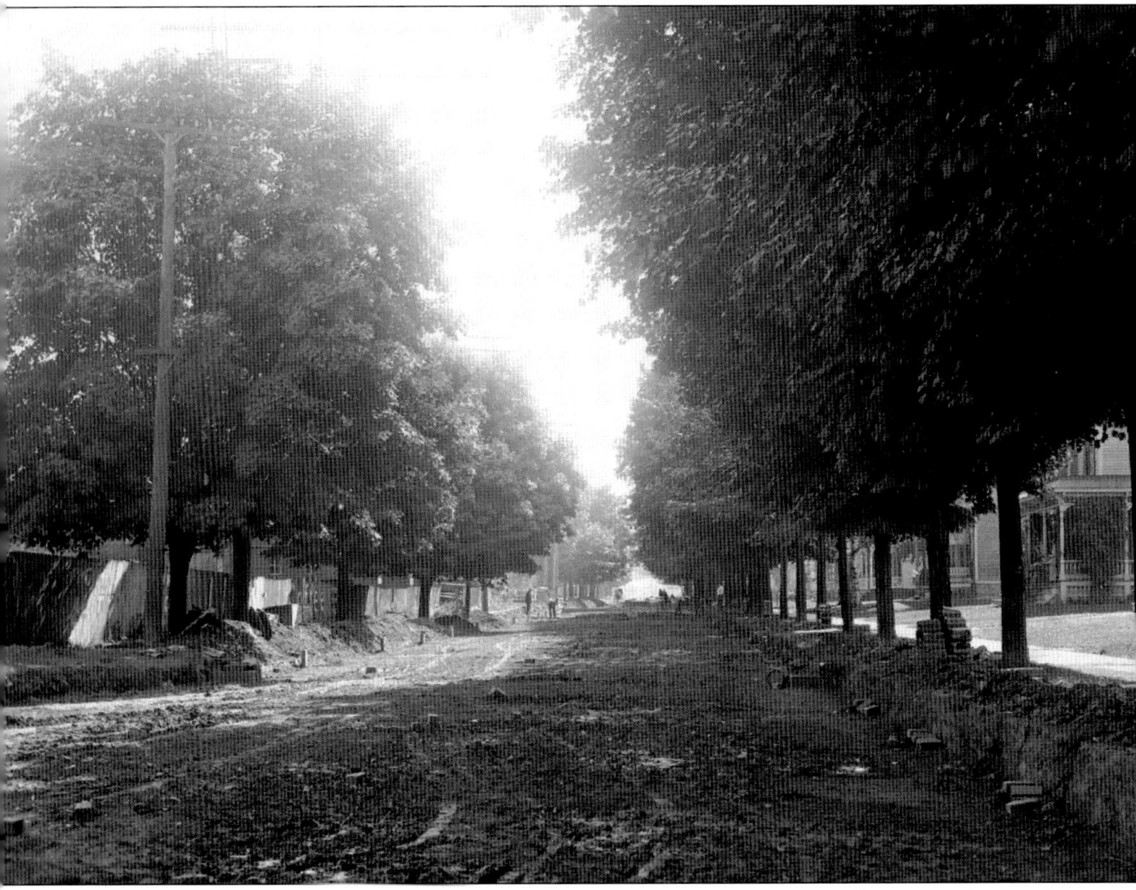

Cleveland Avenue was a major thoroughfare during the first part of the 20th century, but at the time, it was known as Railroad Avenue. The street made its way up to the area of the DAV&P station, which today is near the area of the Fredonia Beaver Club. Travelers using the train usually used this street as their way in and out of the village when riding the *Dolly Varden*. This photograph was taken on August 23, 1909, during the construction project and shows that most of the side streets were completed in the weeks after Main Street and Central Avenue were done.

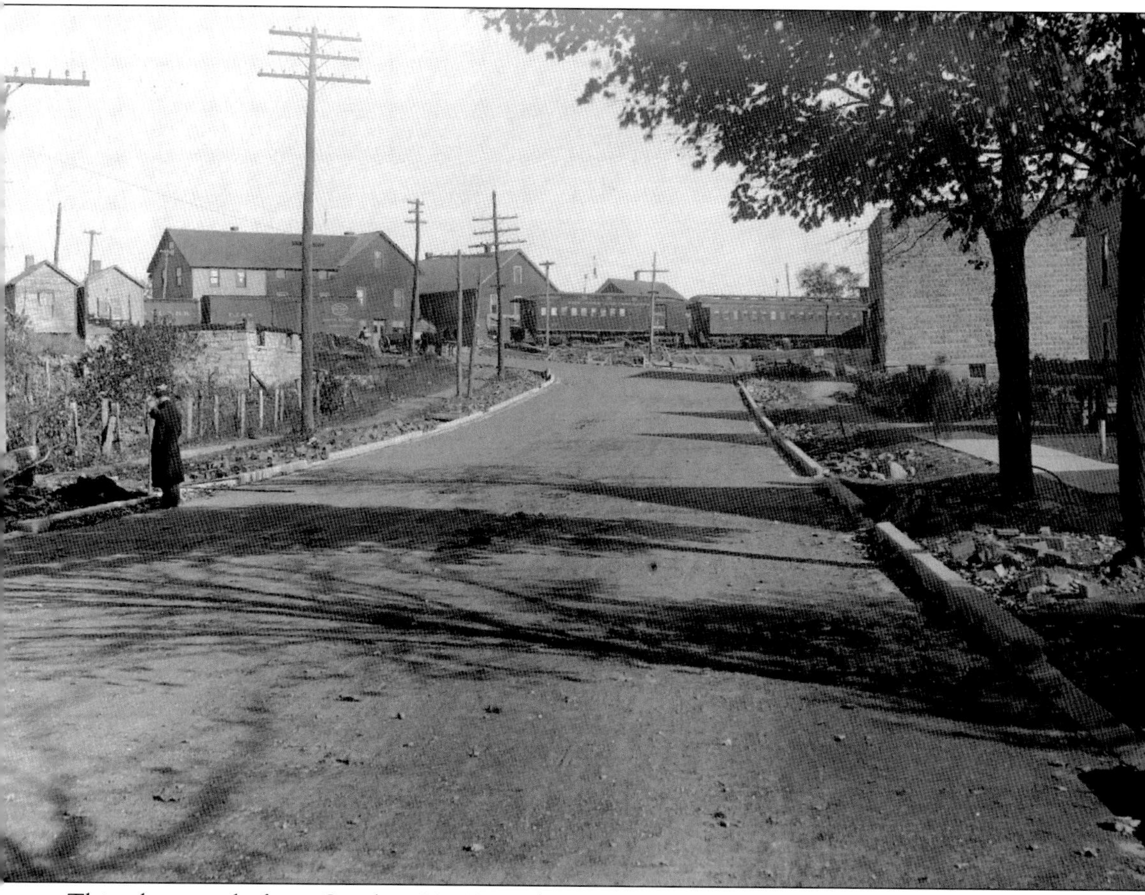

This photograph from October 29, 1909, shows that the upper part of Cleveland Avenue (Railroad Avenue) has still not quite been finished as winter approaches. The railroad cars in the background are crossing exactly at the point where Prospect Street now meets Cleveland Avenue. Reports indicate that this street was probably finished in mid-November when most of the last parts of the project were completed.

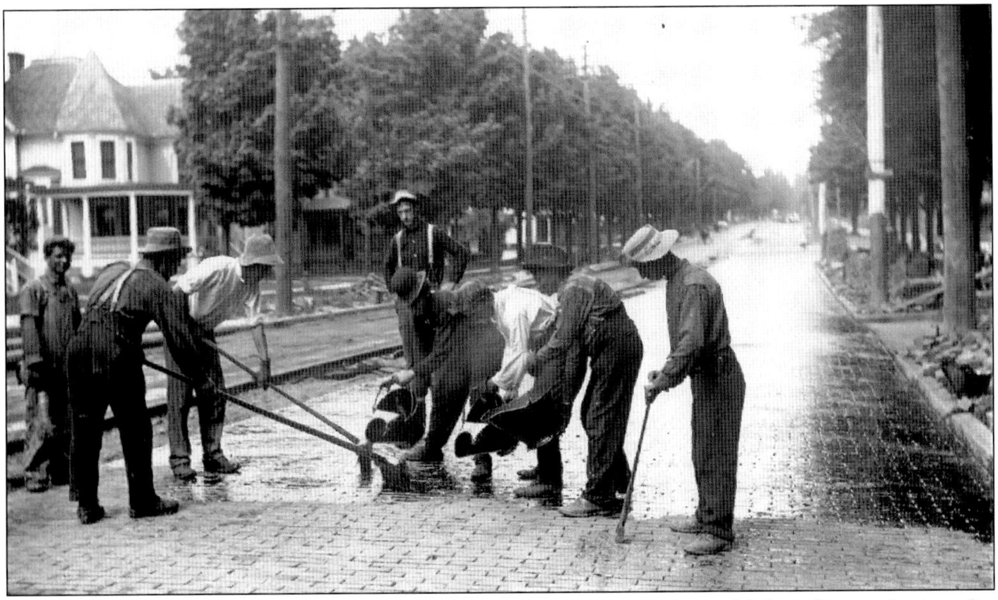

Workmen from the Tom Fitzgerald Company are tarring a portion of Main Street during the 1909 project. The company was the contractor in charge of the project during 1909, with a combination of both local and out-of-town workers. This project was one of the most extensive public works projects completed in the first 100 years of the town of Pomfret. Since this project, many of these streets have been repaved numerous times, but the width of the streets has remained about the same in most areas.

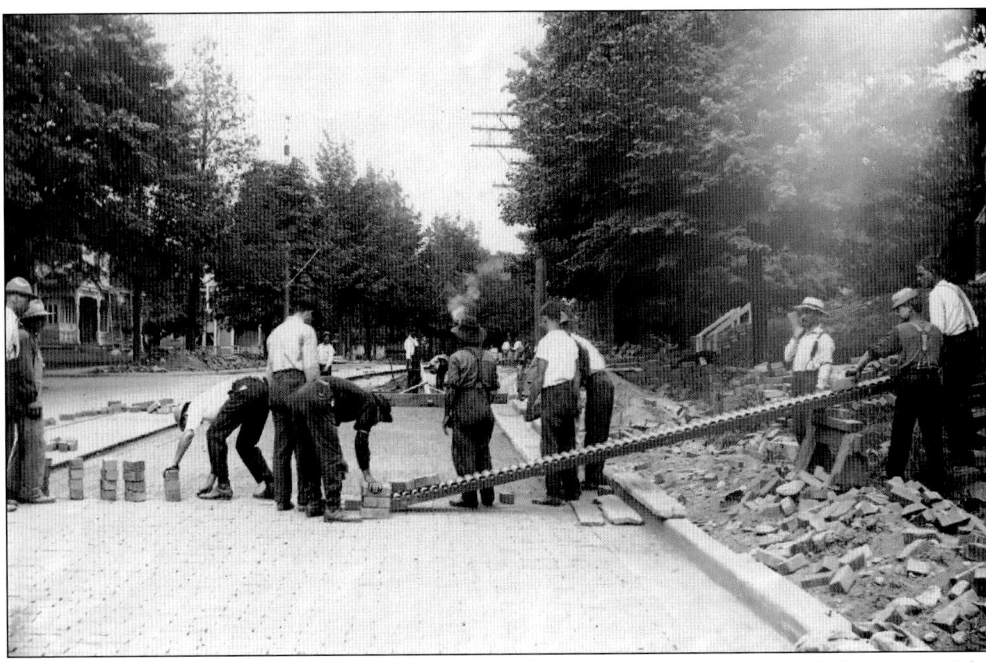

The automatic roller-conveyer machine was used extensively during the 1909 project. The architect for the overall project was D. G. Henry. The beautifully designed wide streets that exist today were necessary due to the presence of the trolley lines that ran on the street during the first part of the 20th century.

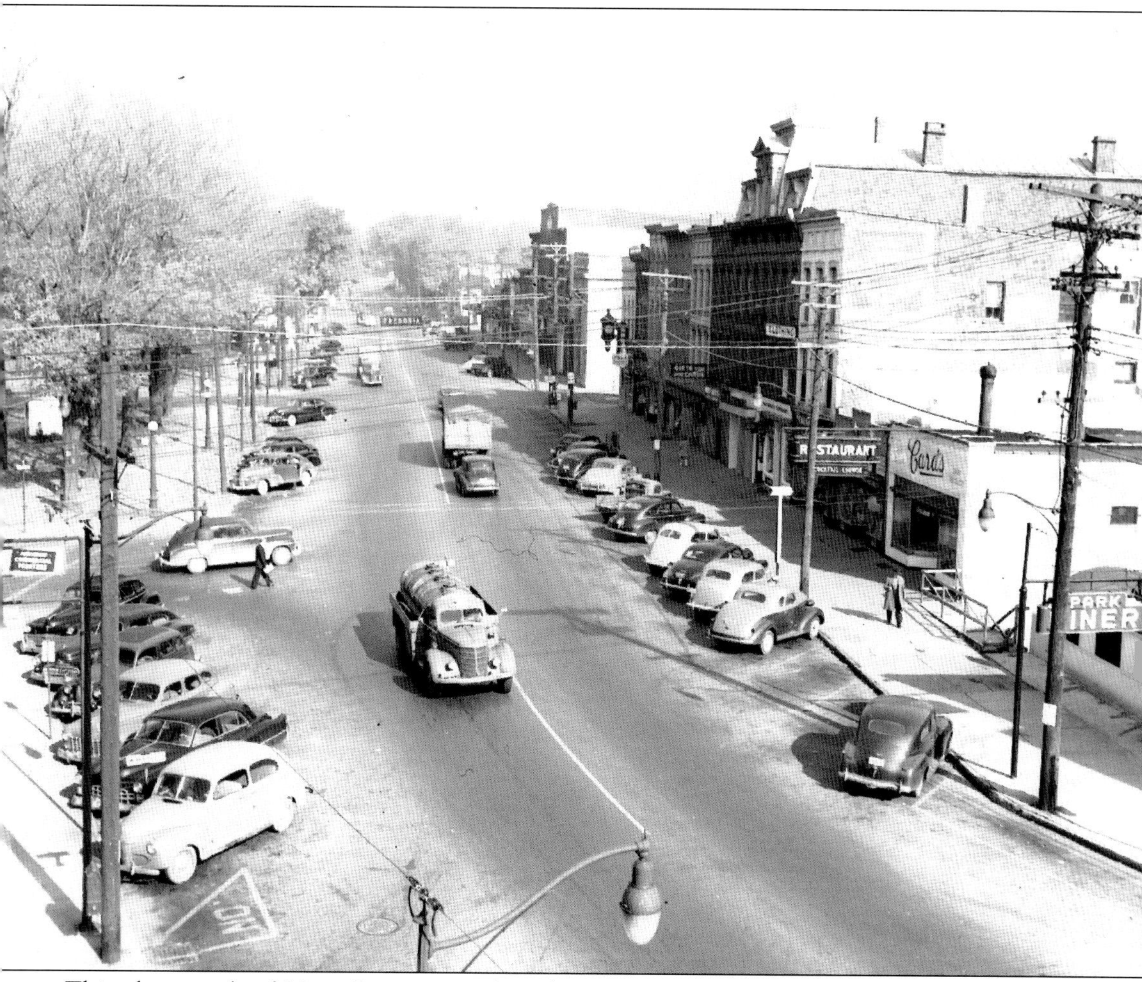

This photograph of Main Street was taken during the early 1920s. Traffic was not a major problem in the village, but that eventually changed as the village became busier during the mid-20th century.

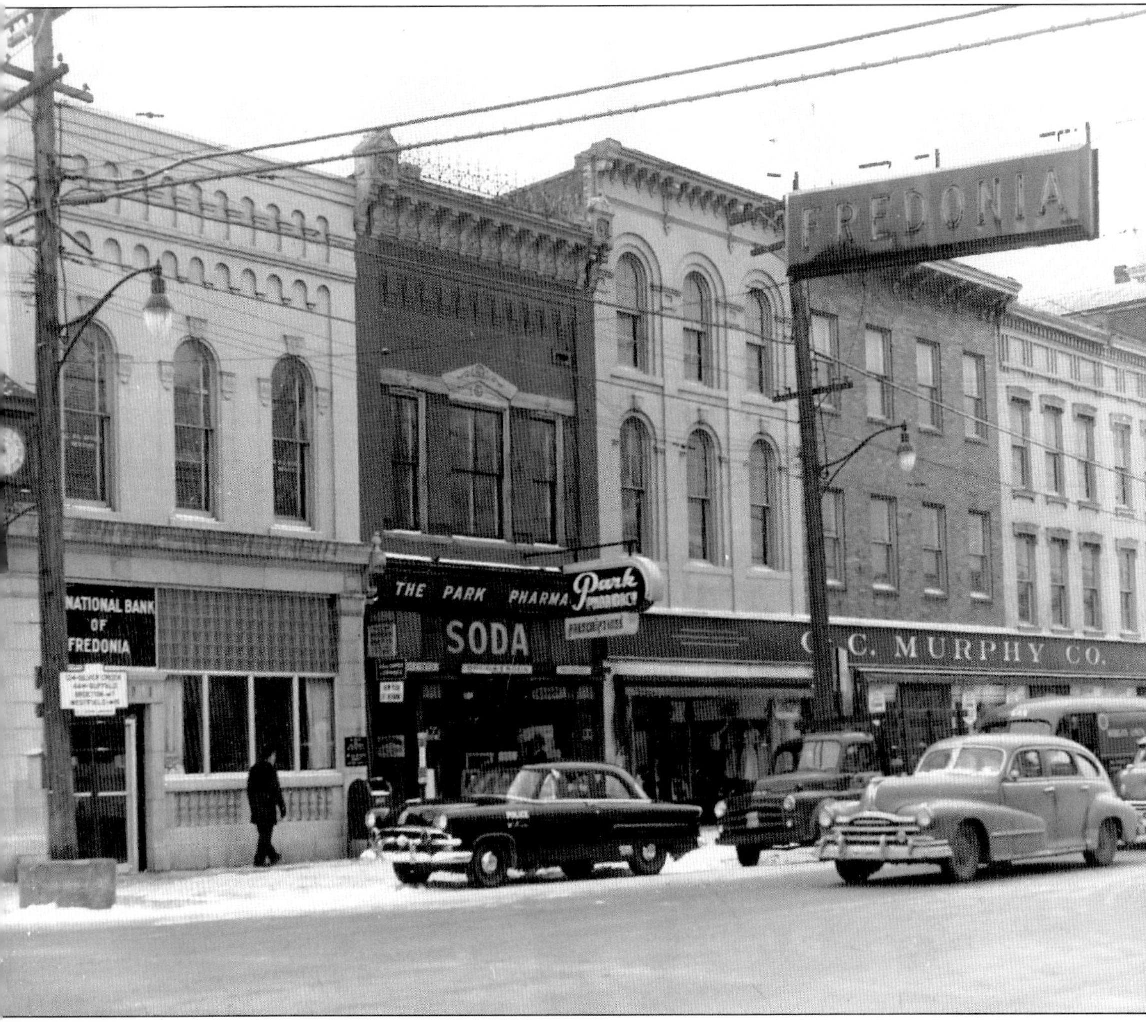

The G. C. Murphy store shown in this photograph was a popular place to visit in the village during most of the 20th century. The store was one of the typical small town variety stores that were in every village before the big chain stores came into existence. It carried everything from penny candy to gardening supplies, as well as clothes, food, and household items. Today office space and the new home of a Jamestown Mattress store have replaced the building. The original building was renovated and turned into Costello's Music before it collapsed and was eventually removed in favor of the new buildings.

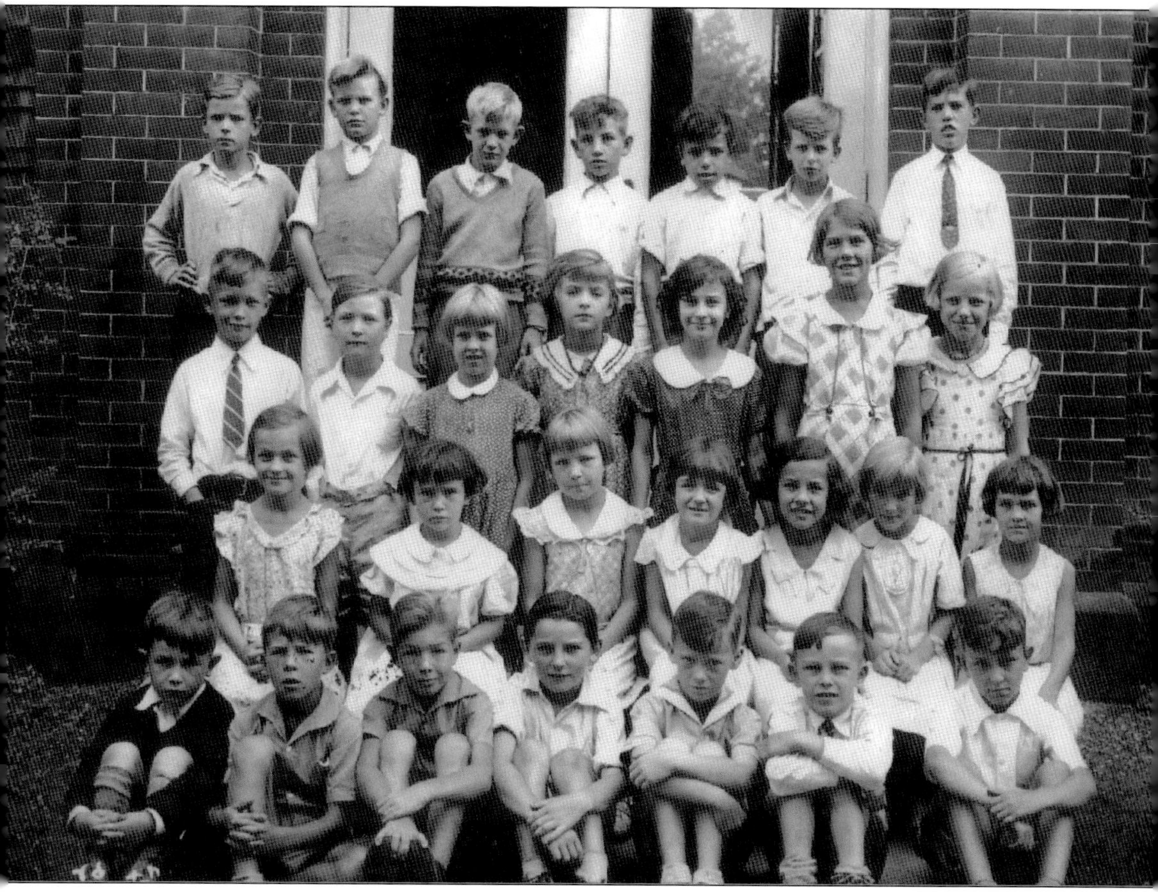

This photograph shows the third and fourth grades at the old Seymour Street School in the late 1930s. Most of the children in the photograph are unidentified, but one that was identified, Richard Saden, who is second from the left in the front row, is still an area resident.

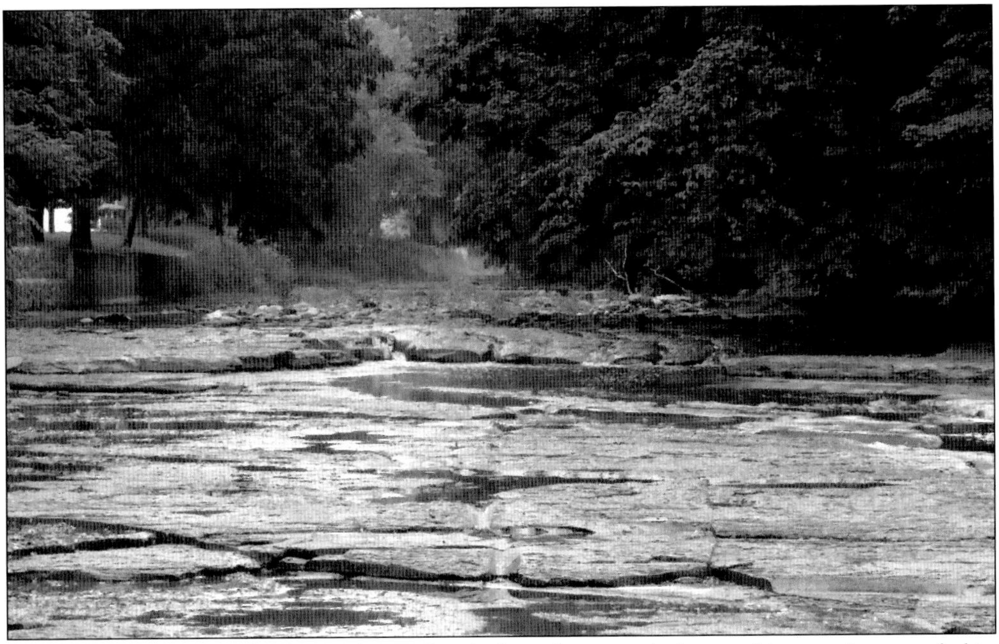

This modern photograph of Canadaway Creek shows how much the creek's water has receded in recent decades. The photograph was taken from the Risley Street bridge looking back towards Main Street. The creek was much larger at the time that Zattu Cushing settled here in 1805. It was often traveled by small boats to transport crops to Lake Erie for transfer to larger ships.

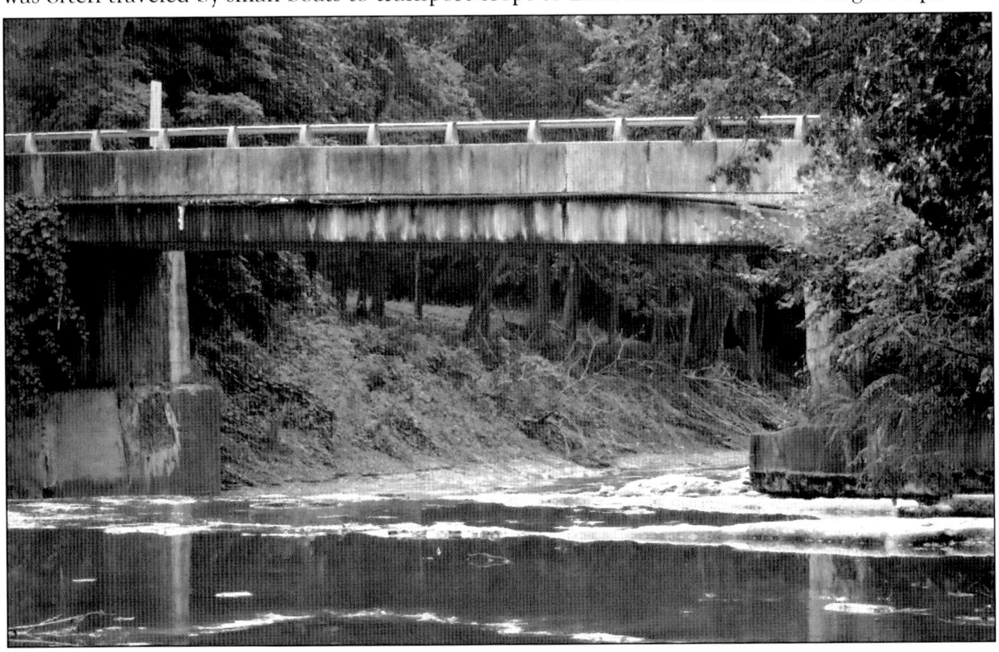

This photograph of the Canadaway Creek shows the Reinhoudt Bridge, which is the most recent bridge that crosses Canadaway Creek on Risley Street. The bridge was named in honor of Don Reinhoudt Sr., who was the District 2 county legislator from 1972 to 1976, and his son Don Reinhoudt Jr., who was a power lifter that held the title of the "World's Strongest Man" in 1979. Don Jr. is currently the director of the Chautauqua County Youth Bureau.

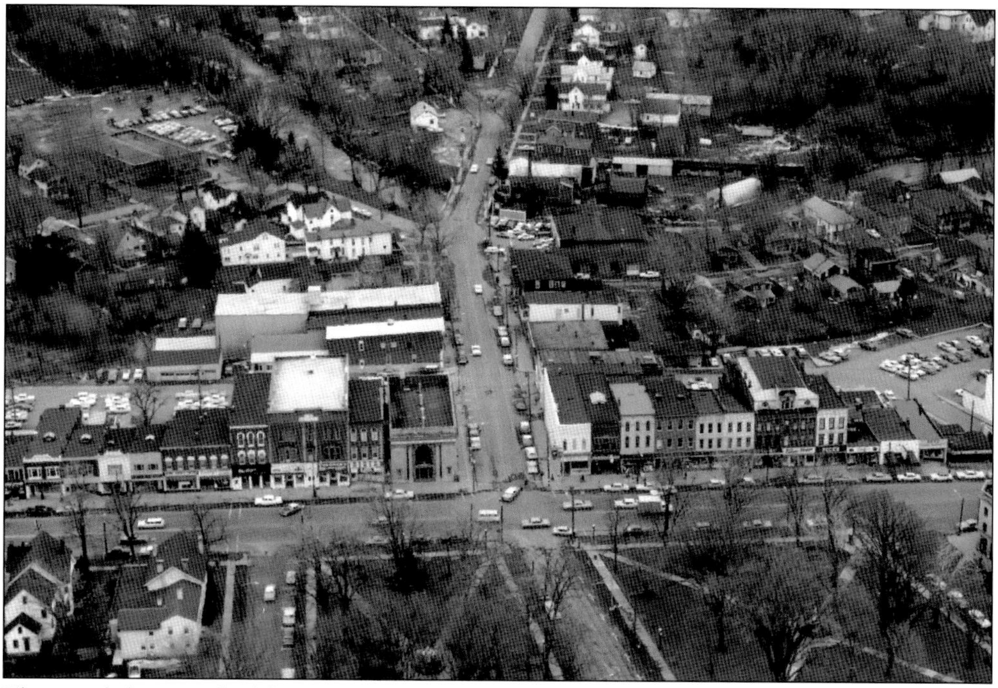

This aerial photograph of the center of the village was taken for the 1960s study of parking problems within the village. A lack of parking has long been a concern for the many businesses in Fredonia because of the number of vehicles traveling through the area on Main Street (Route 20).

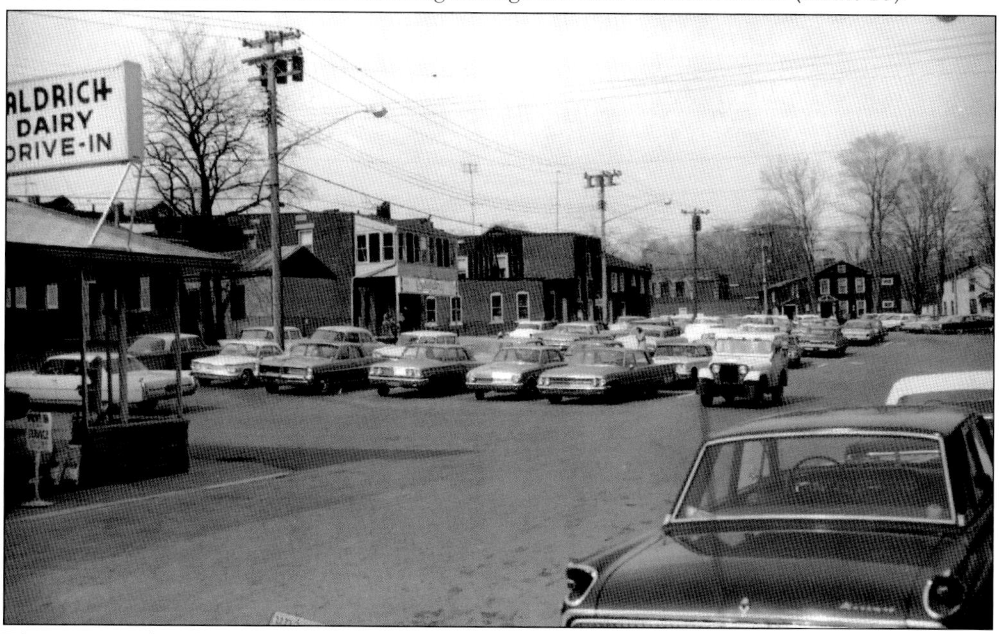

The municipal parking lot behind East Main Street and M&T Bank was a big part of the study concerning parking problems in the village in the 1960s. The configuration of parking spots has remained unchanged in this area to the present day, as a better alternative has never been found. The village is currently looking at options for reconstructing the elevated sidewalk in this area, so a change in the parking configuration may be the result of this makeover.

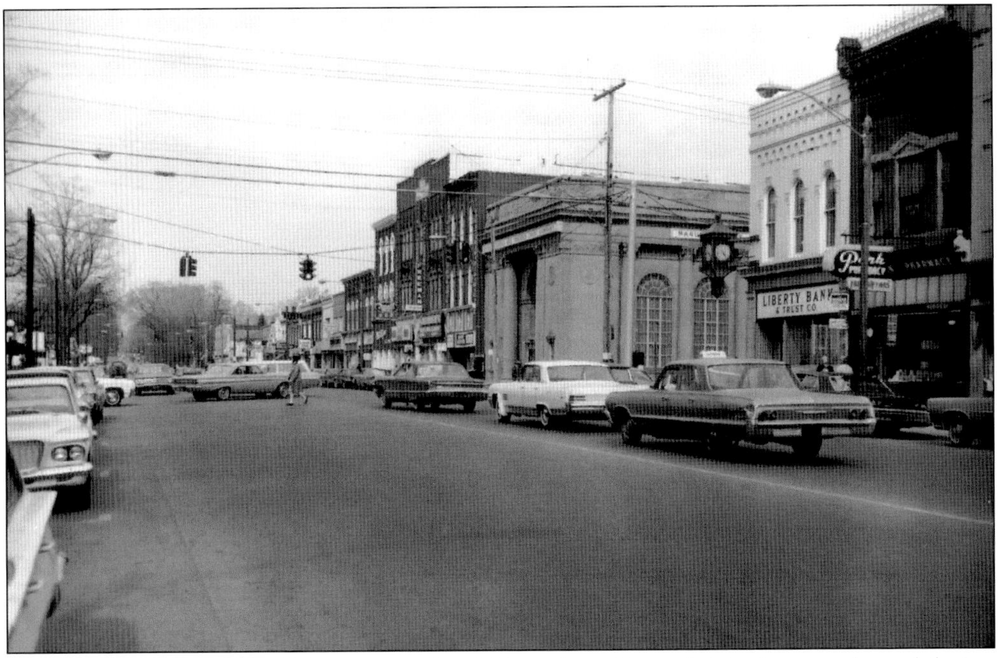

Rush hour in the middle of Fredonia in the 1960s is the subject of this photograph used during the parking study in the village at that time. Notice the clock showing that it is 4:45 p.m. when this photograph was taken. It depicts what the traffic and parking situation is like at its peak of the day.

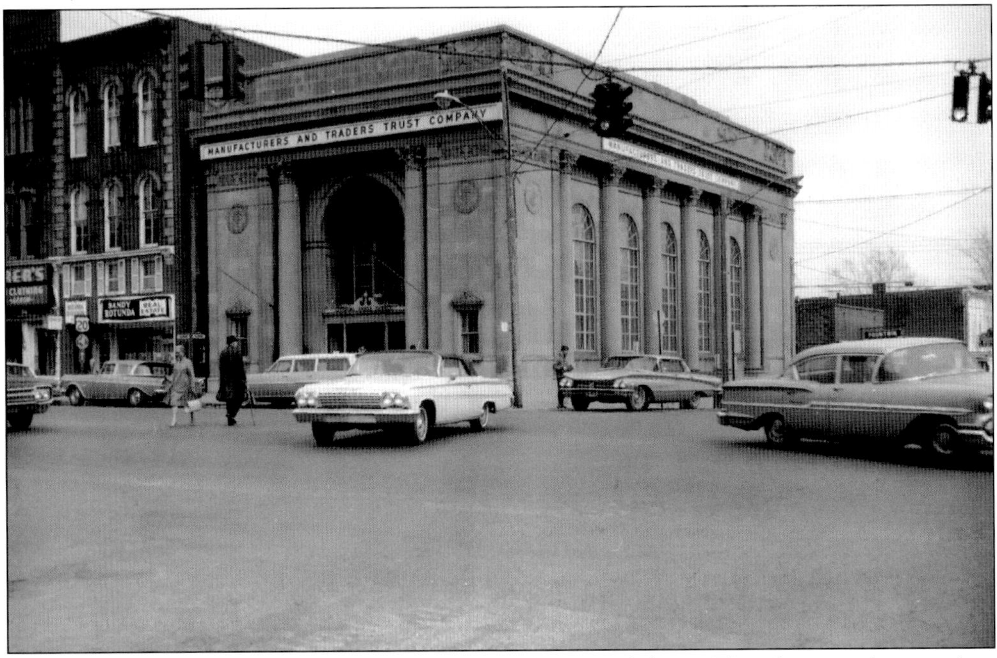

Here is another picture of the middle of Fredonia during rush hour. This photograph was taken within a few minutes of the other photograph on this page, as many of the same parked cars are shown. This photograph was not staged, but it was taken with an attempt to show how cars and pedestrians must maneuver around each other at peak times in the village.

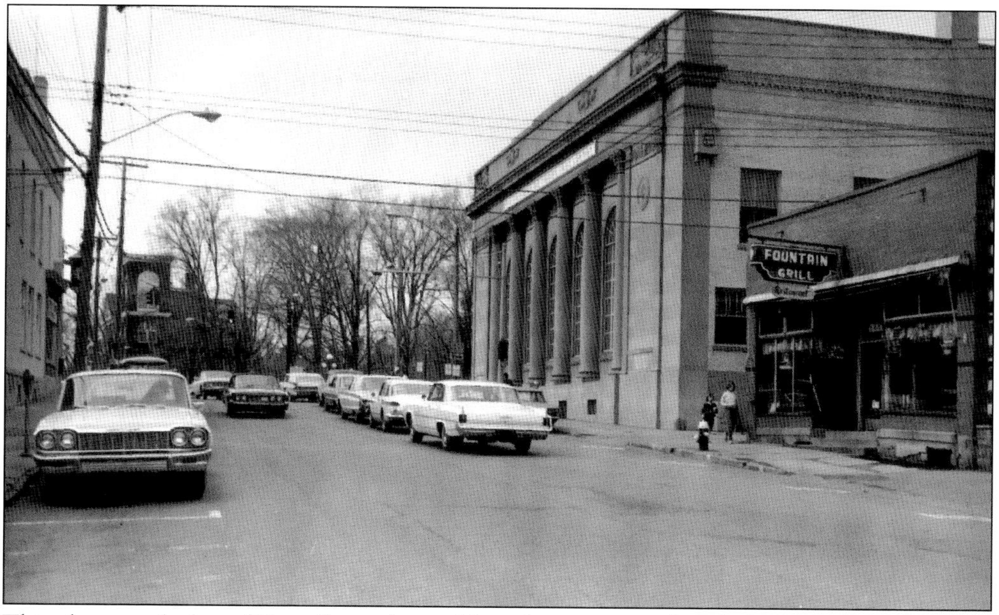

This photograph shows Water Street facing Main Street as seen from below. The Fountain Grill is shown on the left, which was owned and operated by the Pacos family for many years. Today the Fountain Grill has been renovated and changed into Valentine's Bar. The intent of this photograph might have been to show how much traffic enters the intersection at Main Street from Water Street.

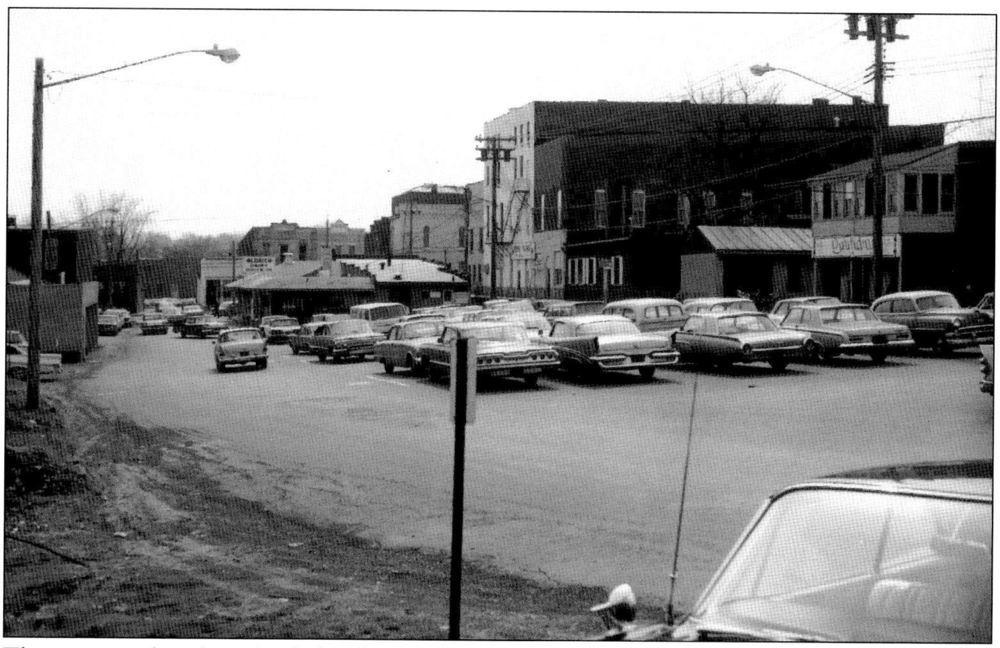

The municipal parking lot behind East Main Street seemed to be one of the major topics of discussion during the parking study in the 1960s. This view of the lot facing west shows a full parking lot with cars entering to look for a spot that does not exist. No real changes were made following this series of photographs taken to study the problems. There is probably no easy solution, as this question has been discussed many times in the village up to the present day.

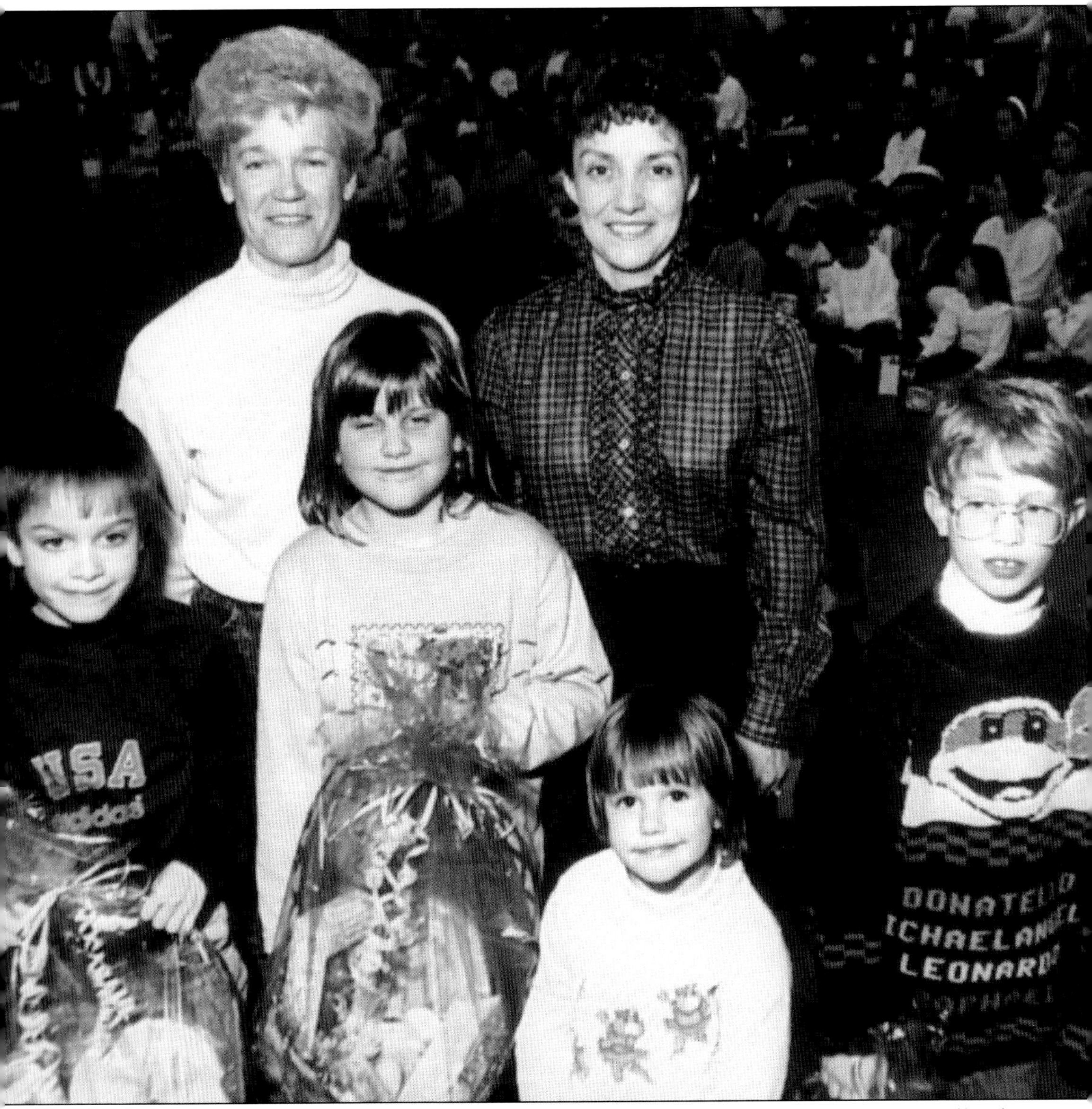

The Town of Pomfret and Village of Fredonia have worked together for many years to offer the children in the area a number of programs like the Easter programs, which continue today. This photograph from 1991 shows two local government representatives that have been involved in improving the community for years. Pictured from left to right are (first row) John Siskar, Jill Berner, Jessica Bartkowski, and Jeffrey Galley; (second row) village trustee Sue Marsh and Pomfret councilwoman Roberta Valentine. Most residents know Valentine today as the town clerk.

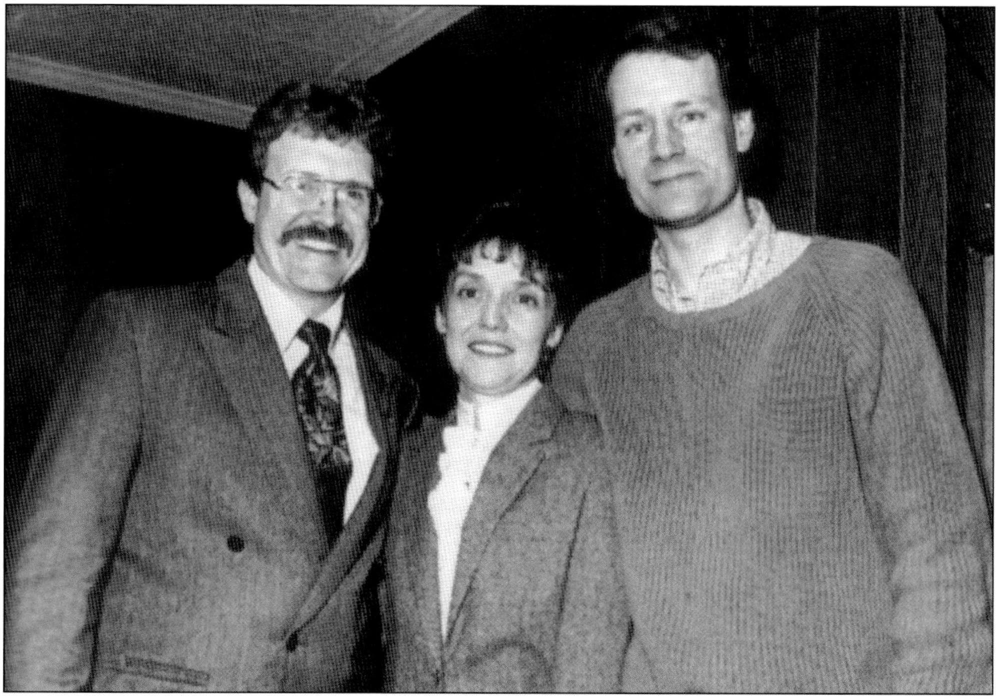

The November election of 1991 saw newcomer Mark Thomas (left) win a seat on the Pomfret Town Council. At center is Valentine, who won her reelection bid for her council seat. Thomas eventually became the town supervisor in 1994 followed by successful terms as county executive from 1998 to 2005. At right is victorious county legislator Michael Bobseine from Fredonia.

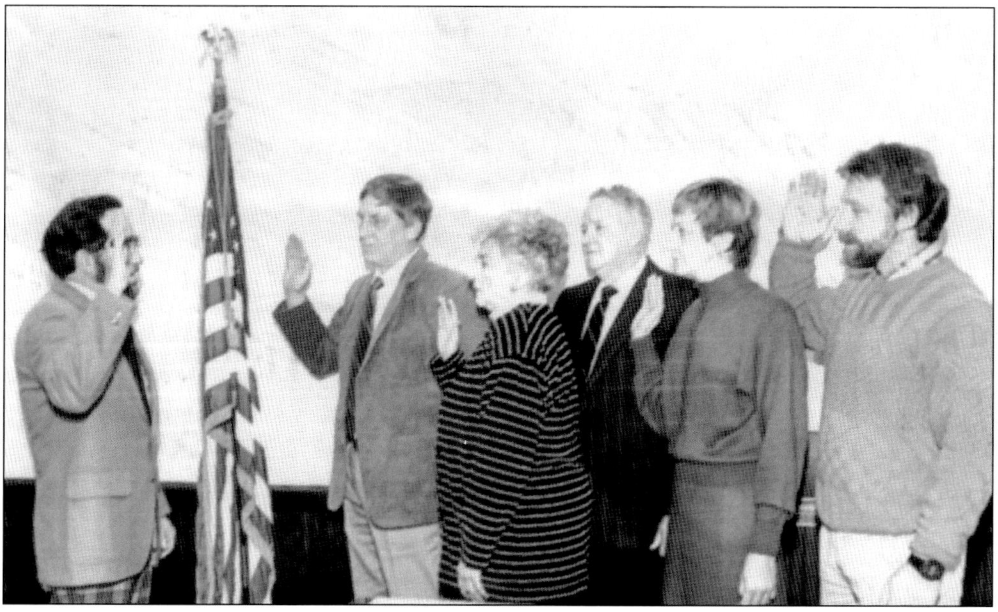

January 1 is typically the day when new public officials are sworn in to begin their term in office. In 1990, the representatives being sworn in, from left to right, included Richard Whipple, Roger Ruckman, Claire Penfold, Kenneth Horey, Beverly Swyers, and James Oakes Jr. Oakes still serves the town as highway supervisor today.

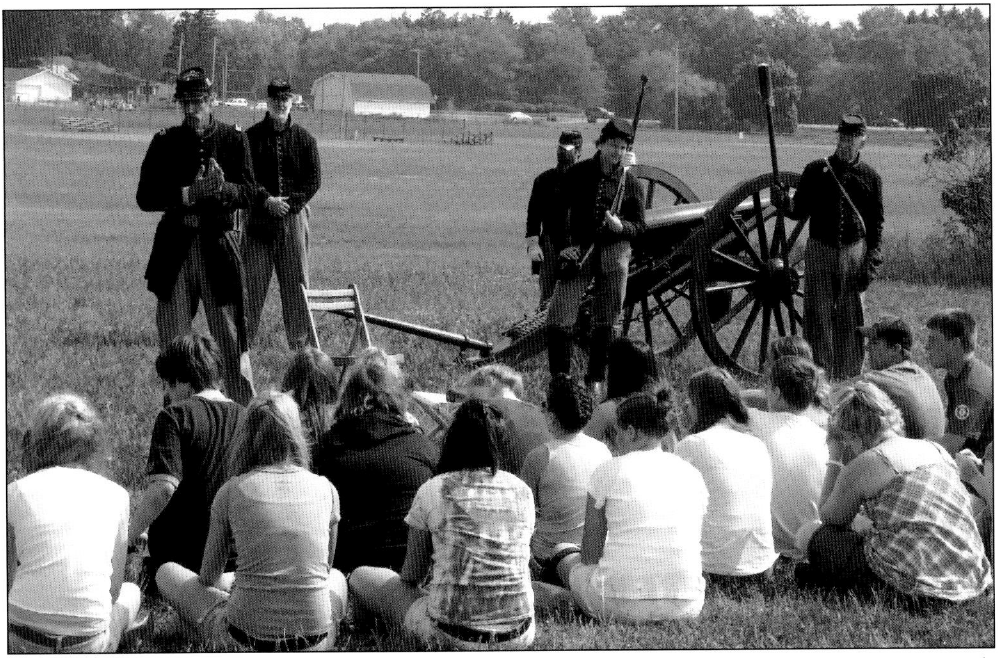

This photograph is of the Cushing Memorial Civil War Camp that is held at Fredonia High School at the end of each school year. The camp brings students into town from many different school districts around Chautauqua County. Included in the full-day schedule is a trip to the Darwin R. Barker Museum, which teaches the visitors a little more about the area's history.

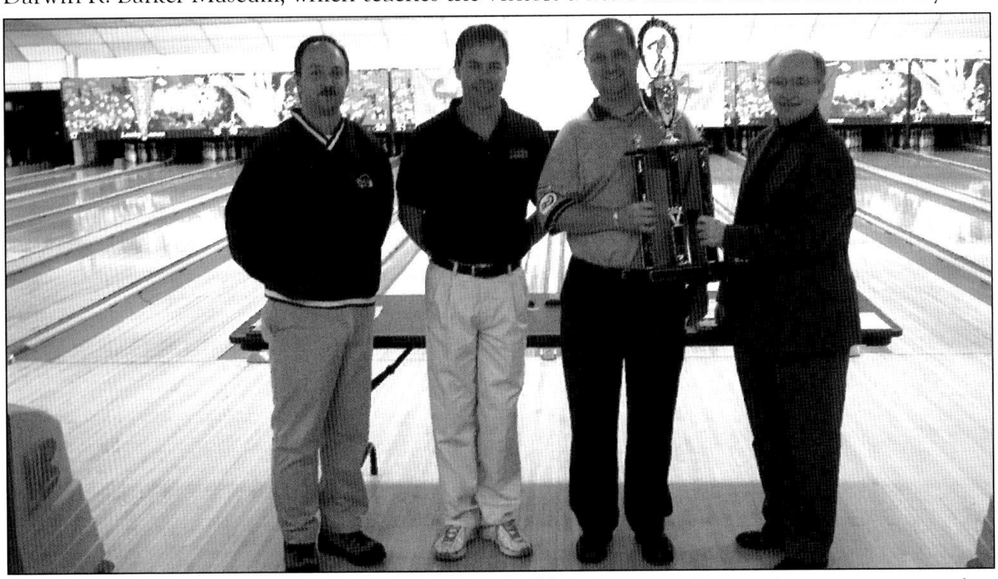

Not many towns the size of Pomfret can boast of hosting a professional sporting event, but Pomfret can, courtesy of Lucky Lanes on Route 60. In 2005, the Professional Bowlers Association Eastern Region hosted a tournament at the 40-lane bowling center in town, featuring the best bowlers in the world. The pro-am tournament was well attended by area bowlers, while the professional competition saw standing-room-only crowds at times. Shown from left to right is the author, Lucky Lanes owner Paul Nocek, tournament champion Brian Kretzer, and Professional Bowlers Association Eastern Region director Russ Mills.

Five

MONUMENTS AND IMPORTANT PLACES

Pomfret has a wide variety of monuments and important places to be proud of. Many of the monuments are located within a short walk of the center of the village of Fredonia. Many monuments were the work of the local chapter of the Daughters of the American Revolution (DAR). Their work in preserving the past is outstanding.

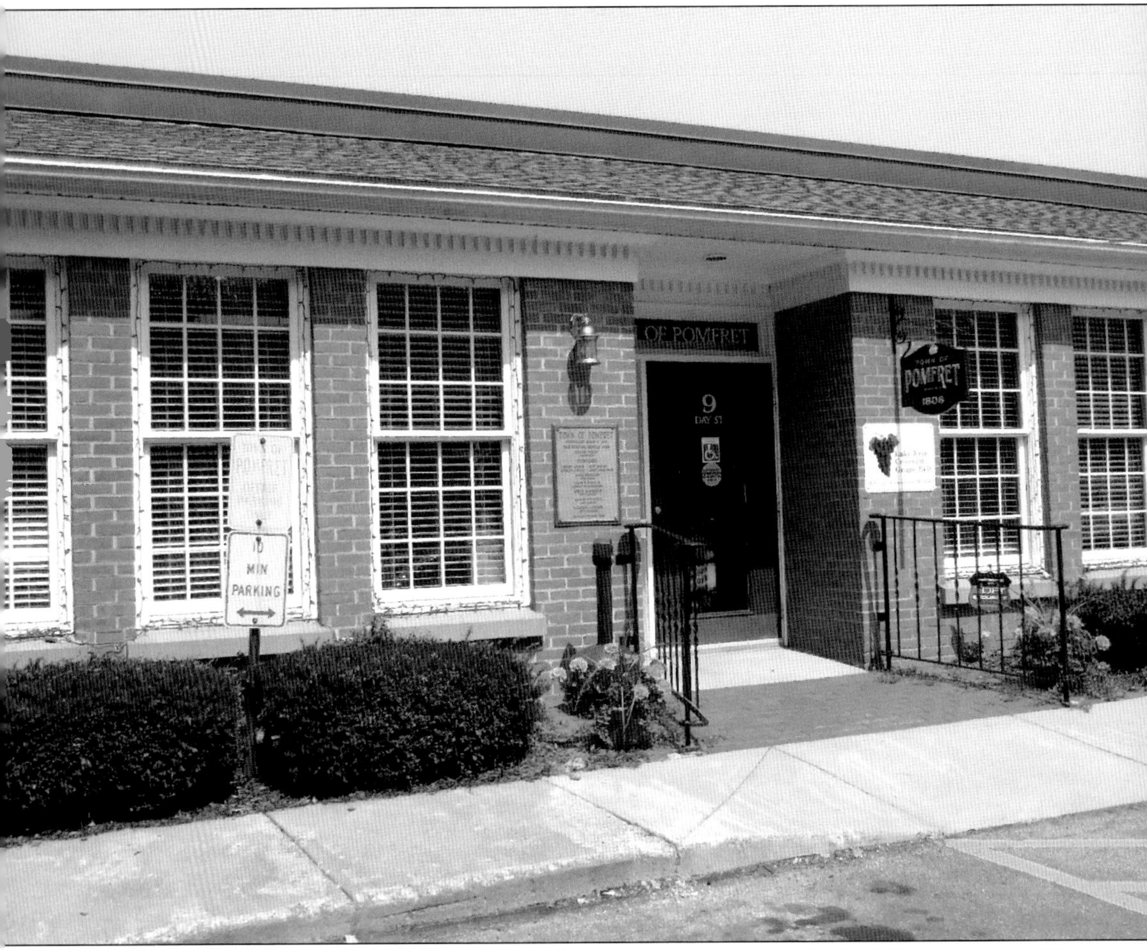

Today's version of town hall is much more decorative than how it looked 40 years ago. The building has been completely renovated to allow for offices and meeting space for all town officials. The left side of the building is where the assessor's office is now located, while the right side of the building is the town clerk's office. Kevin Muldowney (assessor), Kathy Ludemann (clerk of the assessor's office), Roberta Valentine (town clerk), and Carol Stafford (deputy town clerk) work in town hall as of 2007.

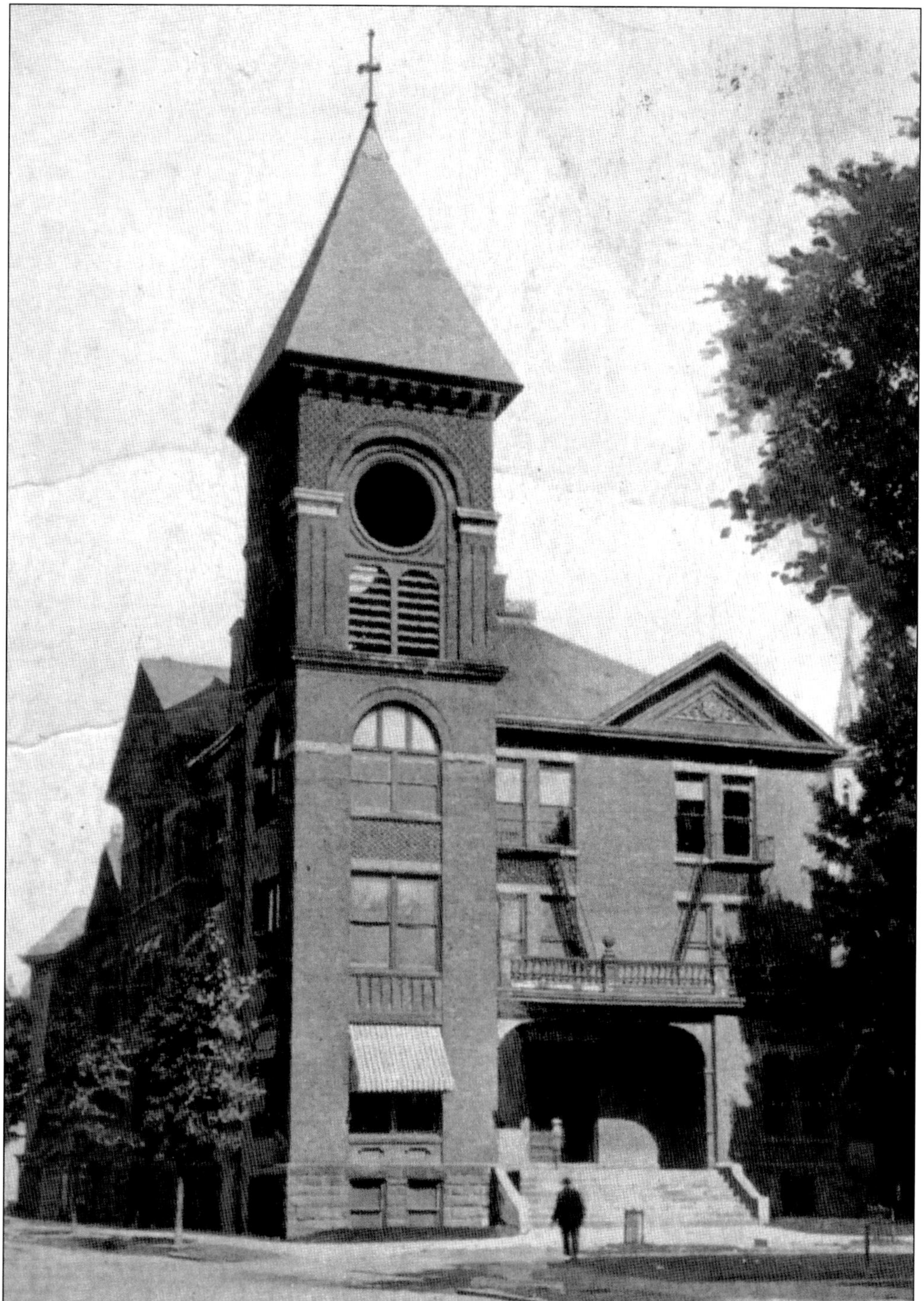

Here is the village hall as it looked at the beginning of the 20th century. This photograph was the most popular one of the hall for many years, as it appeared on postcards sold throughout the village for a long time. Note the church steeple just to the right of the photograph. Today the church is gone and a parking lot is in its place.

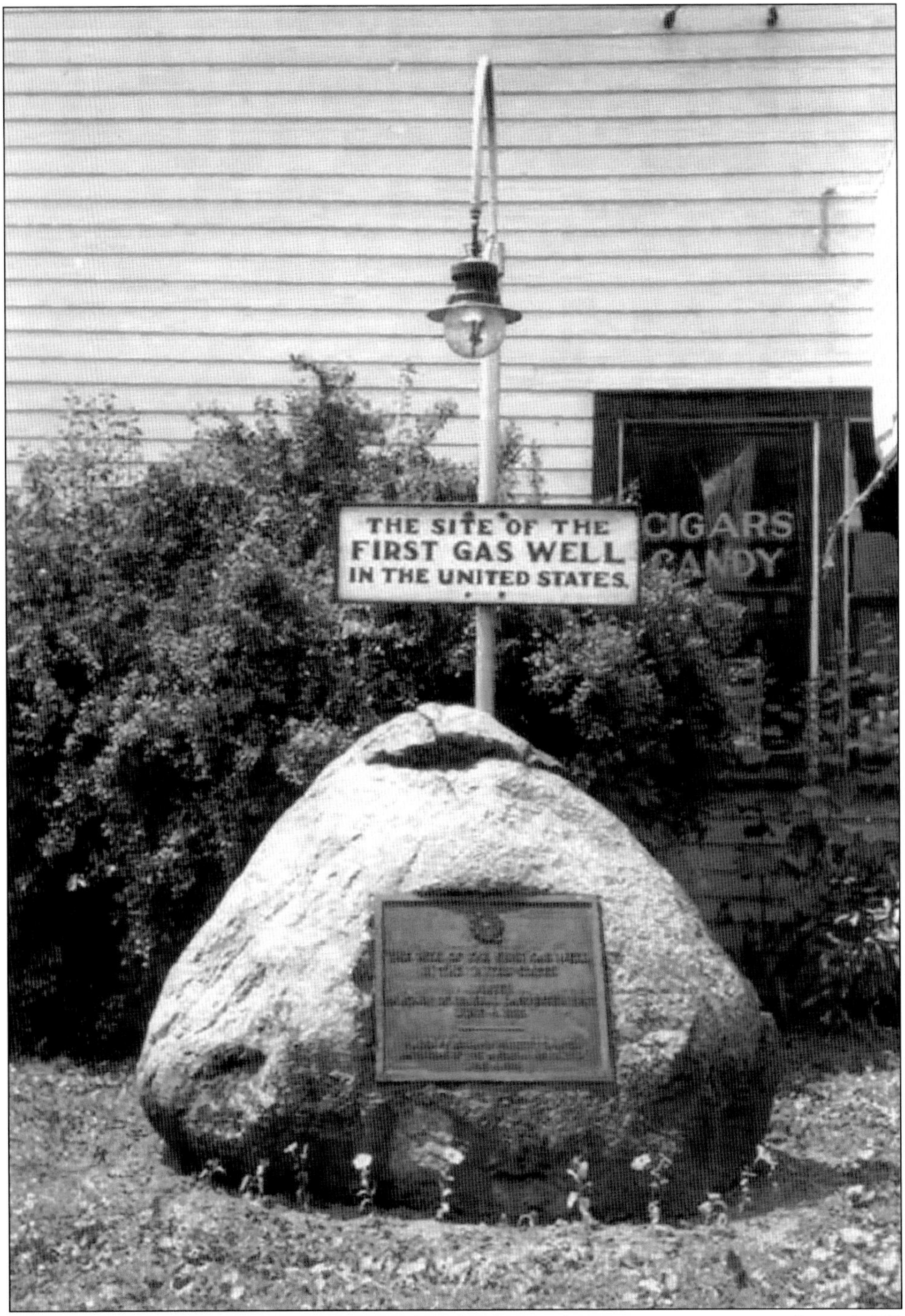

This is a photograph of the gas well marker shortly after its dedication ceremony on June 4, 1925, by the DAR. This monument is still one of the most visited places in the town of Pomfret. For many years, schoolchildren were brought to visit the monument, taking the short walk from one of the elementary schools while hearing about the importance of the discovery and the reception for the Marquis de Lafayette.

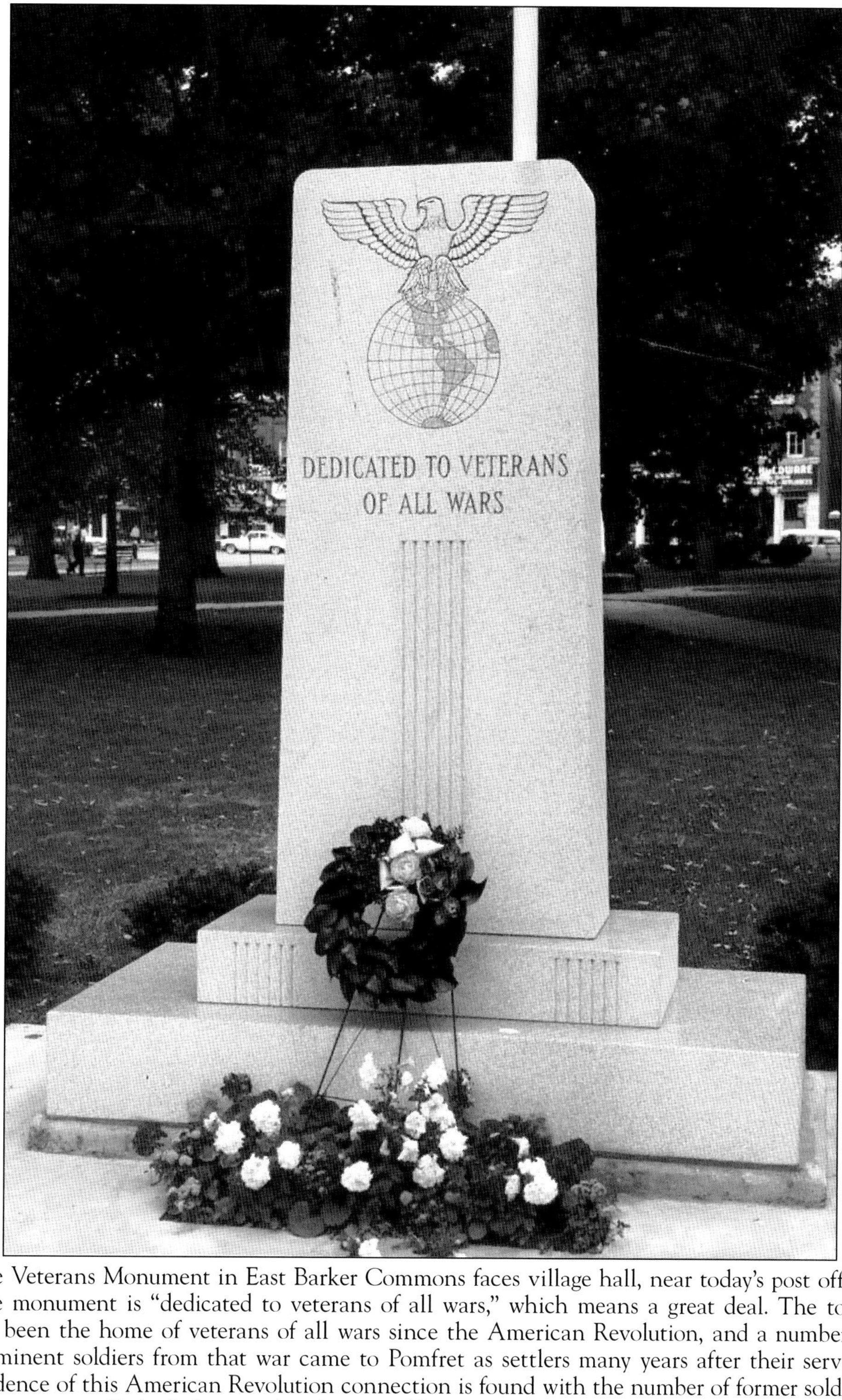

The Veterans Monument in East Barker Commons faces village hall, near today's post office. The monument is "dedicated to veterans of all wars," which means a great deal. The town has been the home of veterans of all wars since the American Revolution, and a number of prominent soldiers from that war came to Pomfret as settlers many years after their service. Evidence of this American Revolution connection is found with the number of former soldiers known personally by Lafayette when he visited here in 1825.

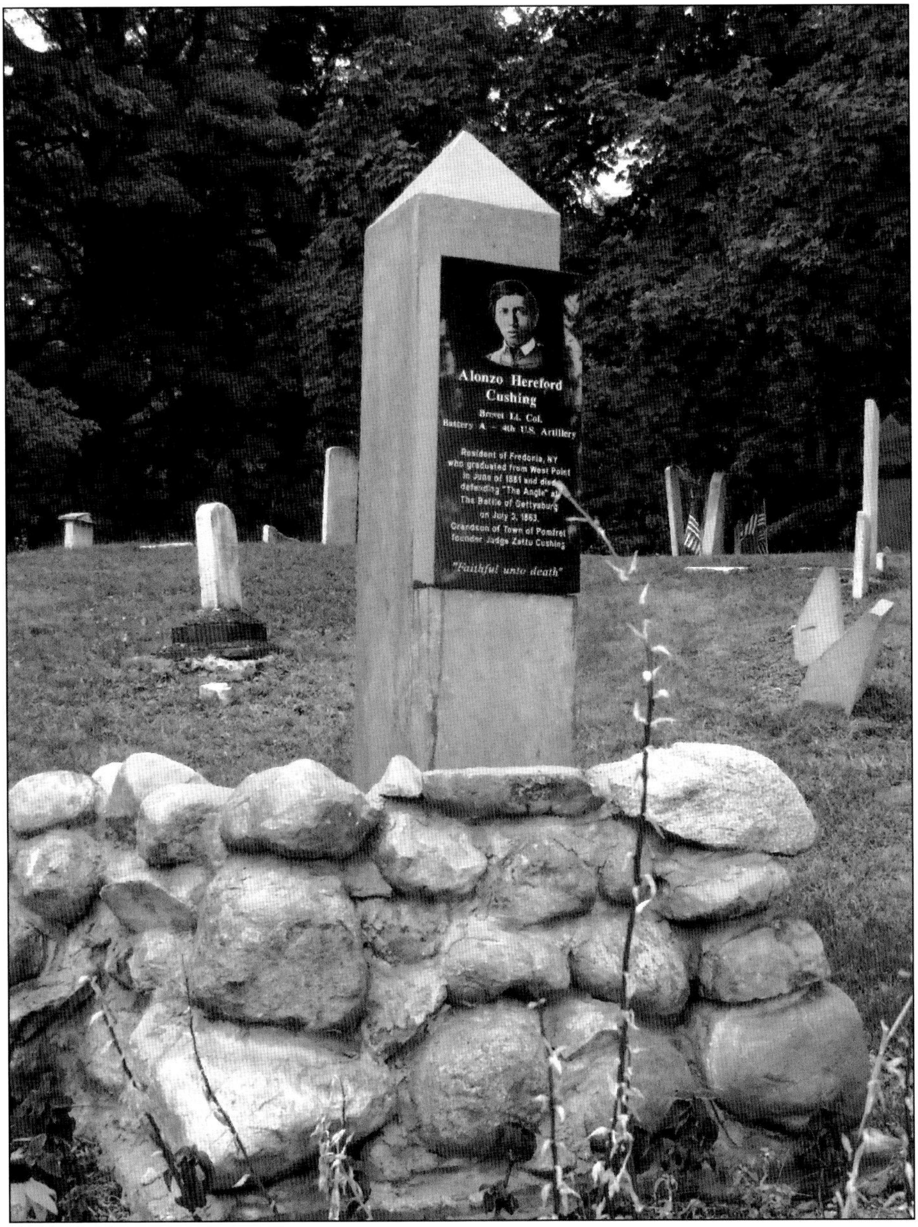

The Alonzo Hereford Cushing Monument stands in Pioneer Cemetery facing the sidewalk on the western edge of the property. The monument was designed and constructed by students from Fredonia High School under the direction of technology department teachers Roger Pacos and Greg Haase. The grant-funded project was dedicated on June 10, 2006, during a ceremony presided over by the author. Pomfret town supervisor Don Steger spoke on behalf of the town while village trustee Joseph Cerrie spoke on behalf of the village of Fredonia. Local resident Richard Ryan also assisted on the project, as coordinator of the Cushing's Battery reenactment group that attended the ceremony and performed a firing display. The monument was dedicated in memory of Cushing, a brevet lieutenant colonel who died at the Battle of Gettysburg on July 3, 1863. The monument was placed only 30 yards from the grave of Cushing's grandfather and town founder Zattu Cushing.

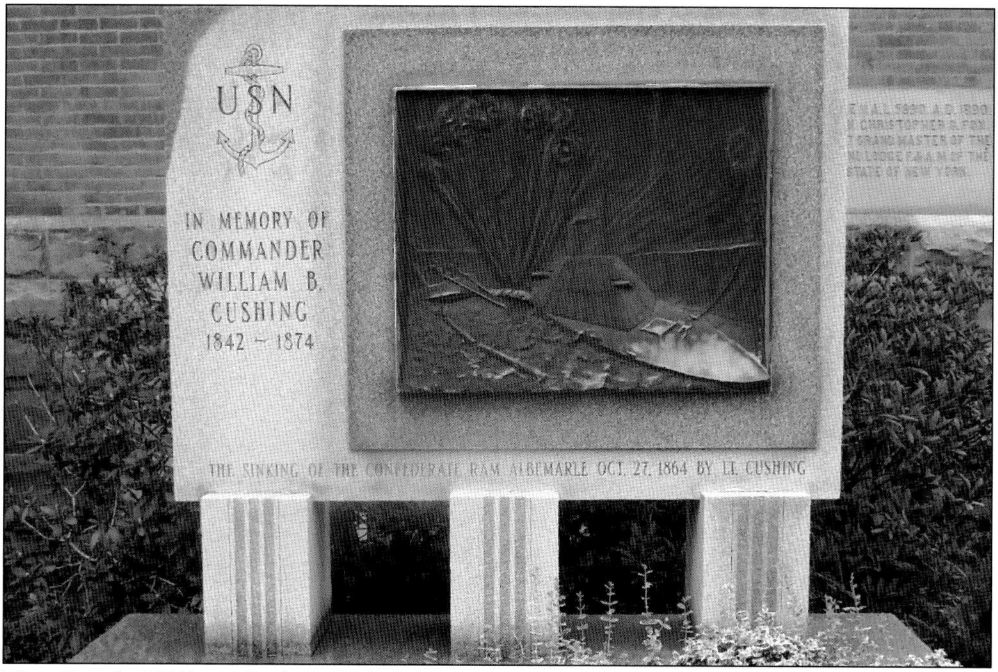

The Comdr. William Barker Cushing monument is located near the front of village hall facing the East Barker Commons. It was dedicated on June 14, 1968. He led an attack on the Confederate ironclad the CSS *Albemarle* and sunk the vessel with a specially engineered torpedo on October 27, 1864. His heroics earned him the thanks of Congress, as well as those of Pres. Abraham Lincoln. He survived the war and continued on in the navy until his death due to the stress of his wounds on December 17, 1874. He also might have been suffering from the effects of tuberculosis, which was a common illness in the Cushing family. His home was at 23 Forest Place in the village, where the house still stands today.

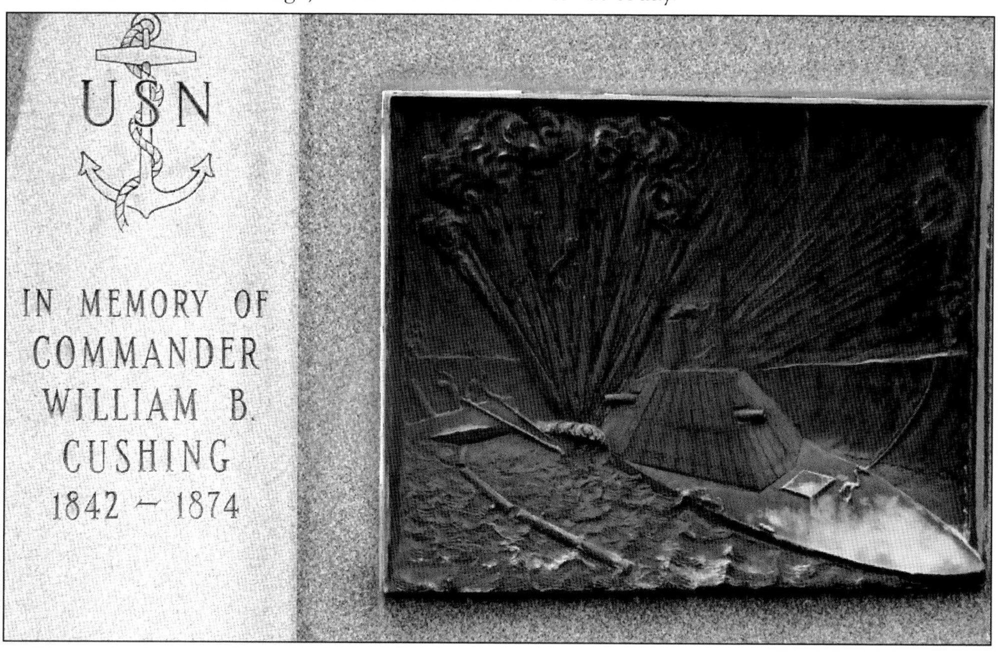

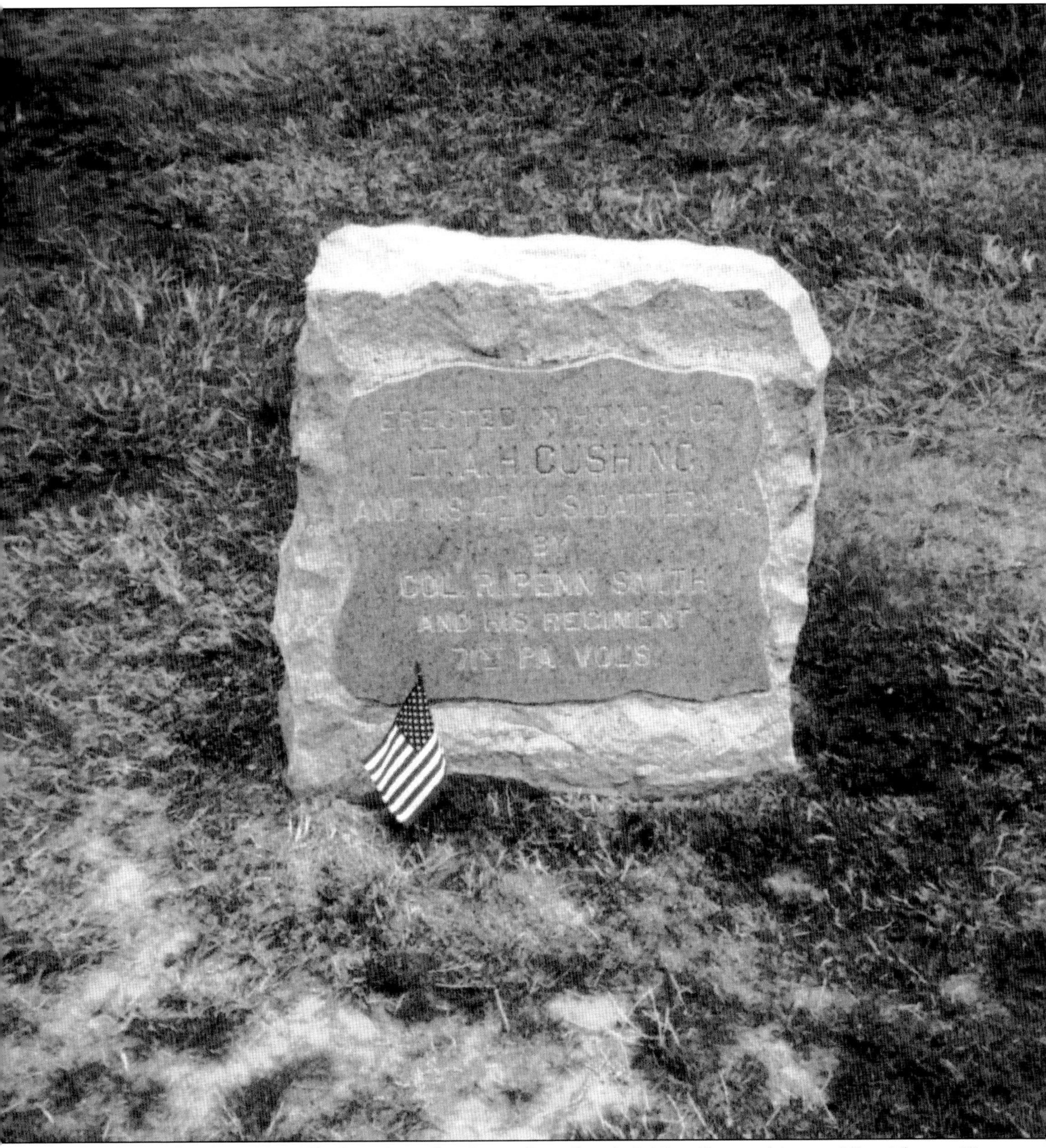

This monument is actually found on the Gettysburg battlefield in Pennsylvania. The Alonzo H. Cushing Monument at Gettysburg is dedicated to Fredonia's hero of the Battle of Gettysburg, who defended "the angle" against the Confederate forces during Pickett's Charge. He was wounded three times during the day's fighting, but refused to leave his post despite orders to do so. He is buried at West Point Military Academy.

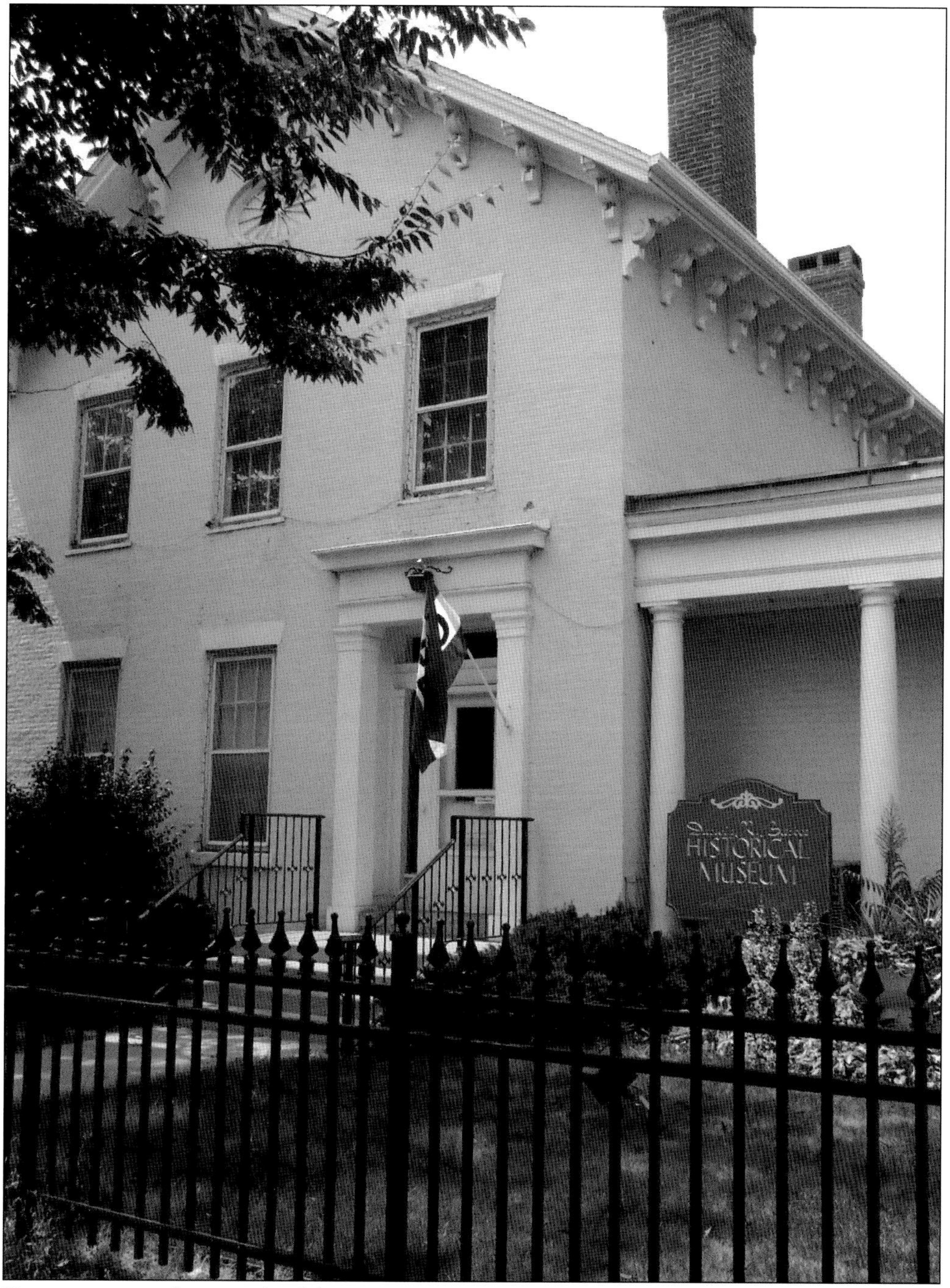

Here is a recent photograph of the Darwin R. Barker Museum on Main Street in Fredonia. The house was built in 1821 by Leverett Barker and later donated by his son Darwin for the purpose of housing a library in the village. Today a new library addition has been constructed and the house has become the home of the Darwin R. Barker Museum. It is connected to the Darwin R. Barker Library.

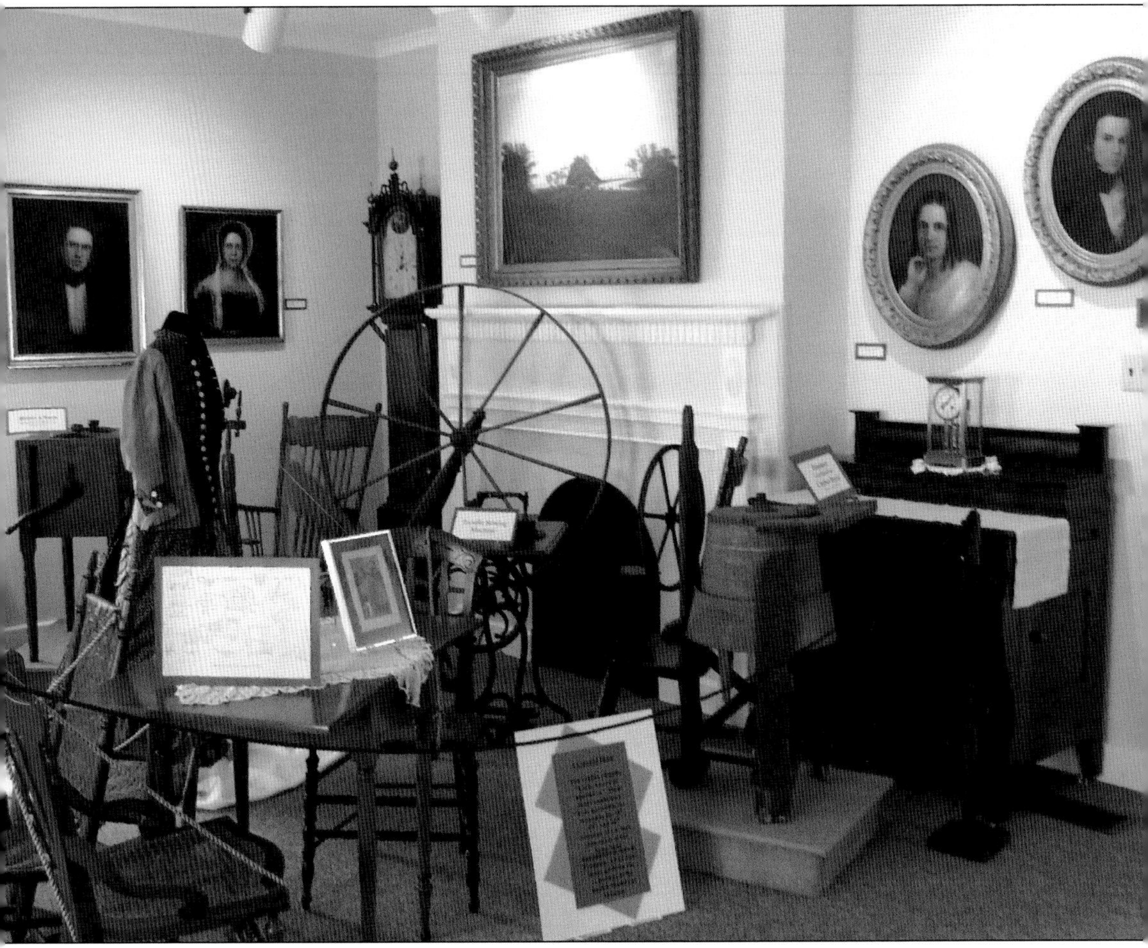

One of the best places to visit in Fredonia to learn about early residents is the Belden Gallery located inside the Darwin R. Barker Museum. The gallery features the portraits of early residents, many of which have been featured in this book. One of the most prominent portraits in the gallery is that of Dr. Squire White, the first physician in Chautauqua County.

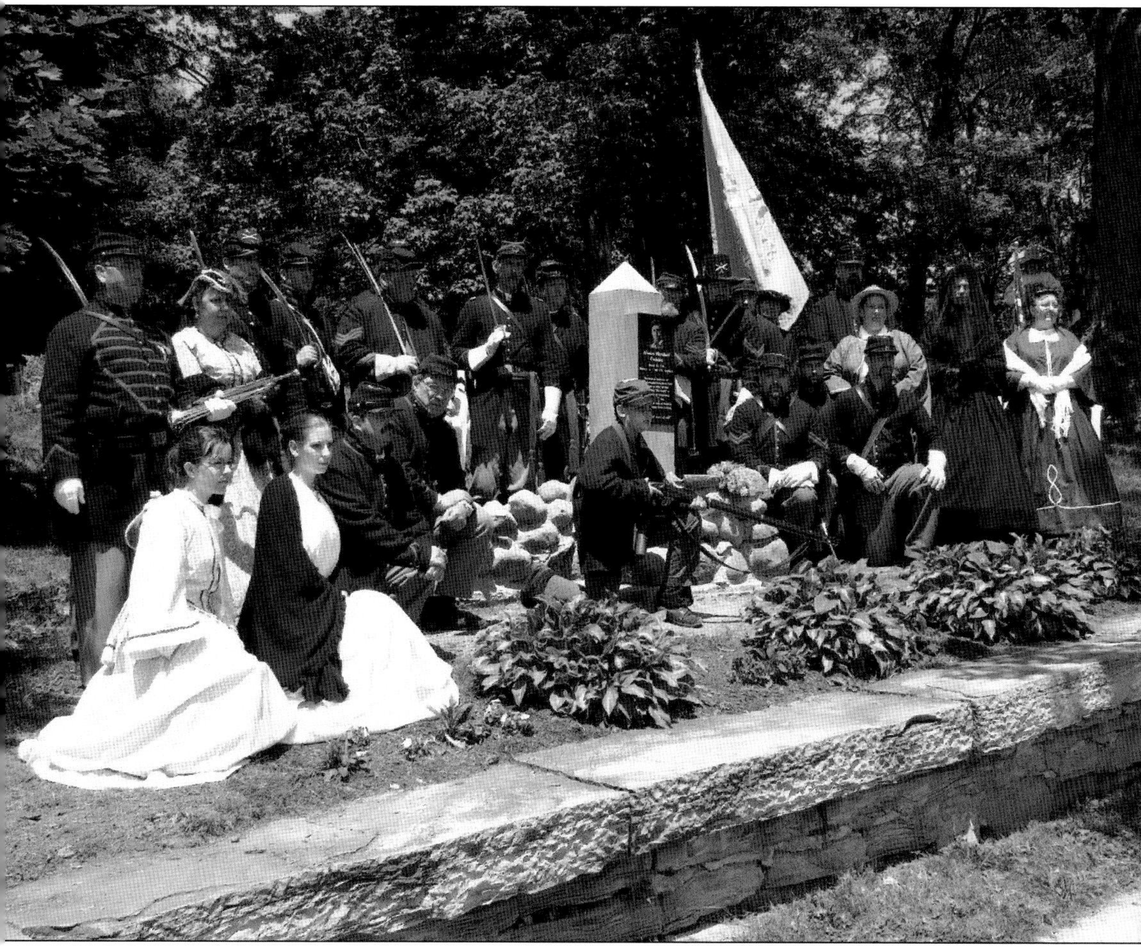

The Cushing's Battery reenactment group made the Alonzo Hereford Cushing Monument dedication ceremony one of the most memorable in the history of the town. The unit camped in Barker Commons the night before the ceremony and performed firing demonstrations throughout the weekend for area residents. The unit has returned to the area recently as part of the Cushing Memorial Civil War Camp hosted by the author at Fredonia High School.

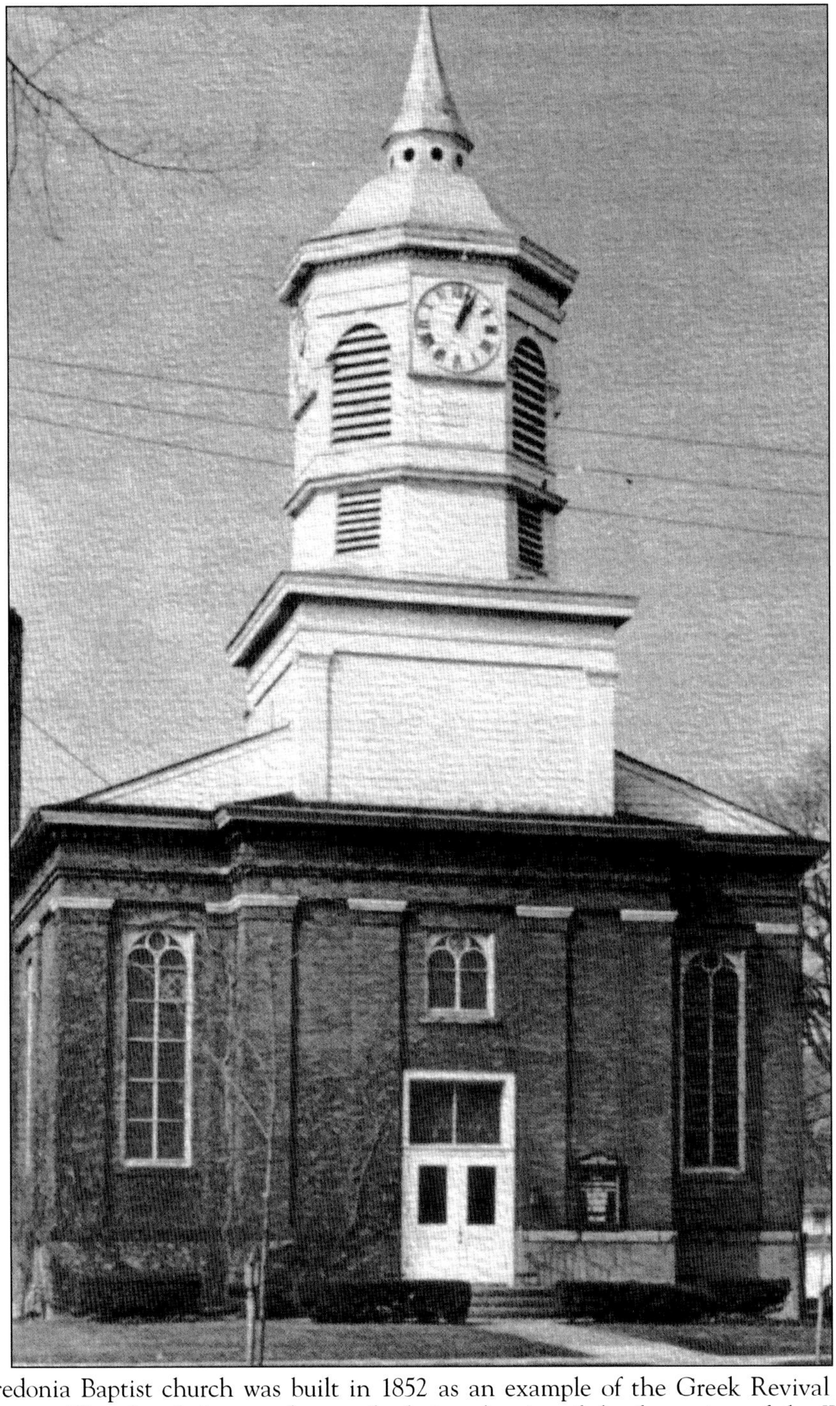

The Fredonia Baptist church was built in 1852 as an example of the Greek Revival style of architecture. The church is most famous for being the site of the formation of the Women's Christian Temperance Union on December 15, 1873. Many prominent early settlers were members of the Baptist Church in Fredonia, although not all of them attended services in this building. Prominent families that were members of the church included the Cushings, the Barkers, the Websters, and the Risleys.

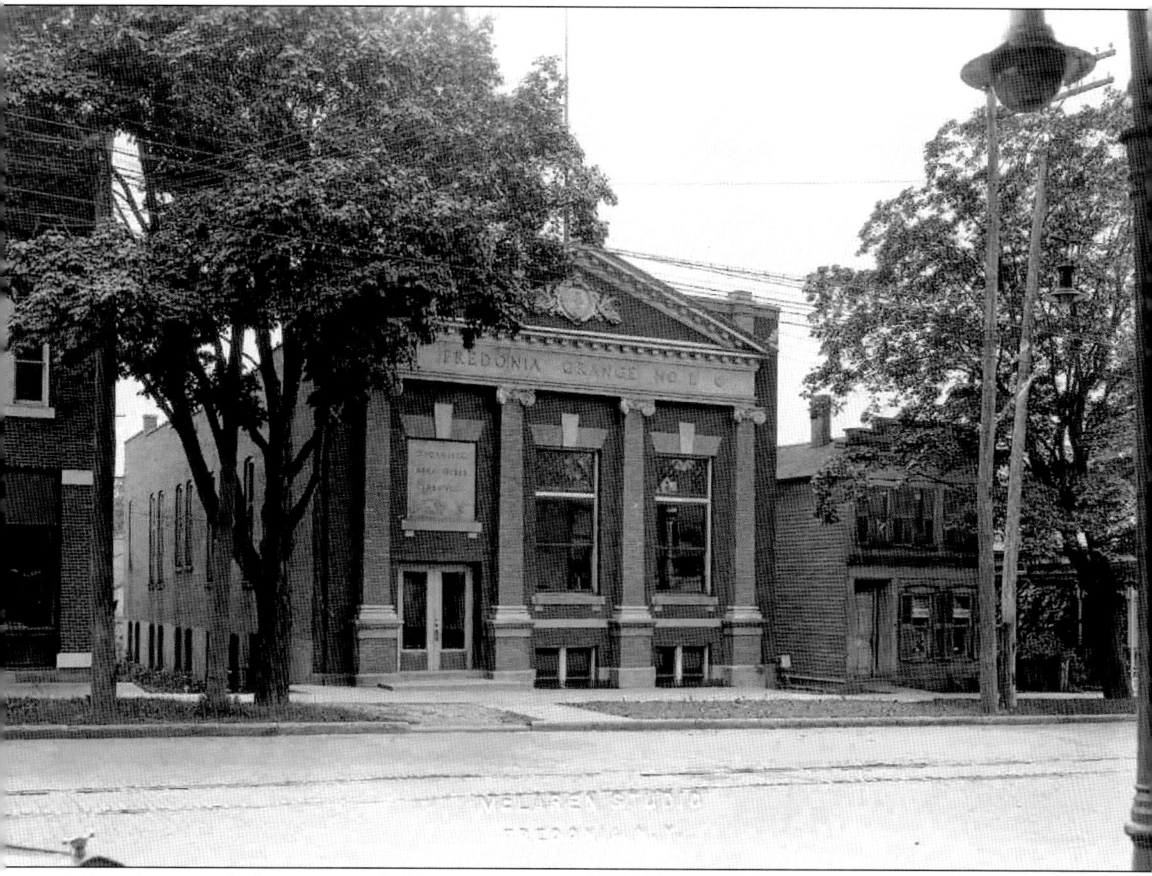

The first regularly organized Grange was established in Fredonia in 1868, although the organization itself was founded in Washington, D.C., the prior year. Fredonia Grange No. 1 is still located on West Main Street in the village, as seen in this photograph. The Grange was an organization of farmers that grew out of the Civil War period, as the need arose for a group to represent the interest of farmers on a national level. The organization still exists today, but in much smaller numbers than its heyday in the 1870s. The Grange is nonpartisan and only supports issues rather than political parties. Today anyone is welcome in the Grange as the number of farmers in the country has dropped dramatically.

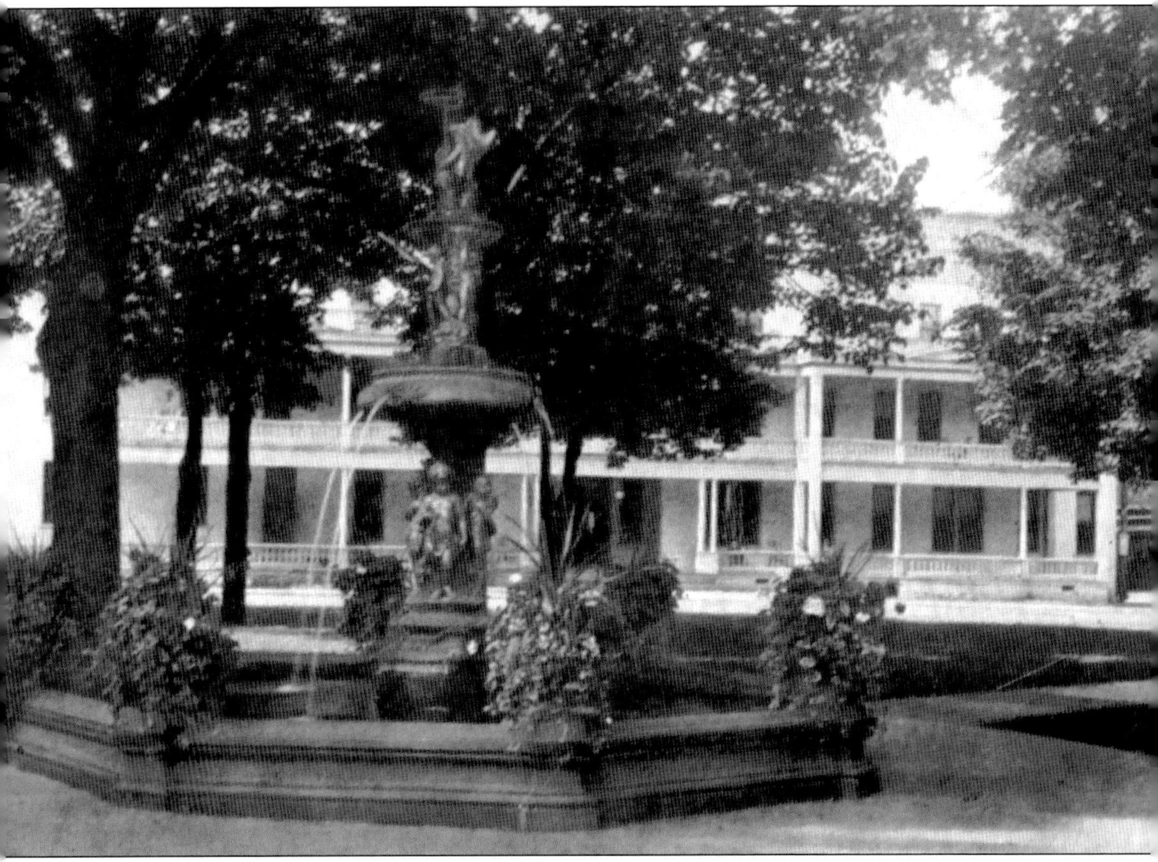

This photograph is of Lafayette Park, with the Columbia Hotel in the background, as seen at the beginning of the 20th century. The park, also known as West Barker Commons, was given the name Lafayette Park after the Marquis de Lafayette visited in 1825. He was received at a specially constructed platform near this location. A tablet commemorates this location and its importance to the community's history.

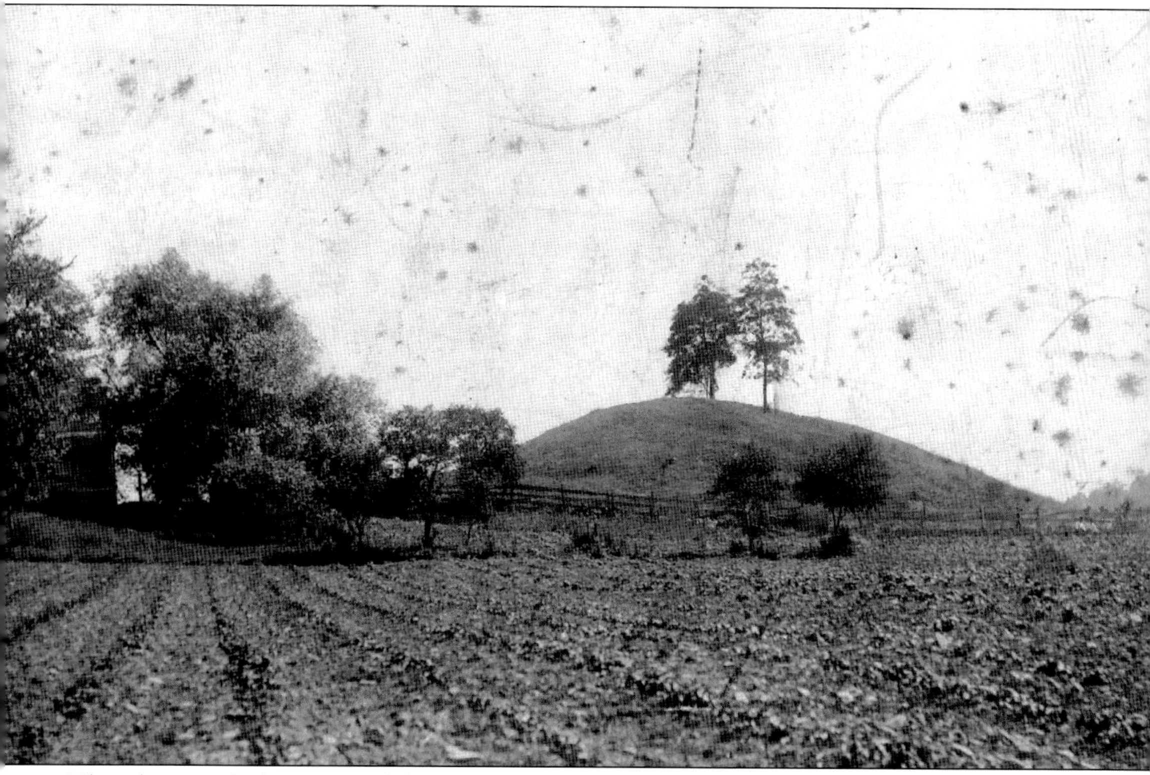

This photograph shows one of the mysterious Native American mounds seen around the town by residents in the 19th century. This photograph was taken in July 1894, but the location of this particular mound is not known. Archaeologists excavated these mounds on a number of occasions and found not only bones but also many other Native Americans relics. The dating of the artifacts established that they were not the remnants of the Iroquois, as most had thought, but they were from a much earlier people that had lived in the area hundreds of years before the Iroquois. Not much more is known about these mounds, as most have been cleared by farmers over the years and little remains except for the items collected by archaeologists during the first digs over 100 years ago.

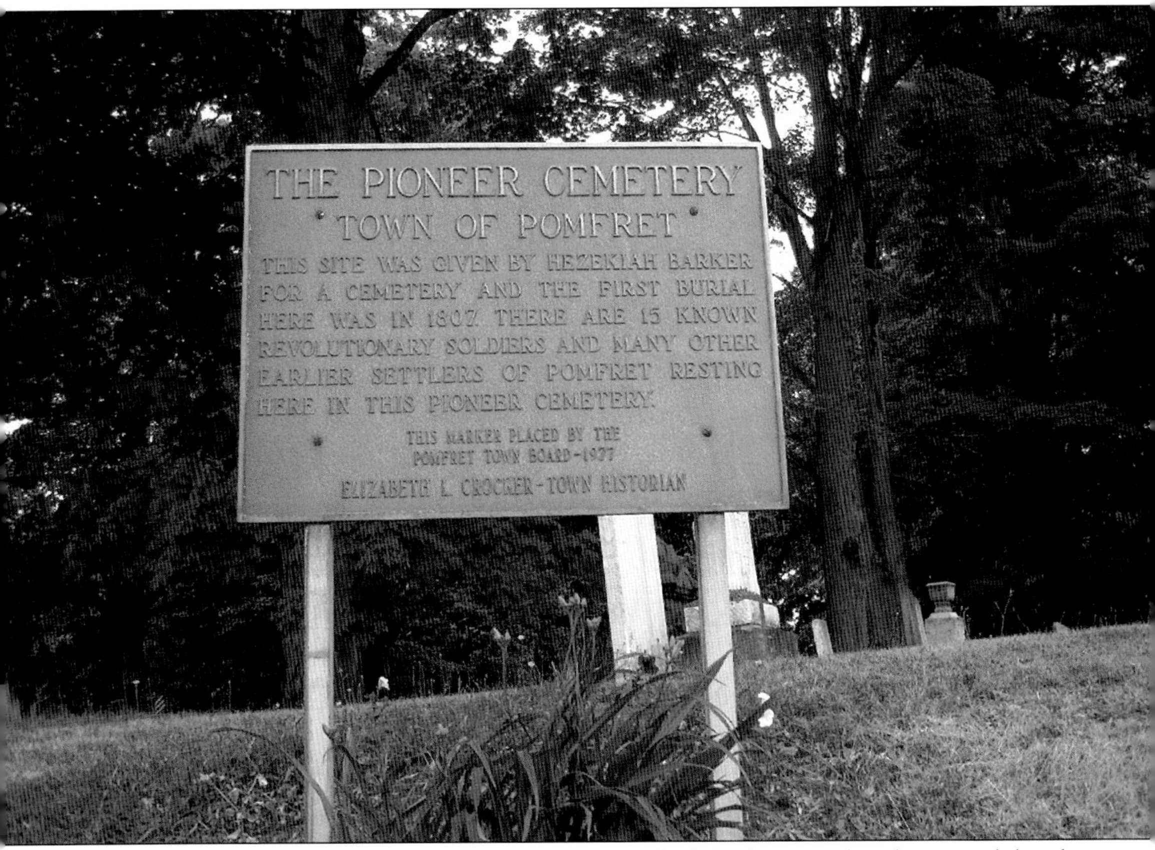

The Pioneer Cemetery was a gift to the town from Hezekiah Barker, a settler who arrived shortly after founder Zattu Cushing. Barker also donated land for the town park, today known as Barker Commons. At one time, Barker owned almost all of the land that is now the center of the village of Fredonia within the town.

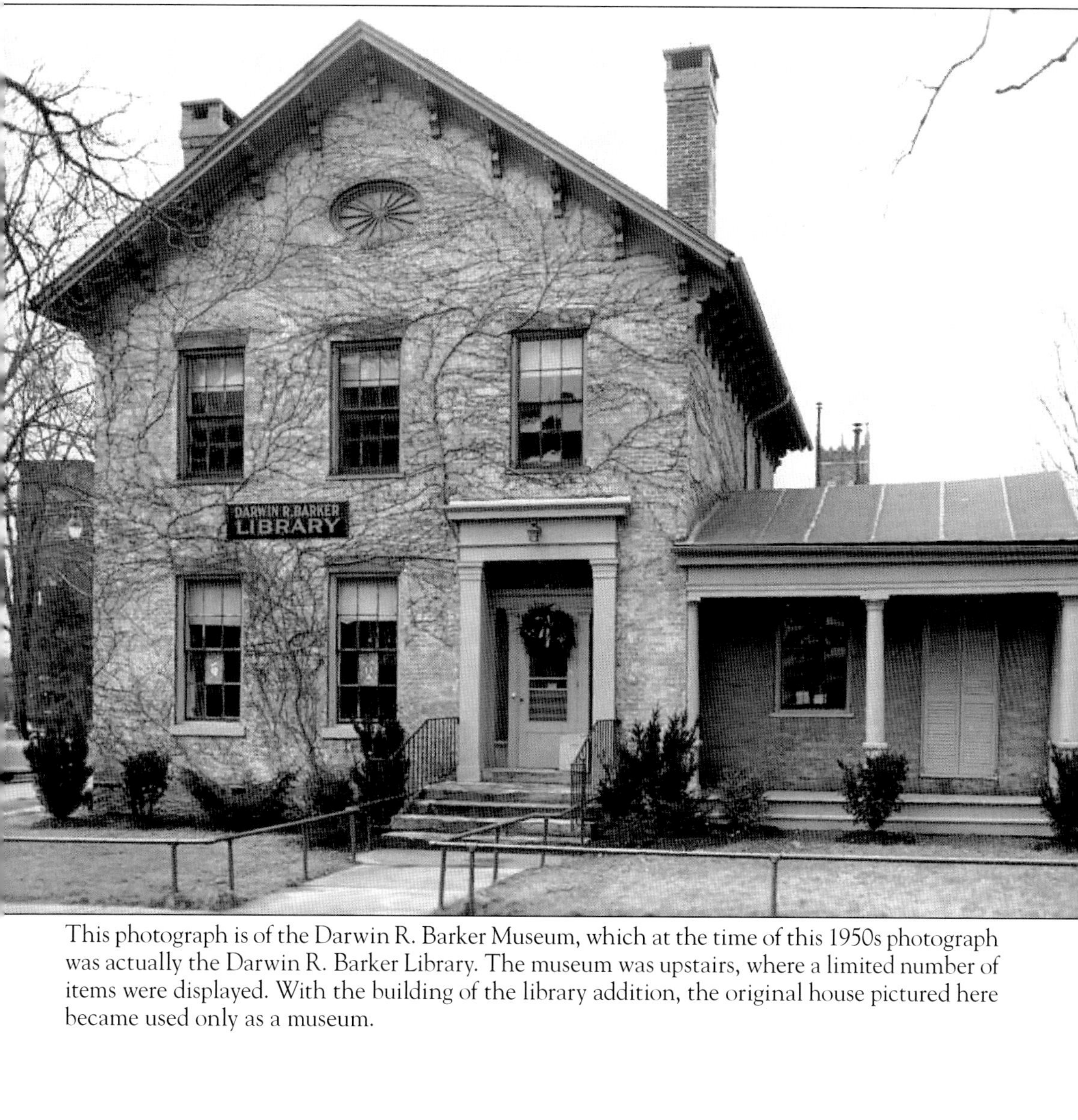

This photograph is of the Darwin R. Barker Museum, which at the time of this 1950s photograph was actually the Darwin R. Barker Library. The museum was upstairs, where a limited number of items were displayed. With the building of the library addition, the original house pictured here became used only as a museum.

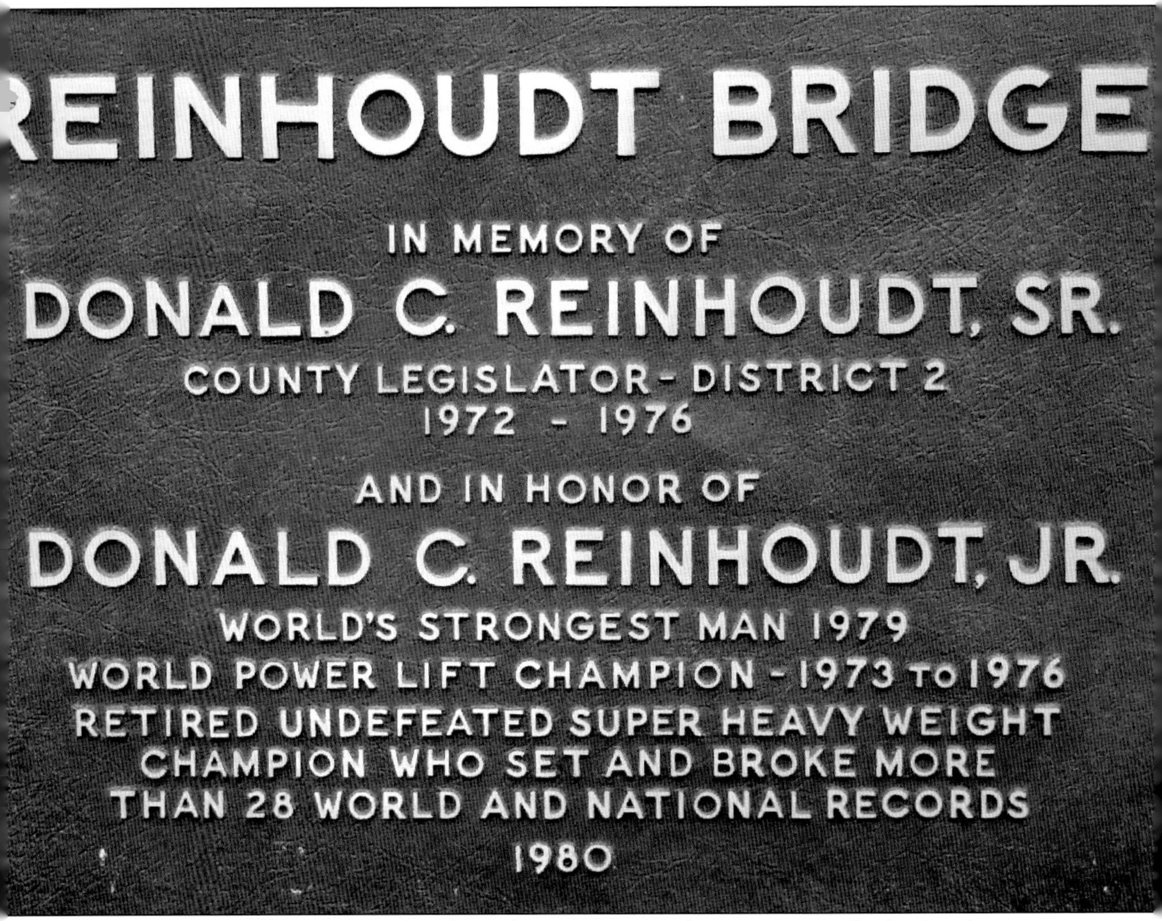

The plate dedicating the Reinhoudt Bridge is seen near the entrance to the bridge that crosses Risley Street in the village. The Reinhoudts are well known throughout the town, with Don Reinhoudt Sr. serving as a county legislator and Don Reinhoudt Jr. becoming the world's strongest man. Don Jr. is well known by the youth of the community as the director of the county youth bureau, who visits schools regularly to perform his amazing feats of strength. Both Reinhoudt men have been fine examples of service to the community for many years.

Six

Modern Era Town Supervisors

The town of Pomfret has been in existence officially since 1808, during which time many great supervisors have served the residents of the town by providing leadership in both good times and bad. This chapter is dedicated to the modern-era supervisors, beginning in 1931 and ending in 2007. Discussed are the years that they served and the important local and national events they may have faced throughout their terms in office.

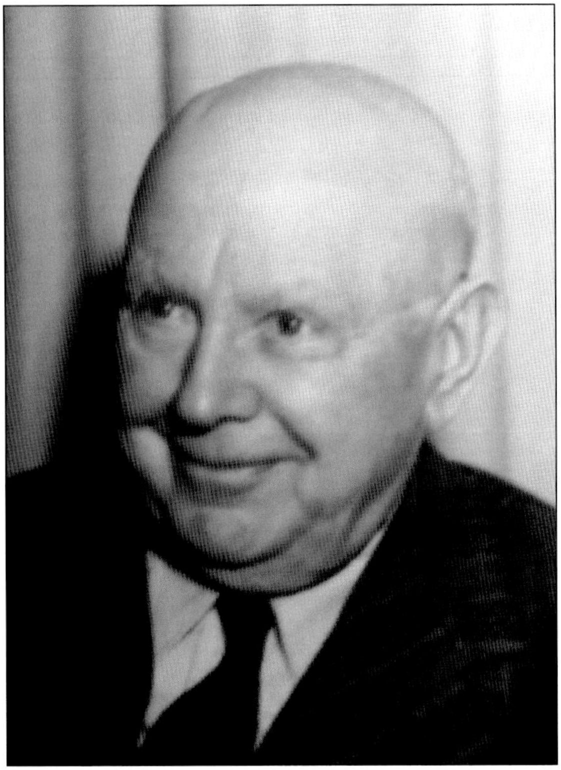

Arthur R. Maytum was town supervisor from 1931 to 1937. Maytum was already an important figure in the area prior to becoming town supervisor because of his involvement with the Fredonia Normal School for many years. His term in office was difficult due to the Great Depression, which had a great effect on Pomfret.

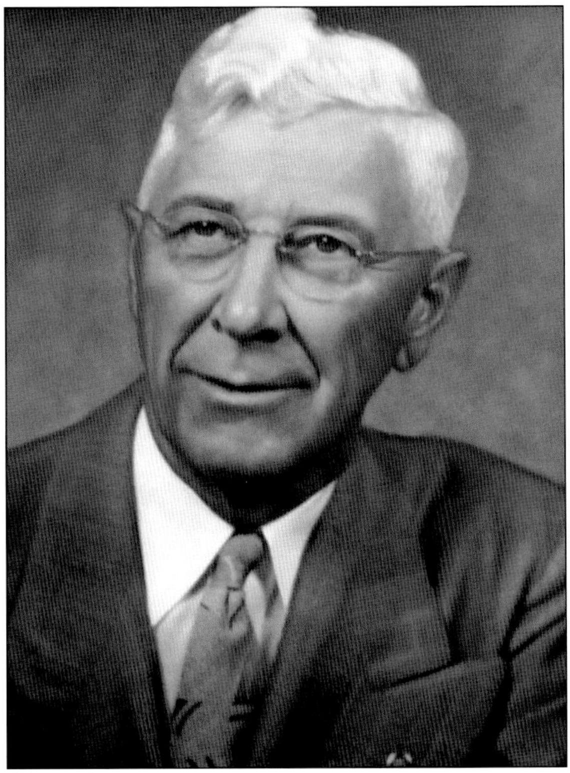

Florian Spoden served as town supervisor from 1938 to 1963, from the end of the Great Depression through the turbulent times of the 1960s. During Spoden's lengthy term, the Fredonia Normal School became a state university college, leading to the tremendous growth that has led to the existing campus today.

Stewart Dudley served as town supervisor from 1964 to 1985. Dudley's term saw tremendous building projects on the SUNY Fredonia campus, as well as a number of new facilities locally. His term may have been one of the largest periods of growth in the town's history.

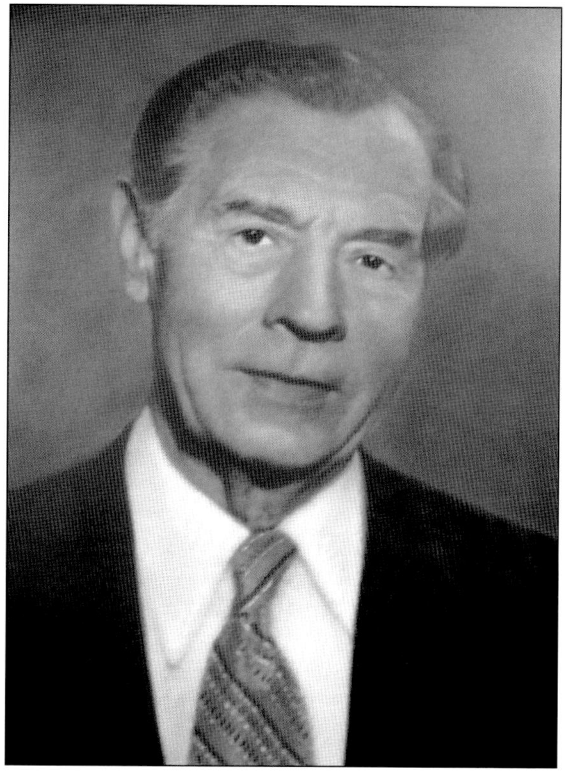

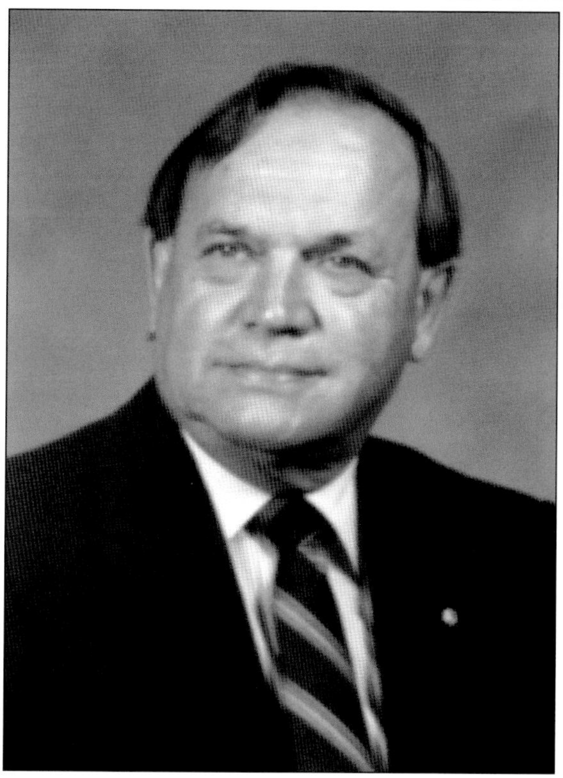

Larry McQuiggan served as town supervisor from 1985 to 1989. McQuiggan was known as an extremely detailed person, who was a reliable administrator. A great deal of expansion took place during his term in the area of Route 60, which looks much different today than it did even during his term only 20 years ago.

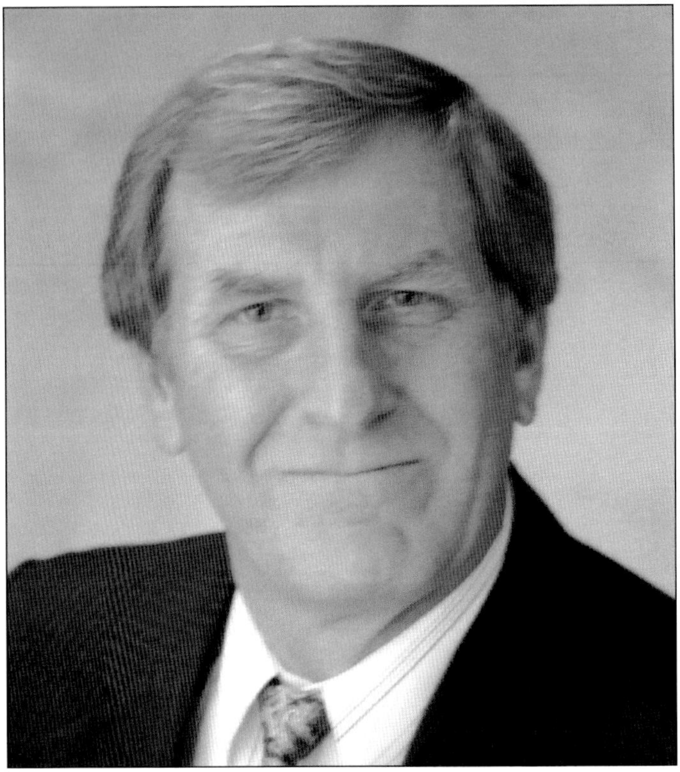

Roger Ruckman served as town supervisor from 1990 to 1993. Ruckman's term saw a number of new projects undertaken at SUNY Fredonia, as well as numerous construction projects revolving around the roads within the town.

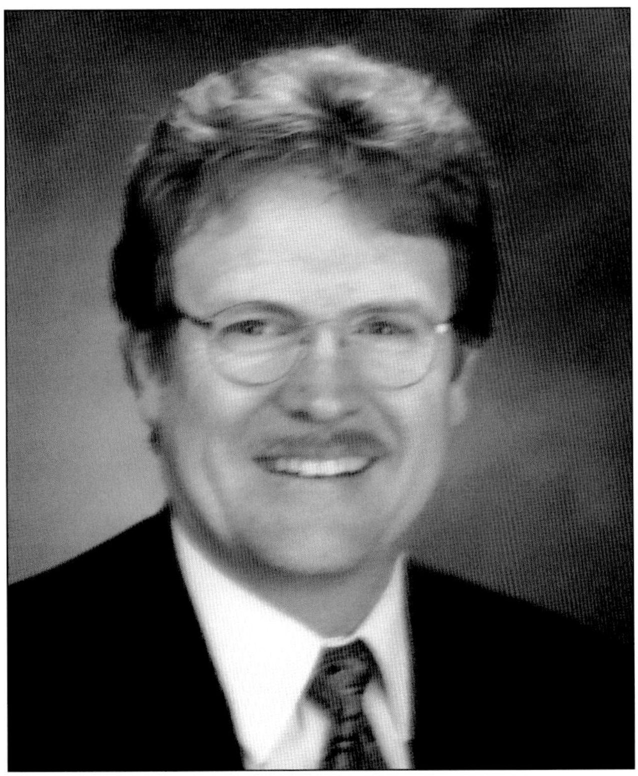

Mark Thomas's term as town supervisor was from 1994 to 1997. Thomas gained a great deal of praise as an administrator during his terms leading to his election as Chautauqua county executive in 1998, an office he held until 2005. Thomas has recently been the project manager for the Regional Intermunicipal Services Project.

Edward "Bud" Woloszyn served as town supervisor from 1998 to 2001. One of the main events of Woloszyn's term was the Vision 2000 project that was undertaken at the Fredonia Central School. This project provided the latest advancements in education for students in area schools.

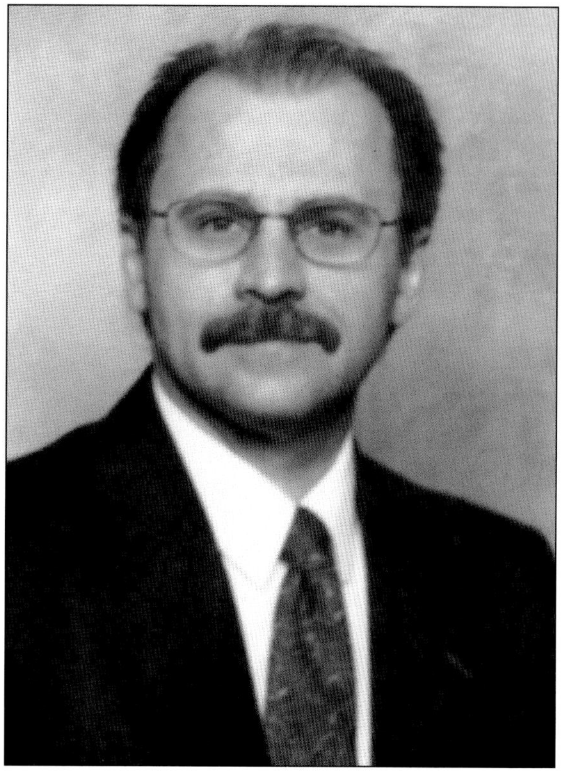

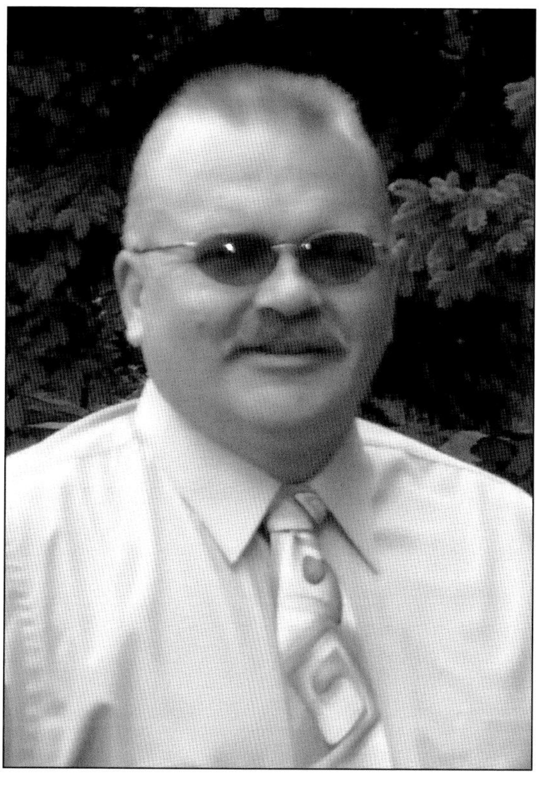

Don Steger began serving as the town supervisor in 2002. Steger has had a number of projects come across his desk in recent years, including the question of a property reevaluation, water districts, and wind energy. Steger has provided strong leadership in a time of change within the town, as it continues to look for ways to grow in the future.